War in the Western Theater

Favorite Stories and Fresh Perspectives
from the Historians at Emerging Civil War

Edited by
Sarah Kay Bierle & Chris Mackowski

The Emerging Civil War Series

offers compelling, easy-to-read overviews of some of the Civil War's most important battles and stories.

Recipient of the Army Historical Foundation's Lieutenant General Richard G. Trefry Award for contributions to the literature on the history of the U.S. Army

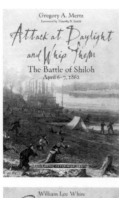

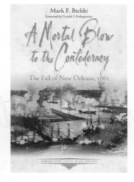

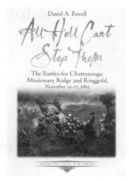

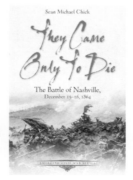

For a complete list of Emerging Civil War titles, visit www.emergingcivilwar.com.

War in the
Western Theater

Favorite Stories and Fresh Perspectives
from the Historians at Emerging Civil War

Edited by
Sarah Kay Bierle & Chris Mackowski

SB

Savas Beatie
California

First edition, first printing

ISBN-13 (hardcover): 978-1-61121-596-0
ISBN-13 (ebook): 978-1-95454-713-1

Library of Congress Cataloging-in-Publication Data

Names: Mackowski, Chris, editor. | Bierle, Sarah Kay, editor.
Title: War in the Western Theater : favorite stories and fresh perspectives from the historians at emerging Civil War / edited by Chris Mackowski, and Sarah Kay Bierle.
Other titles: Favorite stories and fresh perspectives from the historians at emerging Civil War | Emerging Civil War (Blog)
Description: El Dorado Hills, CA : Savas Beatie LLC, [2024] | Series: Emerging Civil War anniversary series | Summary: "Often relegated to a backseat by action in the Eastern Theater, the Western Theater is actually where the Federal armies won the Civil War. In the West, Federal armies split the Confederacy in two-and then split it in two again. This book revisits some of the Civil War's most legendary battlefields: Shiloh, Chickamauga, Franklin, the March to the Sea, and more"-- Provided by publisher.
Identifiers: LCCN 2023023734 | ISBN 9781611215960 (hardcover) | ISBN 9781954547131 (ebook)
Subjects: LCSH: Southwest, Old--History--Civil War, 1861-1865--Campaigns. | Mississippi River Valley--History--Civil War, 1861-1865--Campaigns. | Gulf Coast (U.S.)--History--Civil War, 1861-1865--Campaigns. | United States--History--Civil War, 1861-1865--Campaigns.
Classification: LCC E470.4 .W37 2023 | DDC 976.8/04--dc23/eng/20230522
LC record available at https://lccn.loc.gov/2023023734

SB

Savas Beatie
989 Governor Drive, Suite 102
El Dorado Hills, CA 95762
916-941-6896 / sales@savasbeatie.com / www.savasbeatie.com

All of our titles are available at special discount rates for bulk purchases in the United States. Contact us for information.

Printed and bound in the United Kingdom

Sarah:
To Mark and Cheryl Schoenberger.
You are some of my dearest friends in the "far west,"
and your stories of exploring battlefields
and re-enacting in the actual Western Theater
always bring joy.

Chris:
With thanks to my friends at El Patron Mexican Restaurant
in Spotsylvania Court House,
where I spent many enjoyable afternoons
editing all the books in this series
while nursing giant margaritas.
Cheers!

We jointly dedicate this book
in memory
of our friend and colleague
Meg Groeling,
the founding member of ECW's
"Western Department."

Chris Heisey

www.emergingcivilwar.com

Table of Contents

List of Maps

Editors' Note

Emerging Civil War serves as a public history-oriented platform for sharing original scholarship related to the American Civil War. The scholarship we present reflects the eclectic background, expertise, interests, and writing styles of our cadre of historians. We've shared that scholarship not only on the Emerging Civil War blog, but also in the pages of the Emerging Civil War Series published by Savas Beatie, in other general-audience and academic publications, at our annual Emerging Civil War Symposium at Stevenson Ridge, on our monthly podcasts, and even through social media.

Our Emerging Civil War 10th Anniversary Series captures and commemorates some of the highlights from our first ten years.

This compendium includes pieces originally published on our blog; podcast transcripts; and transcripts of talks given at the ECW Symposium. It also includes an assortment of original material. Previously published pieces have been updated and, in most cases, expanded and footnoted. Our attempt is to offer value-added rather than just reprint material available for free elsewhere.

Between the covers of this series, readers will find military, social, political, and economic history; memory studies; travelogues; personal narratives; essays; and photography. This broad range of scholarship and creative work is meant to provide readers with a diversity of perspectives. The combined collection of material is *not* intended to serve as a complete narrative of events or comprehensive overview. Rather, these are the stories and events our historians happened to be interested in writing about at any given time. In that way, the collection represents the sort of eclectic ongoing conversation you'll find on our blog.

As a collective, the individuals who comprise ECW are encouraged to share their own unique interests and approaches. The resulting work—and the respectful discussions that surround it—forward ECW's overall effort to promote a general awareness of the Civil War as America's defining event.

Another of ECW's organizational priorities is our ongoing work to identify and spotlight the next generation of "emerging" Civil War historians and the fresh ideas they bring to the historical conversation. (Some of us were "emerging" when ECW started up ten years ago and have perhaps since "emerged," but the quest to spotlight new voices continues!)

Most importantly, it is the common thread of public history and the ideals of interpretation that so strongly tie our seemingly disparate bodies of work together. America's defining event should not be consigned to forgotten footnotes and dusty shelves. As public historians, we understand the resonance and importance history's lessons can have in our modern world and in our daily lives, so we always seek to connect people with those great stories and invaluable lessons. Emerging Civil War remains committed to making our history something available for all of us—writers, readers, historians, hobbyists, men, women, young, old, and people of all races and ethnicities—and by doing so, making it something we can engage, question, challenge, and enjoy.

Please join us online at www.emergingcivilwar.com.

A Note About This Volume:

As we plotted out the Emerging Civil War 10th Anniversary Series, we identified a lot of excellent material that didn't necessarily fit into one of the themes we'd settled on. We still wanted an opportunity to showcase some of that work, though. This volume does just that.

It is *not* intended to be comprehensive. Like the Western Theater itself, there is too much territory to cover. ECW writers write about the topics they happen to be interested in at any given time, so this anthology is necessarily limited by that process of self-selection. Many fascinating stories at many favorite battles are not included simply because no one in our stable of contributors has opted to write about them yet.

Sherman's efforts through Georgia and the Carolinas are not included in this volume but will, instead, appear in a planned future volume. An additional forthcoming volume on the fall of 1862 will also touch on some of the actions not covered here.

Stories in this collection are organized in roughly chronological order. Beyond that, there's no narrative through-thread, so the book lends itself to either a front-to-back reading or to "sampling."

Acknowledgments

First and foremost, as editors, we'd like to thank our colleagues at Emerging Civil War, past and present. ECW has always been and remains a team effort. We've worked with some wonderful historians, writers, and "emerging voices" over the past decade, and we're proud to show off some of that work here.

Thanks, too, to Theodore Savas and his entire team at Savas Beatie, with a special thanks to our editorial liaison, Sarah Keeney, and production manager, Veronica Kane. Ted took a chance on ECW when we were still a young blog, accepting Kris White's pitch for the Emerging Civil War Series. That proved to be a game-changer for us. Together, ECW and Savas Beatie have produced some great work, and we're thankful to Ted for agreeing to help us celebrate ECW's tenth anniversary by allowing us to produce more great work. We thank everyone at Savas Beatie for all they do to support the work of Emerging Civil War.

Sarah Kay Bierle, as ECW's managing editor, manages the content on the blog on a daily basis. Her work made it a lot easier for us to collect the material we've assembled in this volume. Our official un-official archivist, Jon-Erik Gilot, has helped us make it easier to access our past work.

Cecily Nelson Zander, as our chief historian, provides overall quality control for our work. She joins a list of distinguished historians—Kristopher D. White, Christopher Kolakowski, and Dan Davis—who have served in that role. Our thanks to all of them over the years for ensuring a high bar for our writers in service to our readers.

Thanks to Patrick McCormick, who reviewed the text and made valuable suggestions and observations. And a big thank-you to Chris Heisey for always being willing to contribute *one more* photograph as the design of this book and this series, continued to evolve.

Finally, a special thanks to co-founders Chris Mackowski, Jake Struhelka, and Kristopher D. White, whose brainstorming over beers, cigars, and history led to ECW's creation. To quote Kris's wife, "Not too bad for three idiots sitting on a porch."

* * *

Sarah:

Sending thanks to Dan Davis, who taught me a lot about blog editing in my early days at ECW and who has remained a good friend and colleague through the years.

Much appreciation to the authors at Emerging Civil War who have kept content on the blog (who have "fed the beast," as we call it) for many years; it's a privilege to work with all of you!

Thank you to my parents, Shawn and Susan, for letting me follow my adventurous calling into the Eastern and Western Theaters of Civil War history. Finally, thank you to my brothers and sisters-in-law, Josiah & Lexis, Nathan & Katelyn, for always being just a phone call away and asking, "What are you writing now?"

Chris:

Being a guy from "the East," I am indebted to the many gracious and remarkable historians and preservationists who opened "the West" to me: Garry Adelman, Mike Bunn, Charlie Crawford, Dan Davis, Steve Davis, Jim Doncaster, Curt Fields, Rachel Finch, Will Greene, Todd Groce, Parker Hills, Eric Jacobson, Bob Jenkins, Gordon Jones, Jim Lewis, Jim Ogden, Dave Powell, Joe Ricci, Tim Smith, Greg Wade, Kris White, Lee White, Brian Wills, Terry Winschel, and Jim Woodrick. I've had wonderful battlefield adventures with all of them.

My thanks to my dean, Aaron Chimbel, for the support he constantly offers. I also thank the Jandoli School of Communication at St. Bonaventure University, as well as my colleagues in the university's Office of Marketing and Communications.

Finally, my thanks to my wife, Jenny Ann, and my children, Steph and her husband, Thomas (and my granddaughters, Sophie "the Pip," and Gracie); Jackson; and Maxwell James. Family is everything.

The Dead Angle at Kennesaw Mountain—which does not appear in this book. Tales from the Atlanta Campaign, the March to the Sea, and the Carolinas Campaign will appear in a planned future volume. *Chris Mackowski*

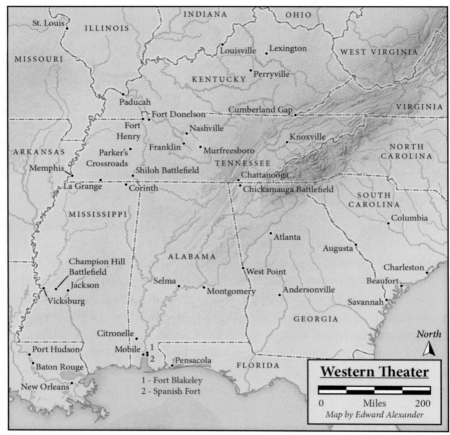

WESTERN THEATER—Space: the defining feature of the Western Theater. The vast geographic distances created a far different strategic and operational picture in the west than in the Eastern Theater. This map points out the locations of towns and sites mentioned by name in the stories collected for this volume. See Phill Greenwalt's final essay in the book for a rubber-meets-the-road exploration of this idea.

Foreword

by David A. Powell

Each of the American Civil War's three main theaters—East, West, and Trans-Mississippi—have a unique character. The Eastern Theater was the "Cockpit of War," a tightly confined space where the contending armies fought largely over the same Virginia terrain for four years. Even Confederate General Robert E. Lee's two northern forays to Antietam and Gettysburg traversed only small portions of Maryland and Pennsylvania in campaigns that ran for weeks, not months. Famously, the distance between the two opposing capitals was just one hundred miles. Within this space, both the Federals and Confederates raised very large armies. The Union routinely fielded forces topping 100,000 men, with many more tied up in support elements and garrison troops. And though Rebel numbers often fluctuated more dramatically, the Confederates did not lag far behind: during the Seven Days in 1862, Lee's force and supporting troops amounted to nearly 110,000 men, and at Fredericksburg, almost 90,000 troops filled his ranks. Had either side managed to achieve a truly decisive Napoleonic victory in Virginia that shattered the other's main force, the war might have ended quickly. Instead, stalemate resulted.

In the Trans-Mississippi, of course, the space was vast, but the troops far fewer. Texas alone encompassed nearly 270,000 square miles, making up more than one third of the whole Confederate land mass. But those states west of the Mississippi were also part of the expanding frontier, barely settled, lacking the infrastructure to support modern war on a large scale. Accordingly, an army of 20,000 men was a veritable horde. Battles were waged with brigades and divisions, or very rarely, corps. Nothing like a truly war-ending battle was possible, given those conditions.

Which left the Western Theater—which in the Civil War meant that territory between the Appalachians and the Mississippi, south of the Ohio River. This region was also vastly larger than the East but, having been settled a generation earlier than the frontier states, it possessed the infrastructure to support large armies. A network of navigable rivers supported an enormous traffic in vessels of all kinds: most famously the grand steamboats of Samuel Clemens's childhood, but also barges, rafts, and other transport. In the decade before war erupted, railroads expanded rapidly, supplementing but not yet replacing that riverine traffic. Thus, on both water and land, the steam engine revolutionized the transportation industry—and warfare itself.

The four Confederate states comprising this region—Georgia, Alabama, Mississippi, and Tennessee—were, along with Kentucky, critical agricultural and population centers vital to the Southern war effort. Both sides committed large numbers of troops to the theater, though given the space they needed to defend and control, those forces were always destined to be much more dispersed than in Virginia. Army strengths in the west rarely equaled their eastern counterparts, but they came close: field forces of 50,000 to 80,000 men were not uncommon, and large, bloody battles were frequent.

One argument holds that by depriving the Confederacy of these resources, the Federal government won the war in the West. Perhaps that is true; certainly, it is correct that the Armies of the Cumberland and the Tennessee achieved more measurable successes in 1862 and 1863 than did their eastern counterpart, the Army of the Potomac. By the end of 1863 virtually all of Tennessee as well as large swaths of Mississippi and Louisiana were in Federal hands, whereas in Virginia, the Rapidan and Rappahannock still defined the boundary between Lee and Meade. However, Lee's need to defend Virginia as well as his hard-hitting, offensive style of warfare required enormous resources in manpower, livestock, and materiel. If more of those resources, not to mention leadership, had been diverted to the west, would the outcome in that theater have been different? It is unreasonable to view the Western Theater in isolation, overlooking the sacrifices made in Virginia, Maryland, and Pennsylvania. The war was not won or lost by a single battle, or in a single theater.

Historiography has not been so balanced. For many years, the Eastern Theater dominated the thoughts of historians. Books and articles covering aspects of the war in Virginia far outnumber those documenting the western struggle. For example, while few of the men who commanded corps in the East on either side of the conflict lack modern full-length biographies, many, if not most, westerners do. Fortunately for our ongoing study of the war, that imbalance is changing, but there is still room for growth.

The following essays explore all facets of the war in the Western Theater, from Secession to surrender. Military, political, cultural, and socioeconomic aspects each get a nod. One important theme is the rise of western leaders, exemplified by Ulysses S. Grant, the last and by far most successful of a procession of Federal generals brought east to "win the war." Grant was the man who finally succeeded. Conversely, some name-brand easterners—James Longstreet and John Bell Hood, to name just two—discovered that waging war on the far side of the Appalachians was considerably more complicated than doing so in Virginia. Their reputations were diminished rather than enhanced as a result. It is no accident that perennial punching-bag Braxton Bragg appears more than once; Bragg had one of the longest tenures in command of any army of the war, leading the Army of Tennessee from June of 1862 until the beginning of December the following year—18 months, the second-longest tenure of any army commander on either side behind only Lee. As such, he is a central player in the western drama, for much of the Confederate west fell into Federal hands on Bragg's watch.

In keeping with that effort to expand our knowledge of the theater, the essays included here demonstrate the breadth and scope of Emerging Civil War's coverage. We at ECW hope that they shine additional light on the events described, inducing readers to take Horace Greeley's advice and "go west."

Above: The crossroads at Corinth *Chris Heisey*

xxvi-xxvii: Water Oaks Pond at Shiloh *Chris Heisey*

xxviii-xxix: Overlooking the Yazoo Bypass Canal and original bend of the Mississippi
River from the bluffs north of Vicksburg *Chris Heisey*

xxx-xxxxi: McGavock Cemetery at Franklin *Chris Heisey*

xxxii: State capitols in Montgomery, Alabama (top)
and Nashville, Tennessee (bottom) *Chris Heisey*

I. *Photographing the Western Theater*

by Chris Heisey

Given I live at the apex of the triangle of the great Eastern Theater battlefields of Manassas, Antietam, and Gettysburg, my 50 years of studying the Civil War always seems to favor these rich places where, historic lore has it, the war was won and lost. Truth be told, the Civil War was lost in the Western Theater, where the Confederacy could ill-afford to lose the vast core of territory. That region—consisting of the first states to choose to leave the Union early in 1861—was the heart of the South, where its most rabid Secessionists made their wealth.

While I still find true solace in photographing the heavily monumented hallowed grounds near our nation's capital, my most cherished memories and experiences, so seared into my photographic conscience, remain my excursions to battlefields deep in the heart of Dixie—battlefields like Shiloh, Stones River, Fort Donelson, Chickamauga, and the many parcels of Civil War battlefields that surround the megalopolis of Atlanta and southeast, where the tentacles of the Union armies crippled the Confederacy's belief that it could obtain a negotiated peace.

In Richard McMurray's thoroughly thought-provoking book *The Fourth Battle of Winchester: Toward a New Paradigm*, Dr. McMurry posits an entertaining counterfactual history to poke fun at how Civil War historians have been blatantly Eastern-centric in their answers to the great question: Why did the Confederacy lose the Civil War? Never of course did the fourth Battle of Winchester occur, and the mere title politely lampoons those who believe the war's outcome rested in the east.

"The western paradigm shows us at a glance the reason for Confederate defeat. The matter is brutally simple," McMurray points out. "The secessionists lost the war because they lost the key battles." More specifically, the Confederacy lost because it lost the key campaigns in the west: Shiloh, Perryville, Vicksburg, Chattanooga, and ultimately Atlanta. Gone were the resources of the southern frontier as the conquest by Union armies led to a military occupation that crippled the Confederacy's heartland. Wars are most commonly won by fighting—no matter the historical contortions to prove otherwise. The fight was lost, not won, out west.

That makes visiting our great Western Theater battlefields all the more enriching. Stand high atop the bluffs at Vicksburg as pummeling summer rains quell the boil of Deep South summer heat. It is easy to see that the Confederacy simply could not afford to lose the Mississippi River and still supply its armies and populace. Losing at Shiloh cost the Confederates any hope at holding Tennessee. The loss of Chattanooga ultimately gave Sherman's army the conduit to Atlanta, then Savannah, while spreading destruction along the way.

Shiloh remains my favorite battlefield because it just feels like 1862. Fog there dances as to remind one of the unseen spiritual world that flits about suddenly seen. At Shiloh, you can see it, and it's a memorable experience no matter the season. There is a quiet at Shiloh not matched at any other Civil War battlefield I have photographed. Yet, stand at the Hornet's Nest in the center of the battlefield on an early April pre-dawn, and it is quite easy to picture the guns booming and the bedlam of combat that many a soldier clad in blue and gray experienced as their first terror-filled hours of combat. That some 24,000 wounded and killed fell there sobers me. The mass burial trenches of Confederate dead that dot the hallowed landscape there in the nook of southwestern Tennessee is enough to give you the chills even on a very warm spring afternoon.

One of my favorite haunts is the old Sheldon Church near Beaufort, South Carolina. Resting neatly in the Spanish moss-draped live oaks of the southern coastal plains of the Palmetto State, this church—now in ruins—is a photographer's paradise. Shadow and light fight each other amidst the oaks. Stately columns and humble graves offer the camera ample, daylong opportunities to capture images that speak. Images that say something rather than just show something is my main pursuit, and it's a battle sometimes to accomplish the "saying" part. Photography looks easy until you do the

The ruins of Sheldon Church, Beaufort, South Carolina *Chris Heisey*

looking in the viewfinder. A respected photographer said to me a few years ago that it took 150 years of photography to produce a trillion images; now, almost a trillion are taken worldwide daily.

Burned by the British armies in 1779, then rebuilt only to be burned again by Sherman's hordes, this peaceful, divinely rich place is surrounded by old unmarked graves of long dead who have become sadly obscure to our collective American memory. Yet, the whispers of history still to be heard there in the beauty tell me this is where the Confederacy lost the war. No, there was no battle there, yet battles lost on far-off fields—where hard fighting, steep casualties, and the loss of huge tracts of the southern heartland—are why this church stands as a metaphor for why the Confederacy died in ruin.

So, too, did the British in the American Revolution envision a "southern strategy" meant to cripple the colonists' will to fight. Never, however, could the British win enough fights or inflict enough losses in the southern battles to destroy the militias and Continental fighters hell-bent on winning independence. Their burning of Sheldon Church was far different than Sherman's burning. The difference, it appears to me, was in the fight.

2. East vs. West

by Chris Kolakowski and Chris Mackowski

This is an edited transcript of an Emerging Civil War Podcast episode that dropped on August 3, 2018.

Chris M: Welcome to The Emerging Civil War Podcast. I'm Chris Mackowski.

Chris K: And I'm Chris Kolakowski. And today: "East versus West."

Chris M: Everyone seems to pay attention to the war in Virginia. . . .

Chris K: But outside the Old Dominion, a *whole* bunch of stuff happened, too.

Chris M: Where was the war really won? We'll explore that question today on The Emerging Civil War podcast.

*   *   *

Chris M: So, we're here to talk East versus West. And, first of all, I sort of had this set up as a binary, an either or. . . .

Chris K: Is it an "either/or"? I think it's both. It's not one or the other for me.

Chris M: Why is it both?

Chris K: From a political standpoint, the Eastern Theater is the most important. It's what everybody watches, and where the two capitals, Washington and Richmond, are. The two largest armies—the Army of the Potomac and the Army of Northern Virginia—are there, and it's a scene of some of the largest battles in American military history until the twentieth century. However, from a military standpoint, the West is far more important, in terms of resources, scale, and scope.

For example, the international aspect of blocking off Confederate port cities in the West, the taking of New Orleans, and the cutting of the Mississippi River—from a military standpoint, the argument can be made that the Confederacy loses the war in the West.

Chris M: Jim Ogden, the legendary historian at Chickamauga and Chattanooga National Military Park, really opened that idea up for me. He said, "This is where the war was really won." And that was a real gestalt shift for me to start thinking about it in those terms. I one hundred percent believe that's true, and Jim is right.

Chris K: Yeah, I think he's right. If you look at what the East does. . . . Let me put it to you this way: the Confederacy needs to win in the East to win the war. If you look at how the Confederacy can win the war, either through recognition from Britain and France, or from Northern political war weariness frustrating the reelection of Abraham Lincoln in 1864, from a political standpoint, what is the most important area for that? It's Virginia. The North can afford to not win, as long as they don't lose in the East.

Chris M: On a strategic level, they can't lose—because, of course, they rack up loss after loss.

Chris K: They rack up loss after loss, but they always win just enough that Lee is always looking for one more Second Manassas or one more Chancellorsville. He never quite finds it. Whereas in the West, first of all, the North wins most of the campaigns, which is essential to what they're trying to do. You can hold in the East and basically fight back and forth between Washington and Richmond, and it's a stalemate. However, win in the West and you win the war. If you're the Confederacy, you can win everything in the East and lose everything in the West, and you lose the war.

Chris M: Right. I think, just in terms of real estate, you've got that 120-mile stretch between D.C. and Richmond where much of the war shifts back and forth. However, out in the West, we're talking vast tracts of land. Whole states are won and lost, and just the amount of geography the armies have to cover out there is mind-boggling.

Chris K: Well, let me give you three examples, because that's one of the things about the West: the scope is much bigger and broader. Perryville, for example, in Kentucky was the battle for Kentucky. Whoever won that battle was basically going to get the state; they were battling for control of Kentucky.

Chris M: And as Kentucky goes, so goes the Union.

Chris K: Exactly. Then there's Middle Tennessee. Control of Middle Tennessee was contested at Stone's River. That was a third of Tennessee that was decided for Union control at the end of 1862 and the first few days of January 1863.

Finally, Chickamauga, Chattanooga, and Knoxville, they collectively pull East Tennessee into the Union, so the scope is immense.

The other thing about the West—and this is somewhat forgotten—is that you may have multiple armies maneuvering independently or maneuvering in a coordinated fashion, and they're a hundred to one hundred and fifty miles apart. But they're performing the same campaigns, they're supporting each other. For example, the Confederate Kentucky invasion where you have an army moving up from Knoxville and another one moving up from Chattanooga. The scope in the West is just fundamentally different than the East.

Chris M: I think about Grant's Overland Campaign, where he's going move his army across the Rapidan and pursue Lee. While he does that, he's going to send Butler up the James, and he's going to send Sigel down the Valley—but that sort of coordination's been going on in the West for quite some time.

Chris K: Right. That's a Western-style strategy. You're looking at the big picture. What Grant is doing is he's having come from the West where he fought in campaigns—Tennessee River campaigns, Mississippi River campaigns—where he'd learned to look at maneuvering multiple armies toward a common objective. He has to look at the whole state of Virginia as a theater, not just "the Army of the Potomac versus the Army of Northern Virginia" and everybody else as a bunch of bit players that we don't really need to worry about, which his predecessors in the East had done. Grant shows up and says, "We're going maneuver everybody together and put the pressure on and see what we can do."

Chris M: He has a tremendous learning curve that he has to come to that knowledge through. I mean, he's has to work with the navy out west; he needs work with the Army of the Ohio, and later, the Army of the Cumberland. It's not like he wakes up early in the war and says, "Hey, here's what we're going do." He must come to that realization.

Chris K: That's correct. Actually, I'm glad you brought the navy up. The other thing people forget is that Grant, when he comes across the Rapidan River into the Wilderness, takes up the bridge. He abandons his land communications from that direction, toward the Orange and Alexandria Railroad and through central Virginia. Instead, he realizes what an asset it is that the United States Navy controls the Chesapeake Bay and most Virginia rivers up to the navigable portions. There are exceptions, the James River being the most noted, as you approach Richmond. But he understands that "I don't need the railroad, I can use the navy and shift my supply base to the rivers as I maneuver closer to Richmond and, ultimately, City Point at Petersburg."

Chris M: Of course, when he does that, he does not get the same response George McClellan had in 1862 on the Peninsula, who was "shifting his base." He was essentially trying to do the same thing, using the Union control of the rivers to shift his base, but he took a lot of flak.

Chris K: Well, that's true. But the thing is that McClellan was also retreating to the base, not fighting the active, aggressive campaign that Grant is. Grant is hammering it home and not letting Lee have the initiative, whereas what you're talking about during the Seven Days campaign in June and early July of 1862, Lee has the initiative. Lee actually is forcing that change of base in some ways.

Chris M: Right, right.

Chris K: That's a huge difference. But there's no question McClellan is definitely helped by the fact that the navy controls the James and the York to that point. Otherwise, he'd have been in real trouble.

Chris M: One of the key insights I really find important, was that when the war broke out, and the Confederacy is assigning its generals, its senior-most guy, Samuel Cooper, stays in the War Department. The number-two guy, Albert Sidney Johnston, then gets sent West. So, if you think about it from a Confederate point of view, what did they see as the key area? They're sending their best guy west.

Chris K: Don't forget where Jeff Davis is from.

Chris M: Right.

Chris K: He's from Mississippi, and understands the breadth of that theater. Davis and his family had an estate near Vicksburg, a major Mississippi River port, for decades. He understands what's out there, and understands what needs to be done.

You can get a sense, if you study the West and the Confederate struggle for how to manage the war there, that's one of the things they're attempting. They're trying to conquer that space: "How can we shift our resources between middle Tennessee and Mississippi to both keep the river open and stop the Federals from advancing south from Nashville?" They never quite figure it out, but Jeff Davis continually drives those discussions because he understands—from having lived out there and having traveled back and forth to Washington, D.C. when he was a U.S. senator and a high official in various U.S. administrations—what needs to be done. He can feel it in his bones because he's experienced it.

Chris M: But Johnston thought it was completely indefensible. He had to spread his few available troops out over such a distance that he said they couldn't support each other.

Chris K: And that's the problem. Albert Sidney Johnston has too few forces, and too long a line. But the other problem is that he is forced by a variety of concerns, some political from President Davis himself, to adopt a positional defense as opposed to a more mobile defense. You see the Confederates try and do that later, where they have Bragg's army in Tennessee in 1863 and Pemberton's army at Vicksburg, and they try to shift reserves back and forth. The trouble is they never work out the timing.

However, in 1861, they're still trying to figure that out, and it's a positional defense where he's got armies in Western Kentucky and Western Tennessee, and the middle part of Kentucky and the middle part of Tennessee covering Nashville. But on the eastern part on that line at Mill Springs, Kentucky, Federals defeat one of those Confederate armies—they crack the defensive line—and the Confederates are pushed all the way back to Northern Mississippi.

Chris M: Johnston's finally able to consolidate in Corinth, Mississippi, and then he makes that push aggressively toward Shiloh.

Chris K: Right.

Chris M: But then he's over-aggressive on the battlefield. It leads to his death. But finally, he's got that consolidation he'd hoped for. Maybe he overplayed his hand. He's overconfident.

Chris K: I think that's absolutely right. Johnston's strategy of concentrating at Corinth, going to Shiloh, trying to defeat one of the two major Federal armies in West Tennessee—Buell's Army of the Ohio is coming, and, of course, Grant's army of the Tennessee is at Pittsburg Landing—is sound, very sound. Tactically, there's a lot of issues with the conduct of the battle. The biggest thing about Albert Sidney Johnston is he forgets what he's there for. He forgets that he's a strategic leader and becomes a tactical leader. Ultimately, it costs him his life.

I will say this in defense of General Johnston, and of all these early Civil War commanders: what is the largest army an American officer has commanded before 1861?

Chris M: As Winfield Scott is marching through Mexico?

Chris K: He has 15,000 in Mexico, but it's not that one. It's 17,000 in Yorktown. And that is the size of the army corps in the Civil War.

Chris M: Right, right.

Chris K: That's one of the points that needs to be remembered about all this: these guys are doing this—

Chris M: They're making it up as they go.

Chris K: They're making it up as they go. Albert Sidney Johnston, before 1862, or really, the latter part of 1861—his largest command was the Mormon Expedition. That was just a few thousand in 1858-1859. So, you go from that to commanding a large army at Shiloh, and you begin to realize that Johnston falls back on . . .

Chris M: . . . on what he knows.

Chris K: The old frontier-style, personal leadership. Get out there, leaving P. G. T. Beauregard to run headquarters but let me get out there and inspire the troops. That may work in a small expedition into Utah, but when you're commanding the second-largest Confederate Army, on the fields that you have to win, it's a different matter.

Chris M: Yeah.

Chris K: I give him something of a pass because, he's fighting on a scale that nobody's seen before.

Chris M: He has no playbook to fall back on.

Chris K: Exactly.

Chris M: I think of Irvin McDowell when he leads that army toward Manassas in July 1861. He immediately becomes the most experienced commander in the history of the United States Army.

Chris K: Just by marching out to Centerville.

Chris M: And he's like, "Oh, we're green." Of course, Lincoln famously says, "We're all green. Go on out there and do something." No playbook to fall back on whatsoever.

Chris K: Right. They've done this in Europe, which people have studied. Of course, famously, George McClellan had been part of the observer team to the Crimean War in the 1850s. But it's one thing to observe; it's another thing to do.

Chris M: You touched on a point a second ago that I want to come back to because, again, when we think of East–West, certainly in the East, we think of the Army of the Potomac. In the West, though, there are two major armies and several smaller armies.

Chris K: Correct.

Chris M: We sort of lump it together as "the West." But the armies out there have very different characteristics and objectives.

Chris K: That's absolutely right. Actually, I would include the Trans-Mississippi in this.

Chris M: Yeah, we haven't even really touched that. "Trans-Mississippi? What's that?" But that's another, even larger expanse of land.

Chris K: Exactly. In the West between the Mississippi River and the Appalachian Mountains, you have three major Federal armies. Particularly in 1863, you have the Army of the Cumberland in the center advancing from Louisville through Nashville to Chattanooga. The Army of the Cumberland was originally known as the Army of the Ohio, and it's renamed; there's also an army in Eastern Kentucky that advances into East Tennessee that's later known as the Army of the Ohio. Then, of course, you have Grant's Army of the Tennessee, going from Donelson, Shiloh, Memphis, and down the Mississippi River to Vicksburg.

Let's not forget we have the Department of the Gulf, the guys coming up from New Orleans, and Nathaniel Banks takes Port Hudson just a few days after Vicksburg falls. So, actually, that's four.

Four Federal armies right there. If you add the fifth, Samuel Curtis's guys out in—at this point—Northern Arkansas advancing down from Missouri. That's five.

Chris M: I suppose, in the East, we can start talking about the Army of Virginia, you know, Pope's force. We talk about the different forces in and out of the Valley under various commands and names, and eventually Butler's Army of the James. We have other forces out there, too, but everyone seems to fall back on the Army of the Potomac. A fantastic army. What do you like about that army?

Chris K: The Army of the Potomac is a fine group of fighting men, and they fight very well. They are tenacious, which they prove on many battlefields. Leadership is somewhat erratic until later in the war.

I actually think, in some ways, the Army of the Potomac's finest campaign, which proves what that army is truly capable of doing, is the drive to Appomattox and running down the Army of Northern Virginia in the last eight days of the war. I think the way they're able to move and engage, and the leaders that have come up through the crucible of fire in the last three, four years—it's an army at the peak of its powers.

Chris M: That's a very different Army of the Potomac than the one that Grant inherits in early 1864. When Grant first gets there, the army is big and cumbersome and doesn't move like his lean, mean fast-moving westerners.

Chris K: Correct. By the way, his army at Vicksburg was forty percent the size of the Army of the Potomac. When they come to Chattanooga, they're 24,000, which is smaller than the Army of the Potomac's II Corps. The Army of the Cumberland at Chattanooga—George Thomas's force—is 56,000 strong. That's what—half the size of the Army of the Potomac?

So, when Grant gets to the Army of the Potomac, it is maneuvering in a way he hasn't seen before.

Chris M: So, I think by the time of the Appomattox Campaign, they're finally behaving in a way that he's used to—but look how long it took him to get them to that point.

Chris K: That's true. I think part of it, too, is the troops, because remember, one of the salient characteristics of the Federal armies in early 1864. When did most of those guys sign up? How long did they sign up for? They signed up in the spring and summer of 1861 for three years or the war, whichever comes first. You've got about a third of that army that chooses not to take the re-enlistment bounty. They have "short-timer's disease"—there's no other way to say it.

That impacts the combat power of that army. Plus, the repeated battlefield losses as the campaign continues. I mean, they get the job done, but that sword gets duller the more Grant hacks at Lee's army.

Chris M: He also has to cycle through several corps and division commanders to finally get some of the right guys in the right places, too.

Chris K: That's the thing: that leadership flux is tough. Once you get down to it, it's the instability in that army and in the leadership at those key levels. But once you get to Petersburg, the organizational waters are smooth out a little bit.

You've got people that have survived the crucible like Nelson Miles, who comes down and becomes an absolutely outstanding commander at Petersburg and Appomattox—and goes on to become the General in Chief of the U. S. Army during the Spanish-American War.

You get guys like that that have risen up, and they're able to learn their craft at Petersburg and become more proficient, so by the time that they leave the Petersburg trenches, that army, you're right, is a whole new fighting machine than it was even a year earlier.

Chris M: In the meantime, as Grant's affecting that transformation in the East, out West, Sherman is doing some very innovative things as he's moving through Georgia. Again, much smaller armies, but the organization is much different than what we've seen before.

Chris K: It is. Multiple independent armies in a campaign or a field of battle, which, before Sherman leaves Chattanooga, only two other Americans had ever done: Grant at Chattanooga and Lee at the Seven Days in front of Richmond. So, what you've got is three independent armies: McPherson's Army of the Tennessee, Thomas's Army of the Cumberland, and John Schofield's Army of the Ohio. How do you maneuver those? How do you work those?

It's an interesting contrast where you look at how Sherman uses his two smaller armies, Ohio and Tennessee, to move and lure, and then the hammer blows come from the big Army of the Cumberland, which is over half of his army. But the way he maneuvers and uses the roads in north Georgia is a interesting study.

Chris M: Pretty innovative and amazing stuff.

Chris K: Very much.

Chris M: It's funny, because, you know, we set this up as East versus West. I think we're talking as much "early" versus "late" war as we are East versus West as we talk about this evolution. Let me go back to East versus West for a second. Why do you think people tend to focus more on the East today?

Chris K: That is a complicated question, and I think it has two parts. I'll simplify my answer because we only have a limited amount of time. First of all, is Lost Cause mythology. The Lost Cause focused the war on the Army of Northern Virginia.

The other thing is that—particularly from a Confederate perspective—those guys in the West just are not that good. I mean, Braxton Bragg, Leonidas Polk . . . the infighting in the high command of the Army of Tennessee and the wasted valor of the Army of the Tennessee—that makes those guys in the Army of the Potomac look like they were holding hands all the time and singing "Kumbaya."

But even in the West, it's a different style, it's a different type of officer. You've got troops that have a different literacy and education level—generally, not all. You've got a significant number of West Pointers out in both armies, but you've got far smaller percentages in both western armies than you do in the East. Richard McMurray wrote a great book years ago, *Two Great Rebel Armies*, where he compared and contrasted the Army of Northern Virginia and the Army of Tennessee. One of the things he talked about is the Army of Northern Virginia—between VMI, The Citadel and West Point—I think it was two-thirds of the officer corps had some professional military education. In the West, it was twenty-four percent. That alone makes a huge difference.

Chris M: The Army of the Tennessee, a great army, just had terrible leadership. I feel bad for those guys who did some tough fighting.

Chris K: They do.

Chris M: Yet, just never have the leadership to really push them over the finish line.

Chris K: That's exactly right. If you look at the battles between the Army of the Tennessee and the Army of the Cumberland, all through the war—basically from Perryville to Franklin—Confederates repeatedly pushed that Federal Army to the brink of destruction more than once. But because of mismanagement on the senior leadership side, Confederates are never quite able to finish the job. In some ways, that's actually something that the Army of Northern Virginia, for all of its dramatic battles against Union forces in the East, never quite gets. The closest near-death experience for the Army of the Potomac is July 2, 1863.

Chris M: Yeah.

Chris K: But the Army of the Cumberland has Perryville, which is really a third of the army, but the entire army faces it at Stones River. The entire army faces it again at Chickamauga. The entire army faces it once more during the battles for Atlanta. The Army of the Tennessee, as well, almost gets pushed to the brink on the 22nd of July 1864.

So, there's something there. Those guys were tough. But, again, the leadership threw a lot of it away.

Chris M: You mention the literacy level of the armies in the East versus in the West. That ties back to one of the reasons you think the East receives more primacy when we think of the Civil War.

Chris K: Writings. Those guys in the East wrote. They were very educated, and they were close to the northern media centers. We have photographs. You just don't have the photographs, contemporary photographs, in the West like you do in the East. You have some, but it's not like a couple of days after the battle there are photographers going out like they do at Antietam, Gettysburg, or places like that. You don't necessarily have a sketch artist like Alfred Waud there. Again, closeness to the northern media centers.

Chris M: I think that that has been an important carry-over because media centers also tie into population centers. So, after the war, you've got these huge population centers and veterans coming from Philadelphia, New

York, and Baltimore, and they're able to get to these eastern battlefields a lot easier than folks can get to western battlefields.

That tradition carries on and carries on and carries on. It's much easier for people in these eastern population centers to get to the eastern battlefields.

Chris K: That's correct. I agree with that. I absolutely do.

Chris M: But there's so much to explore out West.

Chris K: Absolutely. Traveling through the West provides an interesting perspective. I've always told people: If you study only one of the two theaters, it's like being a baseball fan of the American League, not the National League. You need to know what's going on with both, because then you see the whole picture. It'd be like World War II, where you just study Europe, and you forget that there's a whole war out in the Pacific, or vice versa. Because they interacted with each other, they acted upon each other, and if you don't give that due consideration, some of the things, some leadership decisions, some perspectives that these people have, you just miss. To round out your perspective of the Civil War, you need to look at East and West.

Chris M: Of course, I'm sure there are people out there saying, "What about the Trans-Mississippi?" Which also plays into it.

Chris K: That's a whole other podcast for another time.

Chris M: Thank you for joining us for The Emerging Civil War Podcast. We'll see you online—and on the battlefield.

1. On the Eve of War: Charleston, South Carolina

by Sarah Kay Bierle

Originally published as a blog post at Emerging Civil War
on April 11, 2021

The sound of cannon was not new in April 1861 in Charleston, South Carolina. A few months earlier, on November 10, a celebration cannon was fired after locals heard that the state's legislature planned to convene a secession convention.

Secession was not a new concept in November 1860. John C. Calhoun had ensured that for decades prior as he argued on the national political scene for nullification, state's rights, and slavery as a necessary evil. Though Calhoun died in 1850, his ideas influenced and shaped the next generation of South Carolina politicians and the majority of the state's political thoughts. Many citizens openly showed their support of secession in the final weeks of 1860 by flying homemade flags with symbolism like "don't tread on me" snakes or Palmetto trees. The U.S. flag started disappearing from streets, balconies, and boats.

Major Robert Anderson's arrival in Charleston on November 23, 1860, brought additional changes. He discovered the Federal garrison at Fort Moultrie had allowed citizens to visit whenever they wanted, and cows grazed on the fort's parapet. Sensing the city's mood, Anderson did not

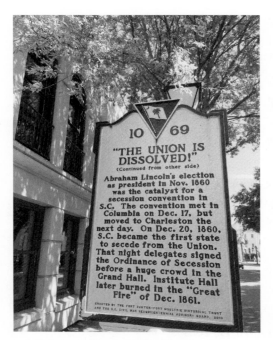

think such loose regulations were appropriate, especially since he had only 81 men and officers at that time and 50 guns total at the fort. Assessing the situation and consulting with other officers, Anderson decided that Fort Sumter was a key position, and considered abandoning the shore fortifications.

Meanwhile, the South Carolina secession convention moved from Columbia to Charleston, attempting to avoid a smallpox outbreak. This pulled more secession sentiment, almost all the state politicians, and national spotlight on the coastal city.

A historic marker on Meeting Street in Charleston indicates the one-time location of Institute Hall, where delegates voted to secede. *Chris Mackowski*

On December 20, 1860, the secession convention met at St. Andrews Hall, voting unanimously to leave the Union. Charleston crowds cheered when they heard the news. Local businesses closed to celebrate, and celebratory cannons were fired. The *Charleston Mercury* newspaper threw broadsheets out their office windows, announcing, "The Union is Dissolved!" That evening, the South Carolina legislature and governor declared their state an independent republic.

Celebrations lasted for days while state and national politicians discussed what to do next. One of the first steps involved transferring Federal property to the "new independent republic." Major Anderson's removal of his garrison from Fort Moultrie to Fort Sumter altered some of the circumstances and discussions.[1]

The situation escalated during early winter, but President Buchanan told Anderson not to risk lives defending Fort Sumter, despite its strategic

---

1   James B. McPherson, *Battle Cry of Freedom*, (Oxford: Oxford University Press, 1988), 264-265.

position for harbor control. Buchanan sent the message down the chain of command, saying, "It is neither expected nor desired that you should expose your own life, or that of your men, in a hopeless conflict in defense of the forts . . . it will be your duty to yield to necessity and make the best terms in your power."

As Anderson contemplated moving his garrison to Fort Sumter and started repairs on that fortification, the South Carolinians built batteries around the harbor. They patrolled the harbor, trying to prevent a Federal movement. It did not work. On December 26, 1860, the garrison moved in the darkness from Fort Moultrie to Fort Sumter.

President Buchanan heard from South Carolina Governor Pickens on January 31, 1861, demanding Fort Sumter's surrender. It started weeks of messages across the harbor with consistent refusals from Major Anderson, and a failed resupply effort. The situation in the harbor stalemated, but communications remained open. Recruits flocked to Charleston, ready for war and anxious to defend the newly formed Confederacy.

By the beginning of April 1861, Charlestonians knew a fleet of ships had been dispatched to resupply Fort Sumter. The first ship was sighted on the evening of April 11th. A delegation rowed to Fort Sumter, demanding surrender. Anderson refused, knowing that he would be attacked.

"Things are happening so fast," wrote diarist Mary Chesnut on April 11, 1861.[2] Perhaps that simple statement reflects much of Charleston's military and political experience on the eve of war, in the final hours before the first shots were fired at Fort Sumter.

---

2 Mary Chesnut, edited by C. Vann Woodward, *Mary Chesnut's Civil War* (New Haven: Yale University Press, 1981).

The Bullard Boys: Tragedy for a Mississippi Family

by Sheritta Bitikofer

Originally published as a blog post at Emerging Civil War on May 26, 2022

A close examination of a single family during the war can reveal information about the struggles and hardships of the average soldier and civilian. One family received a letter from a new volunteer in the 10th Mississippi Infantry. On the cusp of conflict between the newly formed Confederacy and the Union, that soldier wrote from inside Fort McRee, outside Pensacola on April 10, 1861.

> My Dear Ann I write to you again tonight we are well (Arthur Newton & me) Arthur is on guard on the wall of the Fort. I think he is doing well he seems to be satisfied & his health is as good as it has ever been. I had gone to bed & received an order from General Bragg to have the roll called & require each officer & soldier to be present & to caution them to be on the alert as an engagement is daily expected. It has been raining hard to night and the wind is high. The waves of the Gulf lash and foam against the sides of our fort. There is four or five war ships in sight but there are strong men & I think brave hearts in this Fort men that will do their duty under any circumstances. Let me tell you when I look on these warlike preparations (as I do every day and think of my own friends at home and fret of all and above

all my own dear wife and children and feeling that my cause is just my heart [grows] firm almost bold & I feel determined by the grace of god to do my whole duty, have my rights & secure the freedom of my country at whatever cost it maybe.

Our post is one of honor & will be defended bravely. I greatly desire that you keep cheerful and as contended as possible and let me caution you to [take] special care of yourself. Preserve your health and do the best you can every way and remember while I am away from you that you are constantly in my thoughts—no one shall ever say your husband was a coward and I know you had rather I should serve my country.

I have written to you almost every day but have never heard a word from home. Do write & write often give my warmest love to all the children. Kiss Bird Clay for me, tell Benny to be a good boy and take care of Ma till Pa comes home. Tell Perry & Jimmy and Gus to be the best sort of boys & show themselves men.

To Ann Bullard
Your husband till death
James G. Bullard

PS It is nearly eleven o'clock my soldiers are asleep around me. Goodnight"[1]

Captain James G. Bullard, 43, of Company B, 10th Mississippi Infantry, left behind his wife of twenty years, Annis, called Ann, and their five children in Itawamba, Mississippi. He enlisted on February 4, 1861, along with his eldest son, Arthur. They enlisted for twelve months, beginning in March. His company, nicknamed the Ben Bullard Rifles, joined the regiment out of Jackson, Mississippi, in early April, and were assigned to Fort McRee. In the early days of separation, the cause of fighting for "hearth and home" was clear in James's mind as he penned this letter, one of many. According to the 1860 census, the younger Bullard children attended school, and the

1 University of West Florida Historic Trust Archives, Pensacola, FL, Collection #1975.0130.0001.

second eldest son, Lafayette, worked the farm with his father and older brother. One must wonder if, at 17, Lafayette envied the older men of his family as they went off to war, or if he felt obligated to be "the man of the house" for his mother and siblings. The family had suffered the loss of two children, William and Mary Ann, two years before secession, and the death of another, Sarah, in 1847. The fragility of life might have been on James's mind on that stormy night outside Pensacola.[2]

The Florida fortification had been occupied since January 1861, gradually building up its armaments. Though Confederate Gen. Braxton Bragg warned those at Fort McRee to be ready for a fight, the war began far away in Charleston. While Arthur was discharged on April 18, James remained at the fort to see its first bit of action.[3]

A 10th Mississippi detachment fought at the Santa Rosa Island battle that October, though it is unknown if James or his company participated. However, he certainly witnessed the bombardment on November 22 as Fort Pickens, USS *Niagara*, and USS *Richmond* unleashed heavy artillery upon the Confederate fortifications. The Confederates within Fort McRee sustained extensive damage, engaging for only five hours before their guns fell silent under the bombardment's pressure.

The 10th Mississippi evacuated Fort McRee in February 1862, while the rest of the Confederate forces would remain in the fort until May. They reorganized its companies into a "new" 10th Mississippi under Col. Robert A. Smith within Brig. Gen. James Chalmers's Mississippi Brigade, nicknamed the "High Pressure Brigade." In Corinth, Mississippi, Company B became Company C by the same name, Ben Bullard Rifles, and James reenlisted for another two years beginning March 15. His son, Arthur, also rejoined the regiment on March 27, 1862. The Bullard family was once again parted with those they loved, waiting in anticipation for their return.

2 1860 census: 1860 U.S. census, population schedule. NARA microfilm publication M653, 1,438 rolls. Washington, D.C.: National Archives and Records Administration, n.d.; Compiled service record, James Bullard, Captain, Company B, 10th Mississippi Infantry; Carded Records Showing Military Service of Soldiers Who Fought in Confederate Organizations, 1903–1927, M269, record group 109; National Archives, Washington, D.C., roll 0184.

3 Compiled service record, Arthur Bullard, Private, Company B, 10th Mississippi, Carded Records Showing Military Service of Soldiers Who Fought in Confederate Organizations, 1903–1927, M269, record group 109; National Archives, Washington, D.C., roll 0184.

The 360 men of the 10th Mississippi fought at the battle of Shiloh, April 6-7, 1862, positioned on the far right of the Confederate line.[4] Chalmer's Mississippi Brigade enjoyed fleeting success on the first day of battle but retreated with the rest of the army on April 7. The brigade suffered 446 casualties out of 1,739 engaged.

For James Bullard, however, the greatest loss came on April 26 when his son, Arthur, died of disease in Baldwin, Mississippi. He was 19. It is possible James stayed by his son's bedside through his illness, suffering immense anguish as he wrote his wife, telling her of their eldest son's passing. The grief of losing a son and brother in the war was all too familiar by 1862, but that did not diminish the Bullard's bereavement.

Before long Ann, Lafayette, and the rest of the clan heard additional terrible news. The 10th Mississippi entered its next engagement in September 1862 at Munfordville, Kentucky. Part of Bragg's Army of Mississippi, Chalmers marched his men from Cave City, Kentucky, to Munfordville, a station on the Louisville & Nashville Railroad near a railroad bridge that crossed the Green River. The station was garrisoned by Union Col. John Wilder and his three regiments, totaling over 4,000 troops. Unaware he was outnumbered and believing false information that the garrison was not well supplied or manned, Chalmers demanded the station's surrender. When Wilder refused, Chalmers launched unauthorized frontal assaults on September 14. The 10th Mississippi was situated on the left of the first charge. James Bullard, promoted to lieutenant colonel the previous June, was one of 288 casualties that morning. There would be no more letters home to his wife and children.

Bragg continued Chalmer's attempt to take Munfordville, and on September 16, accepted Wilder's surrender of the fort and its provisions. The Confederate victory had little impact on the overall campaign, but the Bullard patriarch's loss would have devastated the family. Ann lost her husband and provider, and the children lost a father that cherished them—evidenced in his 1861 letter. Within one year, the Bullard's lost two men in service to the Confederate Army, but that was not the end of the Bullard's tragedies.

---

4 For a more in-depth read about the performance of Chalmer's Brigade with the 10th Mississippi, see this article by Dr. Timothy Smith (https://www.historynet.com/chalmers-mississippians-shiloh/).

Whether out of retribution or duty, the eldest surviving son, Lafayette, enlisted in Company G of the 10th Mississippi in March 1863. He was in the same regiment in which his father and brother died. Did Ann beg him not to enlist? Did she predict more loss and heartache if her son followed in her husband's footsteps? If she did, it didn't matter. Lafayette went to war. He was wounded at Chickamauga while under the division command of Maj. Gen. Thomas Hindman, participating in the assault on September 20, 1863. He became one of over 18,000 Confederate casualties during the battle, but that one wounded soldier meant everything to the family who waited for him.

Lafayette survived, but was captured at the battle of Franklin in Tennessee in November 1864. He was sent to Camp Douglas in Chicago. The camp, like many POW prisons, was made infamous for its poor sanitation, rampant illness, and crowded conditions, resulting in the deaths of one in seven soldiers. If word got back to his family, it is likely they worried about his safety within the prison. They had every reason to be concerned. He arrived on December 6, 1864 but died of the measles on January 25, 1865. He was imprisoned for 50 days. According to records, he was buried in Block 2 of the city cemetery, grave 572. His name is memorialized on a 30-foot granite monument, along with the 4,000 prisoners who were reinterred in a mass grave at Confederate Mound Oak Woods Cemetery.[5]

Three Bullard men were lost to the war, never returning to the family and state for whom they fought. Only three of Ann's children lived to see the twentieth century. She passed on March 24, 1881, having never remarried. Ann, Fred "Bird Clay," Daniel, and Bennet are all buried in the New Salem Cemetery in Troy, Mississippi.

Their story is not so different from other families that sacrificed sons, brothers, and fathers to the Confederacy. However, the nature of their deaths and service records covers a variety of wartime experiences. The collective experiences of the three include: served at a fort, suffered illness, participated in both successful and futile charges at the order of their superiors, was wounded, captured, and imprisoned. Their stories embody not just events of the war, but the tragedies that could befall a single family.

---

5 Compiled service record, Lafayette Bullard, Private, Company G, 10th Mississippi, Carded Records Showing Military Service of Soldiers Who Fought in Confederate Organizations, 1903–1927, M269, record group 109; National Archives, Washington, D.C., roll 0184; PVT Lafayette Gibson "L.G." Bullard, Find-A-Grave, https://www.findagrave.com/memorial/37530768/lafayette-gibson-bullard.

1. The Fall of Fort Henry and the Changing of Confederate Strategy

by Kevin P. Pawlak

Originally published as a blog post at Emerging Civil War on August 29, 2019

Fort Donelson has "Unconditional Surrender" Grant. It has an early morning Confederate attack, a breakout by Nathan Bedford Forrest, and the stuff that makes good history. However, from this outsider's perspective on the Western Theater, I believe (and have for some time) that Fort Henry, in the grand scheme of things, gets the proverbial short end of the stick.

No, it does not last as long as the operations at Fort Donelson. It does not have the casualties that Donelson witnesses. It does, however, have an impact on Confederate strategy. The Confederacy repeatedly fell back on that strategy throughout the war.

At the war's onset, Commander in Chief of the Confederate States of America, Jefferson Davis, and his subordinates settled on defending all borders of the fledgling nation, encompassing 750,000 square miles of territory. Historian James McPherson calls this the "dispersed defense."[1] Early

1 James M. McPherson, *Embattled Rebel: Jefferson Davis and the Confederate Civil War* (New York: Penguin Books, 2014), 30-31.

in the war, this strategy won political points for Davis and his administration by protecting many points on the periphery of the Confederacy. However, it also made things difficult for the Southern commanders, who vainly attempted to hold vast swaths of land with minimal manpower. Fort Henry's fall on February 6, 1862, changed everything.

The capture of Fort Henry by Union forces opened much of the Tennessee River and its banks to Northern soldiers. Demonstrating the river's dagger-like course through the heart of western Tennessee, a cadre of Federal gunboats proceeded along the river in the wake of Fort Henry's fall into northern Mississippi and Alabama. While the raid failed to destroy several larger objectives, it proved the Northern hypothesis that the Confederacy was a hollow shell—crack its outer layer, and nothing lay in the interior to stop Federal advances.

On February 8, Jefferson Davis began veering the Confederacy away from its dispersed defense. Davis could no longer cave to political pressures while Union forces carved up the Confederacy's boundary. Accordingly, he ordered Southern soldiers to make their way to Tennessee. Mansfield Lovell's soldiers began their trek from New Orleans while Braxton Bragg left Pensacola en route for the Volunteer State. Confederate gunboats protecting New Orleans sailed up the Mississippi River, exposing the Crescent City to Union hands.

While stripping the Confederacy of its exterior defenses, forces began to concentrate in northern Mississippi, poised to strike back at the Federal thrust through western Tennessee. It was a new take on Southern strategy, gathering forces at select points to attack the enemy when advantage seemed in the Rebels' favor. The Confederacy altered its strategy to the offensive-defensive to preserve, as best as it could, the exterior of its hollow shell. This strategy first manifested at Shiloh in early April 1862 and later at places like Antietam, Perryville, and Gettysburg.

One small fort on the Tennessee River and its capture by the forces of Ulysses S. Grant and Andrew Foote in February 1862 changed the Civil War's shape, but not the course, for the next three years.

George Washington Rains, the Augusta Powder Works, and Forts Henry and Donelson: How Union Riverine Warfare Almost Ended the Civil War in 1862

by Theodore P. Savas

George Washington Rains ranks in the top tier of personalities regarding importance and impact on the outcome of the Civil War. Yet only a slim handful of the war's students can articulate anything of consequence about him. His grueling and stressful career may have included logging more railroad miles than anyone in the entire Confederacy. Everything he worked for was nearly derailed early in the war by a series of naval-related events, including the fall of Forts Henry and Donelson in February 1862.

It is impossible to fully appreciate this essay, unless you understand who this man was, and the crucial nature of the mission with which he was tasked.

*   *   *

Rains was born in 1817 in New Bern, North Carolina, the son of Manigault and Ester Rains and brother of future Civil War general Gabriel, better known as the inventor of a land mine and waterborne torpedo used extensively during the war. After an excellent early education George attended West Point. He graduated 3rd in 1842, a stellar class that included such notables as James Longstreet and William S. Rosecrans.[1]

Straight-up engineering bored Rains, who asked for a voluntary demotion to the artillery branch. After a stint at Fort Monroe, he landed a position at West Point to teach chemistry and other scientific courses. Rains chafed at the bit to participate in the Mexican War, and the strings he pulled put him in charge of the supply depot at Point Isabel, Texas. Unsatisfied, he used his friendship with General Winfield Scott to gain a frontline position as a staff officer for General Gideon Pillow. After exchanging Mexican prisoners of war in Vera Cruz (where he spied for Scott and provided him plans of the enemy defenses), Rains saw heavy action that included the siege of Vera Cruz and the battles up to and through the combats around Mexico City, where he was wounded and decorated for gallant service.[2]

Nearly a decade of peacetime garrison drudgery followed the end of the war. In 1856, however, Rains found the perfect solution to the bureaucratic fatigue from which he was suffering by resigning from the service to marry into the Ramsdell family, one of richest in all of New York. Within weeks he was managing a large iron works in Newburgh along the Hudson River. He would remain there for five years. During that span he gained immense practical experience scheduling major projects, handling complex production issues, juggling difficult logistical and transportation matters, and managing employees. He would soon put this practical knowledge to use in a way he could have never foreseen.

---

1 Letter, George W. Rains to Lewis Cass, May 6, 1833, Adjutant and Inspector General's Office, Letters Received, National Archives Microfilm Publication M688, roll 90, Records of the Adjutant General's Office, 1780's–1917, Record Group 94, National Archives and Records Administration, Washington, D.C., hereinafter GWR, Letters, NA. Virtually every source on Rains, including his gravestone, records his birth date as simply "1817." His 1833 letter to Secretary of War Lewis Cass in support of his application to West Point, ibid., is the earliest and one of the few sources to provide his exact date of birth. *Register of the Officers and Cadets of the U.S. Military Academy*, 7.

2 George Washington Rains, Mexican War Journal (partial), 1, Rains Papers, Special Collections, United States Military Academy Library at West Point; See also, *Annual Reunion / Association of the Graduates of the United States Military Academy, June 17, 1871* (West Point, N.Y.: Association of Graduates, U.S.M.A., 1898), 72.

George Washington Rains in a Confederate coat, likely photographed just after the war. *Author's collection*

When his home state of North Carolina seceded, Rains—with a heavy heart and at tremendous emotional and financial cost—bid his Northern family goodbye in June 1861 and headed south.[3]

*   *   *

The Confederacy entered the conflict without a single factory within its borders capable of manufacturing military-grade gunpowder at scale—a fact that surprised even the Confederate Congress. The amount captured in the fallen forts and arsenals, together with the poundage imported from the North or from abroad, would not last long. Hoping for a short war was not a promising strategy. It was President Jefferson Davis's idea to forgo the fickle nature of importation and erect a massive, centralized government mill to supply nearly all of the South's needs. But who had the talent stack to build and operate something like that from the ground up? The answer materialized in Richmond on July 8 with the appearance of George Rains.[4]

3 *Washington Evening Star*, Oct. 6 and 11, 1856; George W. Cullum, *Biographical Register of the Officers and Graduates of the United States Military Academy*, 2 vols. (Boston, MA: Houghton Mifflin Co., 1891), vol. 2, 113; Rains, *Reunion*, 73, 74; *Albany Evening Star*, undated.

4 George Washington Rains, *History of the Confederate Powder Works* (Augusta, Ga.: Chronicle and Constitutionalist Print, 1882), 4; George W. Rains, "Memorandum Relative to the Establishment of a Gunpowder Works at Augusta and the Matter of Material Under Charge of Colonel George Rains, Corps of Artillery on Ordnance Duty in the Year 1861, 1862, 1863, 1864," 2, George W. Rains File, Theodore P. Savas Papers, El Dorado Hills, CA, 2; Josiah Gorgas, "Notes on the Ordnance Department of the Confederate Government," *Southern Historical Society Papers*, 52 vols. (Richmond, 1876-1959), vol. 12, 70; Jefferson Davis, *The Rise and Fall of the Confederate Government*, 2 vols. (New York, NY, 1881), vol. 1, 475. The president played an active role in the conversation with Rains and told him there were "no powder mills except an old one near Nashville and a small affair near Walhalla, South Carolina, neither of which were making powder."

Within 24 hours of his arrival in the new Confederate capital, Rains was in the Spotswood Hotel for a private face-to-face meeting with President Jefferson Davis and the new chief of ordnance, Josiah Gorgas. It was one of the war's most important conclaves, and it would change the course of the conflict. By the time they shook hands and parted a few hours later, Rains had been assigned with what he later described as the "honor of being appointed to take charge of the manufactory of gunpowder." He left the meeting as impressed with Davis and his knowledge of what was required to do the job right, as the chief executive was with him. "No one was so well aware [of the situation] as the President of the Confederate States," the new major later declared, "who, being an educated soldier, was fully alive to the requirements of war, and at once took active measures for the creation of war materiel. Among these, was the erection of a great gunpowder manufactory."[5]

"The necessary works," Rains explained years later to the Confederate Survivors Association in 1882, "were to be erected as nearly central as practical; to be permanent structures, and of sufficient magnitude to supply the armies in the field and the artillery of the forts and defences." Rains was no neophyte when it came to war or industry, so he fully understood the weight of what had just been placed on his shoulders. "Any failure in . . . construction and products would have rested with myself," he acknowledged. "A *carte blanche* had been given," meaning he had complete freedom to act as he wished or thought best. The price tag that came with it was steep, for "there was no one to share the appalling responsibility" should it all go sideways.[6]

Major Rains would eventually settle on Augusta, Georgia, as the home of the mammoth undertaking. By April of 1862, when it first began production, the extraordinary complex would stretch some two miles on either side of the Augusta canal. One of the reasons he selected Augusta was because it was deep inside the Confederacy and safe from the threat of marauding enemy armies and cavalry raids. And it had to be, because the giant mill was intended to serve as the primary source for Confederate powder east of the Mississippi River. The proximity of the Savannah River to his main buildings bothered Rains not at all because Fort Pulaski and other batteries

---

5 Rains, *History of the Confederate Powder Works*, 3.

6 George W. Rains, "Memorandum Relative to the Establishment of a Gunpowder Works at Augusta," 1; Rains, *History of the Confederate Powder Works*, 3.

The Augusta Powder Works was a sprawling complex that faced a daunting task. *Author's collection*

protected the mouth of the waterway around the city of Savannah. Brigadier General Ulysses S. Grant flipped this script at Forts Henry and Donelson.[7]

Nashville, in north-central Tennessee, was the South's primary munitions center in the Western Theater for much of the war's first year. When Rains wasn't overseeing construction efforts in Augusta or riding the rails to examine various arsenals and machine shops, he was usually working in or around Nashville. The munitions hub there began under the watchful eye of Governor Isham Harris and his Tennessee Military and Financial Board, which contracted with various individuals and small factories to supply the growing needs of the state before Rains arrived to take control and nationalize the effort.

Two of the most important Nashville-area facilities were the Sycamore powder mill (about 23 miles northwest of the city), and the Manchester powder mill (some 65 miles southeast in Coffee County). The former was an old facility that produced a small amount of blasting and pistol powder. Unfortunately, production amounts and quality were unreliable, and it did not have the heavy machinery needed to produce military-grade gunpowder.

7 Rains, *History of the Confederate Powder Works*, 10. Augusta was selected a mere ten days after Rains left Richmond. There is good evidence to suggest he only had two or three cities in mind, Augusta included, before leaving Richmond.

The latter mill was a new private facility—more of an idea than a reality by the time Rains stepped foot in Nashville that first July of the war.[8]

Rains contracted with a variety of vendors for the heavy equipment needed, modernized both mills, and filled them with unskilled labor to teach them the complex—and often dangerous—art of making gunpowder. He also built a specialized niter refinery in Nashville to supply the mills with tons of the pure precious mineral. (Niter was but one of the three ingredients necessary for gunpower, the other two being sulphur and charcoal.) Both mills were turning out fairly good gunpowder by the late fall of 1861, though not nearly enough to confront the growing Union threats.[9]

That same fall, President Davis tapped General Albert S. Johnston to assume command of a sprawling department that encompassed everything west of the Appalachian range including Arkansas, Kansas, and Indian Territory, as well as the border states of Missouri and Kentucky. By the time he arrived in the Western Theater that September, Kentucky neutrality had ended, and forces from both sides occupied powerful positions in the Blue Grass State along the Mississippi River. The opening of Kentucky changed the entire calculus of Confederate defensive thinking.[10]

Everything in that theater relied on holding Nashville. As a result, Johnston boldly pushed his front north with its center in Bowling Green, his right in proximity to Cumberland Gap, and his left at Columbus. His entire line was but thinly held, making the advance a bold move that most students and historians still fail to fully understand. According to published correspondence and private reports and letters penned by Rains and others, Johnston's entire command had barely enough gunpowder and ammunition

---

8 Marion O. Smith, "In Quest of a Supply of Saltpeter and Gunpowder in Early Civil War Tennessee," *Tennessee Historical Quarterly*, vol. 56, no. 2 (1997), 98. The Board's membership changed over time. In a report dated Oct. 1, 1861, the Board confirmed there was no functioning "powder mill in operation" in the entire South. One of the board's many successes was the establishment of the Nashville Arsenal in September 1861, which was transferred to the Confederate government and placed under the capable hands of Lt. Moses H. Wright. Once Nashville fell Wright set up shop in Atlanta. He worked closely with Rains for the rest of the war. Dean S. Thomas, *Confederate Arsenals, Laboratories, and Ordnance Depots*, 3 vols. (Thomas Publications, 2014), vol. 1, 731.

9 Rains, "Memorandum Relative to the Establishment of a Gunpowder Works at Augusta," 6.

10 Charles P. Roland, "Albert Sidney Johnston," in Richard N. Current, ed., *Encyclopedia of the Confederacy*, 4 vols. (Simon & Schuster, 1993), vol. 2, 858. Johnston's responsibilities did not include coastal defense.

"to wage an extended skirmish." The only solution was to fool the enemy
and bluff them into thinking they were much stronger than they were. Rains
wrote about this point rather extensively. His full quote—which will truly
drive the nature of the bluff home—was as follows:

> This was a time of great anxiety to all concerned for had the
> enemy moved on General Johnson at that time, he would have
> had to abandon everything as he had not sufficient ammunition
> at that time for an extended skirmish, and there was no remedy
> until I could manufacture it for him. Fortunately the enemy was
> not informed of, or did not believe, this condition of matters, and
> hence waited so long to get prepared to move forward that when
> the movement did take place, our army was sufficiently provided
> with all the necessary ammunition.[11]

His only sources for gunpowder were the Nashville and Coffee County
mills, which were only fitfully producing the substance. A game of bluff was
underway, and Johnston and Davis (and Rains) played it brilliantly.[12]

Other than his inability to pull triggers for a sustained length of time,
Johnston's biggest potential headache were the rivers cutting up his theater.
The Mississippi divided his command and made control and coordination
with troops on the western side significantly more difficult. An obvious
vulnerability awaited 65 miles northwest of Nashville. The broad and
navigable Tennessee and Cumberland rivers flowed north out of Tennessee
into Kentucky to feed the Ohio River. Like giant highways, these twin
avenues of invasion ran deep into the Volunteer State, with the Tennessee
running all the way into northern Alabama and the Cumberland directly to
the capital. Kentucky's initial neutrality had made it politically impossible
to erect forts and other obstructions inside that state to defend the rivers.

---

11 Rains, "Memorandum Relative to the Establishment of a Gunpowder Works at Augusta," 14.

12 Ibid. My research on this subject has uncovered significant evidence, much of it hiding in
plain sight, that the major parties involved were engaged in a dangerous gambit. A defensive
front in Tennessee near Nashville would have been a suicidal decision—especially since the
Sycamore mill was far outside the city and not defensible. Writers since the war have routinely
mocked or criticized the policy without having marshalled the evidence to understand the game
that was afoot. I will present my findings in full, including President Davis's full admission of
the strategy, in my forthcoming biography of George Washington Rains.

Governor Harris had dispatched engineers to scout locations to obstruct the waterways below the Kentucky border as early as May 1861. That effort launched work on what would become Fort Henry (on the Tennessee) and Fort Donelson (on the Cumberland). On a two-dimensional map, the forts projected strength and security. A ground-level observation unmasked this illusion. The forts were poorly located, ineptly designed, lightly manned, improperly armed, and lacked competent leadership. If they fell, Maj. Gen. Leonidas Polk's position at Columbus would be turned, Nashville could be easily flanked and captured, and Johnston's entire attenuated front would collapse. To lose the forts was to lose the game.[13]

In a January 17, 1862, letter to his good friend Major General Mansfield Lovell, the commander tasked with holding New Orleans, Rains discussed a wide variety of issues including a reference to an ongoing military operation. "There is heavy firing going on at Fort Donelson on the Cumberland River, and the enemy are [rumored to be] landing below Fort Henry on the Tennessee, but the country is impracticable for artillery at this time, and hence a general battle I think is out of the question—it is too late in the season."[14]

Rains was misinformed. There was no firing at Donelson, but there was a noisy reconnaissance underway on the Tennessee River against Fort Henry. That operation was part of a two-pronged reconnaissance. Gunboats and troop transports under Brig. Gen. Charles F. Smith spent several days demonstrating in mid-January on the Tennessee against Henry while a second prong, some 5,000 men under Brig. Gen. John McClernand from Grant's command at Cairo, Illinois, reconnoitered in southwestern Kentucky toward Polk's position at Columbus. Neither action portended anything good for the Confederates. The moves strongly indicated that the heretofore mostly quiescent enemy was about to lurch ahead in strength. By early 1862 the river forts and other points along the line finally had enough ammunition, but there was no reserve behind the front; without the Nashville-area mills there was no way to replace what was expended. The

---

13 Steven A. Woodworth, *Jefferson Davis and his Generals: The Failure of Confederate Command in the West* (University Press of Kansas, 1990), 53, 56-57.

14 Letter, George W. Rains to Mansfield Lovell, January 17, 1862, Mansfield Lovell Papers, 1835–1886, Huntington Library, San Marino, California.

Augusta Powder Works Rains was still being built and was still months away from producing powder.[15]

Rains was in Nashville three weeks later on February 10 when he learned that Roanoke Island in Virginia had fallen. More terrible news was at hand: Fort Henry had surrendered, Fort Donelson was in serious trouble, and everything he had worked so long and hard to build in Tennessee was in considerable jeopardy. Unlike the Atlantic coastline, the wobbly Kentucky front was much too close to Nashville for comfort. There was no room for a major mistake or setback there. In his January 17 letter to Mansfield Lovell, Rains had declared that it was "too late in the season" for effective military action. He was wrong.[16]

Ulysses S. Grant had been receiving reports about the vulnerabilities of Fort Henry for several weeks. His superior, Maj. Gen. Henry Halleck, however, had turned down his requests to reach out and take the ill-sited bastion. When Flag Officer Andrew H. Foote, commander of the Western Gunboat Flotilla, voiced his support for Grant's idea and a willingness to take part, Halleck relented and let the brigadier off his short leash.

By February 6, Grant closed in on Henry with 15,000 troops and Foote's gunboats for long-distance punching power. Foote opened a heavy naval bombardment that quickly brought about Henry's surrender. The fort's 3,000 survivors fled to Fort Donelson across the narrow six-mile strip of land separating the rivers. Henry's fall opened the Tennessee River to invasion. Three Union timberclads would churn upriver and penetrate Alabama as far as Muscle Shoals, destroying Southern shipping, capturing supplies, and knocking out the Memphis and Ohio Railroad bridge. Major General William J. Hardee's position at Bowling Green, the center of Johnston's

---

15 U.S. War Department, The War of the Rebellion: *The Official Records of the Union and Confederate Navies*, 30 vols. (Harrisburg, PA, 1987), Series I, vol. 7, 507; E. B. Long, *The Civil War Day by Day: An Almanac, 1861-1865* (Doubleday, 1971), 161-163.

16 "Bad news today about Roanoke Island, and the enemy having captured all our forces there." Letter, Feb. 10, 1862, Lt. L. J. Smith, Augusta Arsenal, to Capt. R. M. Cuyler, Letters Received, Savannah Depot, RG 109, National Archives, Washington, D.C.; Letter, George W. Rains to Mansfield Lovell, January 17, 1862.

extended front, could no longer be held and its garrison began retreating south to Nashville.[17]

The alarming situation deteriorated when Grant marched his infantry across the isthmus to Donelson and besieged the much stronger fort hugging the Cumberland. Lloyd Tilghman, who commanded Forts Heiman, Henry, and Donelson, had made the decision to hold the latter. The fighting began on February 13. Foote's gunboats launched a failed water assault the next day. Heavy land fighting followed. Donelson unconditionally surrendered on the 16th with the loss of nearly 15,000 men, 65 artillery pieces, and tons of munitions (including Nashville-made gunpowder). The major Union victories split Johnston's front wide open and unlocked the twin river arteries into the Confederate heartland. Nashville, with its government niter refinery, factories, warehouses, and satellite powder mills, was fully exposed.[18]

Most did not immediately grasp Nashville's precarious state at the hour of Donelson's fall. Rains, however, fully appreciated the scope of the disaster and its wider implications and was already working to minimize it.

When news of the Federal offensive up the rivers first reached him in Nashville, he had dropped everything to steam down the Cumberland River as fast as possible to reach Donelson in time to witness some of the fighting. He had a deep curiosity to witness the effectiveness of the artillery shells, powered by his gunpowder, against Foote's innovative warships. It was a frightening revelation. When it became apparent that Donelson would fall, he hurried back to Nashville to prepare for the worst.

Rains could not afford to wait and see if General Johnston would fight to hold the city. In what was surely a painful decision, he issued orders to dismantle the government niter refinery and organized rail and wagon transportation to shuttle his priceless equipment and workers out of Nashville before the rising panic—or the approaching Yankees—made such a move

---

17 B. Franklin Cooling, "Henry and Donelson Campaign, in Current ed., *Encyclopedia of the Confederacy*, vol. 2, 764-765. General Johnston and senior officials in Richmond had mostly overlooked the Henry and Donelson "until the moment of crisis." Johnston had left their construction and defensive capabilities to others to pay attention to Bowling Green, and never personally visited the river forts. His and the War Department's negligence regarding their armaments, engineering issues, and manpower is puzzling because the rivers bisected Johnston's front. Losing the forts could only bring about the abandonment of a large swath of Tennessee, with its rich mineral and agricultural resources. It would also, at best, force a major battle for the capital. Since the Sycamore mill was 23 miles outside the city, there was no viable way to defend it.

18 Ibid., 765, 767.

too difficult or simply impossible. This prompt action saved irreplaceable hardware and skilled laborers who would otherwise have been lost.[19]

Major Rains knew the moment Donelson fell that the Sycamore mill was doomed. It was too far away from Nashville to protect, and there was not enough time or transportation opportunities to remove its invaluable machinery. Once he was confident his subordinates understood his wishes, the officer hopped a train for Augusta to prepare the unfinished factory complex for the flood of machinery and personnel that would soon arrive. This was how the Augusta Powder Works, he later explained, was "supplied at the commencement with the necessary means of operation, which could not have been otherwise accomplished." Nashville, meanwhile, was defenseless because Johnston knew he did not have the manpower to save the capital. Instead, he established his headquarters southeast of the city at Murfreesboro and began coalescing his scattered command there.[20]

News of the twin defeats reached Richmond quickly via telegraph, but Johnston had other more important matters to attend to before finishing his report on February 25. "The fall of Fort Donelson compelled me to withdraw the remaining forces under my command . . . and to abandon the defense of Nashville, which but for that disaster it was my intention to protect to the utmost," explained the embattled commander. Indeed, Johnston had no real choice but to do as he had done. The general, who had "not more than 11,000 effective men," risked being cut off and "subjected to destruction." General Buell was moving south from Bowling Green with a much larger Union command, Brig. Gen. George Thomas was flanking him on the east, and General Grant's victorious army and Foote's warships on the Cumberland threatened to move around his left flank and cut off "all communication with the south."[21]

United States forces entered and captured the capital on February 24. The invaluable niter refinery was gone, and the Sycamore Mill was cut off

---

19 Rains, *Confederate Powder Works*, 6–7.

20 Ibid.; Durham, "Nashville, Tennessee," *Encyclopedia of the Confederacy*, vol. 3, 1107. In addition to a regiment under Nathan Bedford Forrest, Johnston sent Brig. Gen. John B. Floyd's brigade to the city to protect it while valuable stores were removed. *OR* 7, 427. See Thomas L. Connelly, *Army of the Heartland: The Army of Tennessee, 1861-1862* (Baton Rouge, 1967), 135–38, for a good description of the chaos that eventually gripped Nashville and the cost in terms of lost supplies to the Southern cause.

21 War of the Rebellion: *A Compilation of the Official Records of the Union and Confederate Armies*. 128 vols. (GPO: Washington, D.C. 1880-1901), vol. 7, 427. See also, Smith, "In Quest of a Supply of Saltpeter and Gunpowder in Early Civil War Tennessee," 106.

from communication and deemed lost. William Whiteman's Manchester mill 65 miles southeast of the capital in Coffee County was not yet under immediate threat. Whiteman and Rains decided to keep the Coffee County mill open and making powder for as long as possible. The Augusta plant was not yet able to produce powder in quantity, and the amount Whiteman could generate in the interim was desperately needed by Johnston's army. Remaining in place in Coffee County was worth the risk.[22]

While all this was unfolding in Nashville, George Rains was enduring what must have been a long and miserable train ride back to Augusta. The sudden loss of the river forts, followed by the collapse of Johnston's long front and the loss of Middle Tennessee and the state's capital had staggering implications for the war effort. The steady production of Sycamore gunpowder was gone, as was the efficient arsenal and the high-capacity niter refinery. The regional niter-producing cave industry was about to be eviscerated. Johnston's hurried retreat marked the unraveling of almost everything Rains and so many others had worked so hard for so long to achieve. But there was something else bothering Rains. He had just witnessed something extraordinary along the Cumberland River, and it weighed heavily on the man.

Rains reached Augusta on February 18, two days after Donelson's fall and six days before the capture of Nashville. One of the first things he did was sit at his desk and respond to a letter that had arrived during his absence from Gen. Robert E. Lee, the commander of the southeast Atlantic coast, concerning the state of the defenses along the Savannah River. It offered the perfect segue for Rains to unburden himself, for he had just witnessed firsthand the strength (and weaknesses) of enemy ironclads attacking fixed positions.

After dealing with issues under previous discussion, Rains shared with the general a host of important facts and figures he had learned by observing part of the river war. "The Gunboats I found on the Western waters were plated with iron, as represented," he explained while referring to a comprehensive cross-section sketch of an ironclad on one side of his letter. Flag Officer Andrew Foote's warships (clad in timber and in iron) had engaged in heavy

---

22 Rains, "Memorandum Relative to the Establishment of a Gunpowder Works at Augusta," 6; Rains, *History of the Confederate Powder Works*, 7. At that time, one mill in New Orleans was making powder for the defense of the Crescent City, and the new Waterhouse & Bowes mill outside Raleigh was only just beginning to produce more than several hundred pounds a day. An explosion would soon destroy the mill.

combat twice during the
campaign, once on February
6 against Fort Henry on the
Tennessee and again on
February 14 against Fort
Donelson's batteries along
the Cumberland. During
his trip to Donelson Rains
had somehow managed to
get close enough during
the fighting to study the
particulars of the strange new
craft and draw and describe

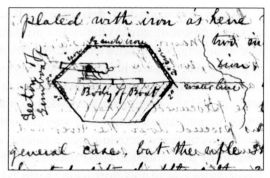

Rains sketched his concerns about Federal ironclads
in a letter to Robert E. Lee, then in charge of coastal
defenses. *Author's collection*

extraordinary details about the hastily built city-class ironclads. His drawing
and letter, which doubled as a poor-man's field report, included such things as
the thickness of their iron, the effect of varying weights of shells fired against
them, and the elevations required for those shells to be effective.[23]

"These boats are proof against ordinary 24 pdr. and 32-pdr [rounds] in
the general case," he explained, "but rifled shot easily penetrated." Rains
had no doubt that when firing from an elevated position, "the 24 pdr. ball
would pass through the iron plates without difficulty because they would be
struck nearly perpendicular to their surface." He turned his attention to the
pair of river strongholds by name. "Fort Henry," he continued, ". . . was on
a level with the water, hence its 24 pdr guns made little impression," while
"Fort Donelson was on higher ground, and thus its shot were much more
effective; indeed, three of the six iron clad gunboats were badly crippled.
In both cases," he added "the Gunboats scarcely injured the forts, guns, or
artillerists at all."[24]

23 Geo. W. Rains to R. E. Lee, February 18, 1862, Department of South Carolina and
Georgia Collection, Rains Papers, Brockenbrough Library, Museum of the Confederacy,
Richmond, Virginia. Rains visited the front as often as he could to witness the effectiveness
of artillery shells and gunpowder, including the battle of Port Royal Sound in November of
1861, Forts Henry and Donelson, and some of heavy bombardments at Charleston during
the summer of 1863, among others. It is possible Rains was present for both warship attacks
(Henry on the 6th and Donelson on the 14th), but given the timing of events it was more
likely only the latter.

24 Ibid.

Rains was confident that heavy rifled guns firing from well-sited elevated positions could challenge and defeat this new style of warship. Unfortunately, he had not a single rifled gun to install on the Savannah River to protect Augusta and his invaluable powder works. Worse still was that no one in Richmond would take his concerns to heart and supply him with the artillery and the manpower he needed to make the river impregnable. The lesson being learned in the field was that when paired with infantry, Union gunboats could reduce and capture almost any static position. If the same version of iron gunboat made it past Fort Pulaski and into the Savannah River, as they were now threatening to do at that very moment, Augusta was doomed. The thought was chilling. The worried major hoped his old friend Lee would realize the danger at hand and help him get what he needed to protect what was about to become the only large-scale powder mill in the entire Confederacy.

"Augusta was selected, for several reasons," explained Rains after the war. "[F]or its central position; for its canal transportation and water-power; for its railroad facilities; and for its security from attack." It was as secure as any location could be from enemy armies or raids. This was especially important, emphasized Rains, "since the loss of the Works would have been followed by disastrous consequences."[25]

The only hope for the long-term survival of the Confederacy rested on a vulnerable complex of buildings lining the Augusta canal along the Savannah River, and an overworked artillery major laboring in the ordnance department "on detached service" determined, somehow, to make it all work.

But he now had grave doubts. Perhaps he had been wrong. Had Union riverine warfare changed everything?

---

25 Rains, *History of the Confederate Powder Works*, 4, 10; Rains, "Memorandum Relative to the Establishment of a Gunpowder Works at Augusta," 13.

7. Persistence of the Mardi Gras Spirit in Civil War New Orleans

by Neil P. Chatelain

Originally published as a blog post at Emerging Civil War on February 16, 2021

Nothing embodies New Orleans more than Mardi Gras. Crowds throng parades, balls, and costumed parties, marking final celebrations before the Catholic season of Lent. Organizations host parades, customizing throws of beads, metallic doubloons, and plastic cups. Though occurring annually, the occasional crisis can stop festivities. Parades stopped because of the pandemic in 2020, the Korean War, World War II, the 1918-1919 Influenza, World War I, and the Civil War. The Civil War era's canceled festivities provide insight into how even a canceled or toned-down celebration can reinvigorate the Carnival spirit with lasting impacts on the future of Mardi Gras.

The first modern parade organization, the Mystick Krewe of Comus, began in 1857. Annually on Mardi Gras day, the krewe donned masks and costumes to "march through the principal streets and . . . afterwards a grand ball would be given" featuring the city's elite.[1] Masked balls were a norm across antebellum New Orleans. Comus adopted this, sparking today's modern Mardi Gras ball tradition.

By 1861, other societies added balls. Louisiana's secession did not stem Carnival celebrations even as the Confederacy organized. Newspapers advertised Mardi Gras balls hosted by numerous societies while the Krewe of Comus marched undeterred. However, troubled signs loomed. Military companies held several balls as fundraisers, and amidst the parading, a collection of enslaved men formed a minstrel group that "marched around, having at their head a comical effigy of Old Abe Lincoln, riding a rail of his own splitting," which provided entertainment as costumed children threw bags of flour onto both one another and the city's African American population, "according to the usual custom."[2]

By Mardi Gras 1862, things shifted. In January and February, papers were full of masquerade ball advertisements and guarantees that the Mystick Krewe of Comus would again "astonish the town."[3] This was not to be. Word arrived of Confederate battlefield setbacks, and nine local regiments marched north, later participating in the Battle of Shiloh. Concurrently, David Farragut's naval squadron ascended the Mississippi River to assault New Orleans. Martial law was declared, and the local militia mobilized. Mayor John T. Monroe issued a directive canceling all Mardi Gras festivities, proclaiming "no masquerade procession or masked individuals will be allowed to parade the streets of the city of New Orleans on TUESDAY, the 4th day of March, 1862, the same being Mardi-Gras."[4] Instead, the day after the canceled festivities, a brigade of militia paraded through the streets.

United States forces quickly occupied the city. With many military-aged men in the Confederate Army and New Orleans under military occupation, 1863's Mardi Gras passed without parades or balls. The largest celebration was a Mardi Gras night performance by a minstrel group of free and enslaved men at the Camp Street Theater. One prominent French-speaking woman lamented

---

1 B.W. Wrenn, *Mardi Gras in New Orleans* (Atlanta: Barrow, 1873), 5.

2 "Mardi-Gras," *New Orleans Daily Crescent*, February 13, 1861.

3 "Balls to Come," *New Orleans Daily Picayune*, February 12, 1862.

4 "Proclamation," *New Orleans Daily Crescent*, March 4, 1862.

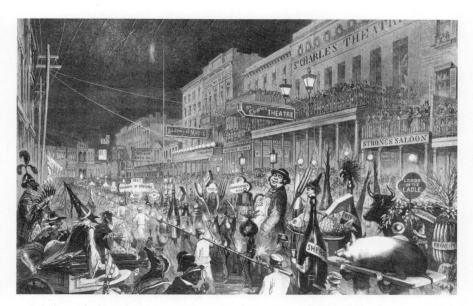

Only improvised parades and impromptu celebrations occurred for Mardi Gras during the Civil War, but just before and after the conflict, parading groups such as the Mystik Krewe of Comus propelled Mardi Gras into the modern phenomenon it is today. *Library of Congress*

to her husband, "Il n'y a pas eu de carnival"—There was no carnival.[5] Despite this, one U.S. soldier witnessed "people dressing themselves up and making fools of themselves generally."[6] A few masqueraders were arrested the week after "for playing Mardi Gras out of season."[7]

1864 found a renewed Mardi Gras spirit embracing New Orleans. Occupiers relaxed rules, and by midday on February 9, 1864, "considerable numbers, attired in every description of costume, in carriages and on foot, began roaming the streets," and an impromptu parade formed as men, "mounted on horses, asses, and mules" pulled carts packed with revelers down

5 Polyxene Reynès to Joseph Reynès, February 19, 1863, *Joseph Reynès and Family Papers*, Louisiana and Lower Mississippi Valley Collections, LSU Libraries, Baton Rouge, Louisiana.

6 Kenneth E. Shewmaker, Andrew W. Prinz, and Henry R. Gardner, "A Yankee in Louisiana: Selections from the Diary and Correspondence of Henry R. Gardner, 1862-1866," *Louisiana History*, Vol. 5, No. 3 (Summer, 1964), 290.

7 "The Maskers," *New Orleans Daily Picayune*, February 26, 1863.

Canal Street.[8] This improvised parade included "King and Queen, Princess, peasants, Satan and fair ladies, beggars and heiresses, clowns, nymphs, Friars, savages, dancing girls, sailors, soldiers, negroes, mulattos, Creoles, octoroons . . . all with one object in view, pure unalloyed, boisterous fun."[9]

United States soldier Carlos Colby wrote home that "all through the day we could see Men, Women, and Children dressed in all manner of styles and all had masks on their faces so you could not tell who it was."[10] Another occupying soldier observed how sacks of flour were employed by children "to whiten any negro who might be found on the streets, with fine clothes."[11] Connecticut soldier Nathan Middlebrook "saw more fun . . . than I have since I came in the army."[12] Three women took the relaxed circumstances to costume in their husbands' old Confederate uniforms while another tore down a United States flag. All were arrested.

New Orleans residents and military occupiers alike seemed anxious to continue the Carnival spirit that year, with one writing home a week later that "some of the Dukes and kings haint got over Mardi-grassing yet."[13] Continuing these festivities and commemorating the newly elected Unionist Louisiana governor, on February 22, 1864, George Washington's Birthday, General Nathanial P. Banks and his wife Mary hosted "a *bal masque* at the Opera House."[14] Acting French Consul Charles Fauconnet attended and recognized Banks' motives to "engender a rapprochement between the two races and serve as a vehicle for amalgamation." Fauconnet remembered the

8 "Close of the Carnival," *New Orleans Daily True Delta*, February 10, 1864.

9 W.S. Hemphill, *Journal of a Trooper*, Vol. 4, 352-353 in Elisabeth Joan Doyle, "Civilian Life in Occupied New Orleans" Thesis, Louisiana State University, 1955, 206.

10 Carlos Colby to Catie Colby, February 16, 1864, *Carlos W. Colby papers, 1821-1937*, Midwest Manuscript Collection, Newberry Library, Chicago, Illinois.

11 "Correspondence of the Gazette," *Lewistown, Pennsylvania, Gazette*, March 23, 1864.

12 Nathan Middlebrook to Sue, February 12, 1864, *Nathan Middlebrook Papers*, Special Collections, US Army Heritage and Education Center, Carlisle, Pennsylvania.

13 Extract from Sam's Letter, February 15, 1864, in John M. Stanyan, *A History of the Eighth Regiment of New Hampshire Volunteers* (Concord, NH: Ira C. Evans, 1892), 355.

14 "The Masquerade Ball Given by Mrs. Gen. Banks," *Frank Leslie's Illustrated Newspaper*, March 26, 1864.

ball as "brilliant with uniforms, dresses, and costumes" but also one where "with very few exceptions, all of the Creole families were absent."[15]

With the war closing, Mardi Gras saw more balls and celebrations on February 28, 1865. The revelry included costumed individuals: "King Richard III . . . walked upon the common pavement. Horace Greeley . . . followed his royal highness in haste while a *Tribune* peered forth, from the depths of his coat pockets. 'Uncle Abe' was following Greeley for the purpose of drafting him."[16] There were no organized parades. However, a crowd gathered on Canal Street, hoping the Mystick Krewe of Comus would appear, but were dispersed by an evening rainstorm. Gen. Edward R. S. Canby attended the evening's masquerade balls. The celebrations prompted trouble, and a freedman was stabbed on the street. The mayor closed bars to prevent further unrest.

The Mystick Krewe of Comus recommenced parading in 1866 with the year's ball themed "The Past, in which the horrors of war were depicted; The Present, which illustrated the blessings of peace; and The Future, over which peace and plenty presided."[17] Carnival grew postwar, influenced by former Confederate leaders moving to New Orleans. In 1892, Winnie Davis, daughter of Jefferson Davis, became queen of Comus. That year, her portrait for the organization marked "her rule simultaneously as the Princess of the Confederacy and the Queen of Comus."[18] Her portrait was used afterward as a model for future portraits and ball gowns, connecting today's Mardi Gras celebrations to the Civil War era.

Race continued to play a part in celebrations. In 1916, the Krewe of Zulu was formed, by the Zulu Social Aid and Pleasure Club. It is famous

15 Acting Consul Charles Fauconnet, March 11, 1864, Carl A Brasseauz and Katherine Carmines Mooney, ed., *Ruined by this Miserable War: The Dispatches of Charles Prosper Fauconnet, a French Diplomat in New Orleans, 1863-1868* (Knoxville, TN: University of Tennessee Press, 2012), 102.

16 "'Mardigras Day' in New Orleans," *Cleveland, Ohio Daily Leader*, March 20, 1865.

17 William H. Forman Jr., "William P. Harper and the Early New Orleans Carnival," *Louisiana History*, Vol. 14, No. 1 (Winter, 1973), 41.

18 Elizabeth Leavitt, "Southern Royalty: Race, Gender, and Discrimination During Mardi Gras From the Civil War to the Present Day," *From Slave Mothers & Southern Belles to Radical Reformers & Lost Cause Ladies: Representing Women in the Civil War Era*, February, 2015, https://civilwarwomen.wp.tulane.edu/.

for black and white members donning blackface and costumes honoring the African Zulus and throwing coconuts to the crowd. This is an interesting turn, considering early Mardi Gras celebrations involved children pelting African Americans with flour, turning their faces white. Recently, arguments over whether the blackface tradition should end emerged, with some claiming they are honoring racist white vaudevillian actors who dressed in blackface in times past, while others claims the Zulu tradition critiques and discredits those very actors. Nonetheless, the tradition continues.

Recent movements against Confederate monuments have impacted Mardi Gras. In 1969, parading krewes distributed metallic doubloons honoring the city's now-removed statue of Pierre G.T. Beauregard. In 2017, the Robert E. Lee statue on Lee Circle on St. Charles Avenue was removed. With this prominent parade-route landmark gone, Mardi Gras beads bearing the statue's likeness began appearing at parades in protest.

Mardi Gras faced its first real challenge in the Civil War. Despite the war, occupation, and cancellations, the citizens of New Orleans maintained Carnival's essence through improvised parading, costuming, and masked balls, albeit via an abbreviated format filled with commentary about the Civil War itself. This challenge helped reinvigorate the Mardi Gras spirit, impacting the celebration's evolution and providing a precedent for how future cancellations can recover by forging cultural additions to the Carnival season.

The 25th Missouri Infantry at Shiloh

by Kristen M. Trout

Originally published as a blog post at Emerging Civil War on April 5, 2019

After mature deliberation [Colonel Everett Peabody] decided to do as above stated–attack, and thus give the alarm to those in our rear, so that they could turn out and make some resistance to the overwhelming force, and not be captured or attacked in their quarters. This move seemed to be the only way to convince General [Benjamin] Prentiss that there was an army between us and Corinth.

In the late 1880s, Union Civil War veteran James Newhard of Company H, 25th Missouri Infantry, recalled his unit's desperate attempt to contact the vanguard of the Confederate Army of Mississippi on April 6, 1862, during the battle of Shiloh. Colonel Everett Peabody, commanding officer of the First Brigade, Sixth Division, sent a small patrol of men from the 25th Missouri and 12th Michigan to establish contact with the enemy and send alarms to the rest of the army.

On the evening of April 5, Peabody's men heard suspicious noises in the woods near their camps. The Union's high command, including Brig. Gen. Benjamin Prentiss, was skeptical that Gen. Albert S. Johnston's Army of Mississippi could be nearby. Unable to sleep, the Missourians' restless brigade commander finally decided to send an additional patrol out the following day. Unbeknownst to many students of Shiloh, several patrols were out on the night of April 5th and the morning of April 6th. On the morning of April 6th, Peabody and his men determined to prove to the high command that the enemy was between them at Pittsburg Landing and the vital railroad juncture at Corinth, Mississippi.

Around 3:00 a.m. on April 6th, Peabody—without orders—deployed his 250-man patrol under the command of Maj. James Powell from the main Federal encampment, scouting the area along the Seay Field Road. Sometime between 4:55 a.m. and 5:15 a.m., at Fraley Field, the patrol clashed with Confederate pickets of the 3rd Mississippi Battalion under Maj. Aaron Hardcastle. Col. Francis Quinn of the 12th Michigan Infantry described the patrol that morning, "Our brave boys marched out, and had not over 3 miles to go before they met the enemy, and immediately a sharp firing commenced, our little force giving ground."

"We quietly passed through our single line of pickets a short distance in front of our camp guard, drove in Johnston's pickets, and fell onto his whole army about a mile and a half from our camp," Newhard recalled. He was right—the Confederate Third Army Corps was in the woodlot in front of them. The battle of Shiloh had officially begun.

As the fight erupted at Fraley Field and the Third Corps under William Hardee advanced to their front, the men of Powell's patrol tried to hold on until safely retreating to the main camp. Private Daniel Baker of Company F, 25th Missouri Infantry, remembered Powell "ordered the men to deploy into line and shield themselves behind trees as well as they could, for they found that the whole rebel army was there . . . I am satisfied that if Major Powell had not made this reconnaissance our army would have suffered much more." Powell sent word immediately to the camp.

Back in camp, "General Prentiss shook himself out of his blankets when he heard the racket, and was shortly convinced that Colonel Peabody was right . . . This move seemed to be the only way to convince General Prentiss that there was an army between us and Corinth." Prentiss viewed Peabody's heroic, yet bold, move harshly, wanting his subordinate court-martialed. However, the chaos of battle forced Prentiss to face the task at hand, particularly in defending the left flank, rather than dealing with insubordination.

A marker shaped like a home plate denotes the camp of the 25th Missouri.
A mortuary monument to Col. Everett Peabody stands in the distance.
Chris Mackowski

With a 9,000-man corps to their front, the 25th Missouri's line was pushed back past Seay's Field. Peabody's Brigade and the rest of the division came to assist but were soon pushed back to their camps. Peabody was shot in the head and killed at the Federal camps. "He was a brave soldier and a good man," recalled Quinn. The men of Peabody's old regiment were unable to get to his body until the next day, as stated by Newhard: "After having driven the enemy back over our ground, we found Colonel Peabody lying on the line of the officer's tents and near the tent where he had passed the night before. It was too bad he was not allowed to live and get the credit he was entitled to."

Unfortunately, Prentiss did not report Peabody's heroic actions in his after-action report. In 1889, the 25th Missouri Infantry veterans wrote in great detail about their fallen, beloved commander in their regimental history, *An Illustrated History of the Missouri Engineer and the 25th Infantry Regiments.* Many quotations by Newhard were out of a larger effort to honor Peabody.

Along with the rest of Prentiss's Division and the Federal line, the men of the 25th continued attempts to make a defensive stand wherever they could. Dozens of Missourians, particularly the officers, became casualties in the first day's fight, particularly the officers. Some included: Lt. Thomas Dunlap of Co. D (killed), Pvt. Samuel L. Leffler of Co. E (wounded), Lt. Fred Klinger (wounded), Maj. James Powell (killed), and Capt. Charles Wade of Co. C (killed).

Shiloh was not the last battle the 25th Missouri Infantry would see. Within one month after Shiloh, the unit saw action at Corinth. They would later serve on garrison duty and fighting guerrillas in Missouri until February 1864. They then consolidated with Bissell's Engineer Regiment of the West, creating the First Missouri Engineers. They would fight throughout the Atlanta Campaign, the March to the Sea, and the Carolinas Campaign.

Selected Bibliography

Daniel Baker, "How the Battle Began." *The National Tribune.* April 12, 1883.

W. A. Neal, *An Illustrated History of the Missouri Engineer and the 25th Infantry Regiments.* (Chicago: Donohue and Henneberry, Printers, 1889).

Report of Col. Francis Quinn, in *The War of the Rebellion: A Compilation of the Official Records of the Union and Confederate Armies,* ser. 1, v.10, pt. 1 (Washington, D.C.: Government Printing Office, 1885), 280-281.

Shiloh:
Preston Pond's Charge at Tilghman Branch

by Sean Michael Chick

Originally published as a blog post at Emerging Civil War
on April 6, 2019

Among the largest brigades to fight at Shiloh was Col. Preston Pond's outfit. It was mostly made up of Louisiana troops, and numbered around 2,600 men. One thousand four hundred of these soldiers formed two regiments, the 38th Tennessee and the Crescent Regiment, a militia outfit made up of wealthy men from New Orleans, primarily Anglo-Americans. By contrast, the Orleans Guard Battalion consisted of 300 men drawn from the Creole elite of the city. The 16th and 18th Louisiana were largely rural outfits, with the 18th Louisiana being mostly Acadian. Capt. William H. Ketchum's Alabama State Artillery joined this brigade with six cannons.

Pond was born in New Hampshire but was raised in the Florida parishes of Louisiana. He was a lawyer and farmer, affiliated with the anti-immigrant Nativist Party. He was also a successful politician and a militia officer who took his task seriously. Pond formed and commanded the 16th Louisiana. His martinet ways made him unpopular. Comically, when he died in 1864, his headstone read that he was "loved by all."

For most of April 6, 1862, the opening day of Shiloh, Pond's brigade marched and fought, suffering relatively light losses. By 4:00 p.m., they and Patrick Cleburne's brigade were the only Rebel infantry on the left flank around Jones Field, although the brigade numbered just 1,000 men. The 38th Tennessee, Crescent Regiment, and two cannon from the Alabama State Artillery stood guard at Owl Creek Bridge, entering the fighting at the Hornet's Nest.

At 4:30, Gen. P. G. T. Beauregard sent Lt. Col. Samuel Ferguson to Jones Field to take over Pond's brigade. It appears Beauregard thought Pond was not in command. Ferguson, a recent West Point graduate, had the reputation of a fire-eater. Young, ambitious, and a troublemaker, he likely embezzled money from the Mississippi Levee Board after the war. On April 6th, Ferguson hungered for glory.

Ferguson reported to Gen. William J. Hardee, who ordered him to capture Battery D of the 1st Illinois Light Artillery, which was shelling Hardee's men from near Cavalry Field. The Alabama State Artillery, Smith's Battery (Mississippi), and the 5th Company of the Washington Artillery (Louisiana) would provide support. Ferguson found Pond's brigade, learning that Pond actively retained command. Pond had earlier made a personal reconnaissance of Gen. John McClernand's division, which was posted east of Tilghman Branch. His absence might have caused Beauregard to think Pond was not in command, thus the reason for Ferguson's assignment.

Ferguson informed Pond of Hardee's orders, but Pond thought that the attack foolish. He sent Ferguson back to inform Hardee, who merely confirmed the order. Pond said "Very well, sir. I will obey the order, but do so under protest."[1] Ferguson later asserted that he led the attack. That is unlikely, but he probably took part in the assault.

Due to the dense terrain, Pond's men did not come under long-range fire. However, Pond attacked en echelon, which allowed the Union to pour fire on the regiments individually. Colonel Alfred Mouton, commander of the 18th Louisiana, protested the order stating: "You will make me sacrifice all my men to no avail."[2] Mouton, though, dutifully led his men up the ravine that divided Cavalry and Mulberry Fields. They advanced in splendid order, but at fifty yards, the artillery opened up. Mouton's horse was shot from under him, and the regiment fled after losing over 200 men.

---

1 L.M. Pipkin Letter (16th Louisiana) Shiloh National Military Park Confederate Regiment Files (Shiloh, Tennessee).

2 Edmond Enoul Livaudais, *The Shiloh Diary of Edmond Enoul Livaudais*. (New Orleans: Archdiocese of New Orleans, 1992), 30.

Never previously published in print: Preston Pond's portrait. *Southern Louisiana University*

Pond pressed on. He ordered, "Orleans Guard, charge!" and the men lunged forward. The battalion moved through the shattered remains of the 18th Louisiana, with Private Edmond Livaudais recalling "it was truly horrendous," and men were "bathed in their blood" and asked "for water and help."[3]

The Orleans Guard made a superb effort. The flag, held up by part of the flagstaff from Fort Sumter, saw four color bearers fall. The fifth, Capt. Alfred Roman, saved it from capture. Major Leon Querouze, the battalion commander, was wounded. The battalion lost 90 men out of 300. The 16th Louisiana, positioned to the rear, did not press its advance. Losses for the 16th were light, although Maj. Daniel Gober had his horse shot from under him and led the men on foot.

Pond lost over 300 men in minutes. Although Pond made good use of terrain, his attack formation was poorly chosen, and he hit a particularly strong part of McClernand's line. Some accused Pond of not being on hand to direct or rally his men. It was not an accusation of cowardice, but rather mismanagement, which likely played a part in Pond not being promoted nor reelected to command the 16th Louisiana. Roman, who later served on Beauregard's staff and helped write his autobiography, particularly criticized Pond. Roman probably shared his feelings with his friend.

The musket era across multiple continents provided ubiquitous evidence of failed frontal attacks on strong positions. One of the most horrendous

3 Ibid.

occurred in Assietta, one of the last battles fought in the War of the Austrian Succession (1740-1748). There, a French army attacked an outnumbered but well-positioned Sardinian army, losing 6,400 men, while inflicting only 300 losses at most. Pond's charge ranked in numerous, if melancholy, company.

Poor communication and commander impetuosity often created these failures. Hardee had not scouted the ground, and with the fighting at the Hornet's Nest intensifying, he likely wanted to help. In the heat of battle, frontal attacks were made on positions far too strong. The musket made defense much easier, and few commanders could consistently win decisive victories. Exceptions across previous eras included Marlborough, Napoleon, and Frederick II (commonly called the Great). What each had in common was a first-rate cavalry force capable of powerful charges and pursuit. Civil War armies generally lacked this type of cavalry support, leading to indecisive battles and a lack of total force destruction.

Nevertheless, there is another reason these attacks happened. Sometimes they worked. Shiloh had already seen Gen. A. P. Stewart make a bold charge across Review Field, piercing the Union line, although with heavy losses. Mouton thought that if the 16th Louisiana and Orleans Guard had advanced with the 18th Louisiana, the assault would have worked. Pond's attack failed, but it did frazzle McClernand's line. Soon after, Patrick Cleburne struck McClernand's flank with his brigade and sent the Federals flying. Coordinating with Cleburne, a Rebel attack with more than half of a brigade might have completely shattered McClernand's men.

Regardless, attacks such as Pond's had low success rates, even if, on occasion, they achieved spectacular results. Those rare successes were arguably seductive. Ulysses Grant, who from 1862 to 1863 mainly avoided frontal assaults on solid positions, was moved by the Army of the Cumberland's dash up Missionary Ridge. It might explain some of his poor tactical choices in Virginia in 1864. Braxton Bragg, who had ordered Stewart to attack at Review Field, would order disjointed and piecemeal assaults on the Hornet's Nest and later at Stones River and Chickamauga.

If the Civil War had ended in the summer of 1862, Pond's isolated attack might be better known among buffs and historians. Sadly, poor assault tactics were too common in the American Civil War.

David Reed:
Shiloh's Veteran Historian

by Kevin Pawlak

*Originally published as a blog post at Emerging Civil War
on April 7, 2020*

Gettysburg has John Bachelder. Antietam has Ezra Carman. Shiloh has David Reed.

Each forever influenced the battlefields they devoted their lives to documenting. Two of them—Carman and Reed—participated in the battles they studied.

I'll admit, Carman and Bachelder were known to me. Until recently, I had never heard of David Reed. His influence on the Shiloh battlefield is still apparent and he forever shaped the way modern historians study the battle of Shiloh.

David Reed celebrated his twenty-first birthday in the camp of the 12th Iowa Infantry at Pittsburg Landing. Four days later, a surprise Confederate onslaught on April 6, 1862, brought chaos and destruction to the woodlots and fields around the Tennessee River landing. Federal soldiers defiantly battled all day, desperately holding back their enemy. No Union defensive position became so mythologized and well-known as the Hornet's Nest—a name given by the buzzing sensation Federal bullets created for the attacking Confederates.

At the Hornets' Nest, along the center of the Union position, young David Reed shouldered a rifle alongside his comrades. Late in the fight, as the Federal

David Reed fought at Shiloh. Later, as historian for the early park, he made sure the battlefield emphasized the parts of the story he thought most important—leading to an enduring Shiloh myth. *University of Tennessee Press*

position began collapsing, a bullet struck Reed in the thigh. Reed remained on the battlefield, writhing in pain and unattended, until the next day.

Despite his wound, Reed rebounded and fought the rest of the war. He returned to Iowa and assumed several government posts from 1867 to 1895. During those years of service, Reed was active in local veterans' organizations, becoming the historian of two of them.

In 1890, the Federal government established the first five national military parks: Chickamauga and Chattanooga, Gettysburg, Shiloh, Vicksburg, and Antietam. Through his network of political connections, Reed received his third official appointment as a Civil War historian in 1895, this time as secretary and historian for the Shiloh National Military Park Commission. To construct the battle's history, Reed turned to the Official Records. However, like Bachelder and Carman, Reed had the tremendous benefit of consulting with veterans.

Reed helped place the scores of monuments that ornament the Shiloh battlefield. He also authored approximately 400 tablets marking troop positions and created two detailed battlefield maps. Lastly, Reed published *The Battle of Shiloh and the Organizations Engaged*, a work still consulted by Shiloh historians today.

Reed's work left a profound impact on the Shiloh battlefield. Despite being felled by a Confederate bullet, he ensured his work was "complete, impartial, and correct" so that his history represented "nothing but the truth."[1]

Understandably, Reed could not escape inputting his own bias, whether he did so consciously or subconsciously. His works and interpretation

---

1 D.W. Reed, *The Battle of Shiloh and the Organizations Engaged* (Washington: Government Printing Office, 1903), 3.

stressed the importance of the Hornets' Nest in the April 6th action and his regiment's role in that fight, assertions now under fire by Shiloh's latest pool of historians.

Despite his interpretations of the battle, Reed's impact on the Shiloh battlefield today is inescapable. His tablets and the monuments he helped place mark the open fields and woodlots of the park as visitors drive along the battlefield's tour route.

The group of historians that included the likes of Reed, Carman, and Bachelder tapped a resource that modern historians dream of, the battles' veterans. Thus, these men laid the groundwork for those who follow in their footsteps.

One cannot study Gettysburg without consulting John Bachelder, or study Antietam without reading Ezra Carman's prose. Historians and enthusiasts cannot learn about Shiloh without utilizing David Reed's resources, including the battlefield itself.

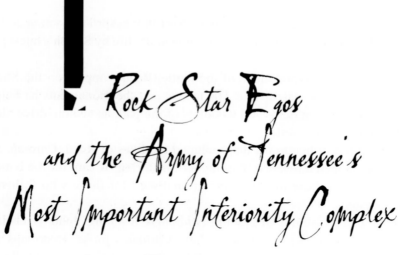

1. Rock Star Egos and the Army of Tennessee's Most Important Inferiority Complex

by Chris Mackowski

Originally published as a blog post at Emerging Civil War on August 7, 2019

In his foreword to Greg Mertz's *Attack at Daylight and Whip Them: The Battle of Shiloh,* historian Timothy B. Smith pointed out a key repercussion of Albert Sidney Johnston's death during the battle: "Confederate command in the West was left for the remainder of the war in a state of turmoil." Greg's book sets the table for that larger story by introducing many key Confederate players. I've been editing the audiobook script of the book and so have been spending some time with these key players lately. Of particular interest to me have been the army's corps commanders.

John C. Breckinridge was a former vice president of the United States and presidential candidate. William Hardee literally wrote the book on infantry tactics, popularly known as *Hardee's Tactics.* Leonidas Polk was the Episcopal bishop of Louisiana. Braxton Bragg was . . . well, Braxton Bragg.

I called my Polish brother, Chris Kolakowski, and laid this out. He's used to random calls from me, when I barely have "hello" out of my mouth before I start bouncing ideas off him.

"Of course, all these guys have egos—that's kind of the story of the command structure of the Army of Tennessee—but it seems like these guys, in particular, have rock star-sized egos," I said of Breckinridge, Hardee, and Polk. They all had accomplishments not just of note but of real significance.

"Polk's a special case," Chris noted. "He's always a special case." While being bishop of the diocese of Louisiana might not sound like a big deal, it's worth noting that New Orleans was the largest city in the Confederacy. Polk's position gave him a noteworthiness that he parlayed into celebrity status. "He laid the cornerstone of the University of the South as recently as 1860," Chris said. "His name was all over the South because of similar dedications he was involved with."

Above the corps level, too, we have to consider Albert Sidney Johnston and P. G. T. Beauregard. Johnston had been the South's most famous military figure at the start of the war. Subsequently, Confederate President Jefferson Davis gave him the most challenging assignment: defense of the vast Confederate west between the Allegheny Mountains and the Mississippi River. Johnston certainly had his ups and downs—mostly downs—during his tenure, but despite setbacks, Davis stuck by him unconditionally. "If [Johnston] is not a general," Davis told detractors, "we had better give up the war, for we have no general."[1]

Think about that for a second: *If Johnston isn't a general, we don't have one.*

That's a bold declaration of faith. We'll never know if Johnston would have lived up to that, but I'm interested in Johnston's position in that particular historical moment: Jefferson Davis saw Johnston as *the* premier general of the South.

Beauregard did not enjoy the same level of support from Davis. However, as the Confederacy's first national hero—for his successful bombardment of Ft. Sumter in April of 1861, then his victory at First Manassas in July of that year—he enjoyed broad public adulation.

---

1 Charles P. Roland, "Albert Sidney Johnston and the Shiloh Campaign," *Civil War History* Vol. 4, No. 4 (Kent, OH: The Kent State University Press, 1958), 356.

Commanders in the Confederate Army of Tennessee thought highly of themselves but not necessarily highly of each other. The command dysfunction that resulted crippled the army's performance and has since become legendary. From left: Braxton Bragg, Leonidas Polk, William Hardee, and John Breckinridge. *Library of Congress*

Now into this mix—two men of significant military stature above him and three "rock-star" peers—let's consider Braxton Bragg.

"He had Buena Vista," Chris Kolakowski said, referencing the battle from the Mexican-American War. "Of the heroes to come out of Zachary Taylor's army, Bragg is one of the most prominent, maybe the most." Then Chris pauses. "But, that was 1847."

"So, there's a 'what have you done for me lately' factor at play," I suggest. "He was a war hero—but a lot of guys we know of today were war heroes. And it was a while ago."

I posit my theory about Bragg's peers' extraordinary level of achievement. Chris adds more to consider into the mix. "Bragg's older brother was the Confederate attorney general and later governor of North Carolina," Chris said. "And there were rumors that Bragg was born while his mother was in jail." Because of those rumors, people picked on Bragg as a child.

"So, he always had an inferiority complex," Chris said.

The other thing Bragg had—dating back to his service at Buena Vista—was the support of Jefferson Davis. Bragg's artillery fought in support of Davis's infantry, a connection Davis forever honored.

Jefferson Davis was friends with Polk, too. Breckinridge would have more influence, and eventually become the Confederate Secretary of War. So, friendship wasn't enough to save Bragg, even if it did sustain him far longer than it should have.

Bragg performed reasonably well at Shiloh, but not without faults. Importantly, it perhaps looked—in the moment—like the old hero of the Mexican-American War might replicate his heroics.

With Johnston dead and Beauregard in command but in questionable health, Bragg held seniority. This made him the ersatz "first among peers" despite the rock-star reputations of other corps commanders. When Beauregard took a convenient absence without leave in June 1862, citing health problems, Bragg ascended to command over corps commanders, all of whom felt themselves to be his better.

Bragg's promotion might as well have come with a sign that said, "Kick me." The angling behind the scenes between him, Davis, and Beauregard cast a shadow of controversy over Bragg's ascension from day one, foreshadowing things to come. Jealousies, petitions, investigations, cabals, and reassignments—controversies, controversies, controversies—would embroil the Army of Tennessee's leadership for the next twenty-one months. Bragg's harsh disciplinarianism would make him deeply unpopular with his men and, through their letters and press reports on the home front. Contrast that against, say, Polk, who was beloved by his men, or Hardee, who was deeply respected.

Later, you'd have the malcontent Daniel Harvey Hill thrown into the command mix—a man so prickly Robert E. Lee effectively banished him from the Army of Northern Virginia. Like Bragg, Hill was a North Carolinian, but that did nothing to endear them to each other. You'd also have James Longstreet parachute into the western theater. As Lee's "Old Warhorse," Longstreet brought a sense of superiority won during high-profile victories in the east, so it's little wonder he looked down on the victory-less Bragg. Chickamauga, Bragg's one victory, came about because of Longstreet's timely exploits during the battle, which did nothing to lessen the tension between the two men.

The grief in the Army of Tennessee wouldn't end until Davis promoted Bragg to a desk job in Richmond in February 1864.

In his 2016 biography of Bragg, Earl Hess credibly called him "The Most Hated Man of the Confederacy." (I highly recommend Hess's book, by the way.) I think of that title in the context of my Shiloh musings. If we consider the most notable achievements of the four Confederate corps commanders—vice president, tactical authority, Episcopal bishop, "most hated"—Bragg achieved a superlative every bit as memorable as his peers, although his ultimate claim was to infamy, not fame.

1. "New Orleans Gone and With It the Confederacy": The Fall of New Orleans

by Patrick Kelly-Fischer

Originally published as a blog post at Emerging Civil War
on May 31, 2022

The signposts of my mental outline of the Civil War have always been major land battles—Shiloh, Antietam, Gettysburg, and Vicksburg. The histories we grew up on are framed around these titanic battles. They're the most popular battlefields to visit, and it would be intuitive to say that the most crucial turning points of a war are its biggest battles.

However, few, if any, of these battles were truly decisive. Some of the largest engagements were a virtual draw. Conversely, some of the most profound, strategic consequences, and missed opportunities resulted from battles that have historically flown under the radar. Glorieta Pass and Monocacy, for example, saw relatively few troops engaged by Civil War standards and are not discussed in many history textbooks, but they were disproportionately consequential. To that list, I would add the capture of New Orleans.

At the outset of the war, New Orleans ranked as the sixth largest city in the country and by far the largest in the Confederacy. At a population of

168,675, it was larger than Charleston (40,522), Richmond (37,910), Mobile (29,258), Memphis (22,623), and Savannah (22,292) *combined*. New Orleans's population alone was larger than the state of Florida (140,424).[1]

But by late April 1862, Confederate Maj. Gen. Mansfield Lovell, a former New Yorker, had only a scratch force to defend the city. The garrison had been stripped bare as the Confederacy sent thousands of troops to reinforce Gen. Leonidas Polk in Columbus, Kentucky, and then to reinforce Generals P.G.T. Beauregard and A.S. Johnston ahead of the battle of Shiloh.[2]

In his report after the battle, Lovell wrote, "every Confederate soldier in New Orleans, with the exception of one company, had been ordered to Corinth, to General Beauregard in March, and the city was only garrisoned by about 3,000 ninety-day troops, called out by the governor at my request, of whom about 1,200 had muskets and the remainder shot-guns of an indifferent description."[3]

The primary obstacle to a naval attack from the Gulf was a pair of forts. A mere 1,100 troops garrisoned Fort Jackson and Fort St. Philip, 75 miles downriver from the city. As early as 1861, Beauregard had predicted: "any steamer could pass them in broad daylight." Having been an engineer in charge of the city's defenses before the war, Beauregard was qualified to speak to its vulnerabilities. He recommended an obstruction be placed in the river to prevent Union warships from sailing through to New Orleans, but Confederate authorities implemented that advice slowly. By the battle of New Orleans in April 1862, a makeshift barrier of small boats had been chained across the river between the forts, but had been damaged as the river ran high in the spring.[4]

Lovell was opposed by Flag Officer David G. Farragut, a Virginian who remained loyal to the Union. This created a scenario in which a Northern-born general led the Confederate defense of New Orleans against a Southern-

---

1 Statistics of the United States Census (Including Mortality, Property, &c.) in 1860, Washington Government Printing Office, 1866, XVII-XX.

2 United States. War Records Office, et al. The War of the Rebellion: a Compilation of the Official Records of the Union And Confederate Armies, Series I, Volume VI, Chapter XVI. 1880, 561, 823.

3 Ibid, 513.

4 Charles Dufour, *The Night the War Was Lost*. Bison, 1994, 29.

born Union flag officer. Never let anyone tell you that the Civil War was a clear-cut affair!

The Union effort started with an attempt to reduce Forts Jackson and St. Philip with a flotilla of mortar boats. However, after several days, they had not succeeded in battering the forts into submission. After sending two ships to open a hole in the barrier across the river, on the night of April 24th, Farragut ran most of his fleet between the forts under cover of darkness.

Captain William Roberston, a Confederate artillery officer in Fort Jackson, wrote, "I do not believe there ever was a grander spectacle witnessed before in the world than that displayed during the great artillery duel which then followed. The mortar-shells shot upward from the mortar-boats, rushed to the apexes of their flight, flashing the lights of their fuses as they revolved, paused an instant, and then descended upon our works like hundreds of meteors, or burst in midair, hurling their jagged fragments in every direction. The guns on both sides kept up a continual roar for nearly an hour, without a moment's intermission."[5]

Successfully running the forts, Farragut sailed north, briefly engaging shore batteries that lacked the position, ammunition, or caliber to stop his fleet. He also received the surrender of several hundred Confederate infantry who found themselves outgunned and, tellingly for the city's defense, occupying low ground compared to the Union warships. After his surrender, Confederate Col. Szymanski lamented, "After losing some thirty men killed and wounded, with no possibility of escape or rescue—perfectly at the mercy of the enemy, he being able to cut the levees and drown me out—I thought it my duty to surrender. A single shell could have cut the light embankment."[6]

Ultimately, Lovell had too few troops, too little artillery, insufficient fortifications, and the disadvantage of being *below* the warships on the river. As it was, Lovell's army had been reduced to reinforce Albert Sidney Johnston in the effort to turn the tide after the losses of Fort Henry, Fort Donelson, and Nashville. Throughout his time in command, there was constant tension and lack of cooperation between the Confederate Army

5 Captain William Robertson, "The Water-Battery at Fort Jackson," *Battles and Leaders of the Civil War*, Vol. 2, accessed via Tufts University Perseus Digital Library.

6 Dufour, 282-283.

and naval forces tasked with defending the city. On March 6, he had written to Confederate Secretary of War Judah Benjamin that, "This department is being completely drained of everything. . . . We have filled requisitions for arms, men, and munitions until New Orleans is about defenseless. In return we get nothing."[7]

Rather than fight it out in the city with, in his words, a few thousand "miscellaneous and half-armed militia of the city,"[8] Lovell abandoned New Orleans and retreated toward Baton Rouge. Major General Benjamin Butler's 15,000 Federal troops moved into the city, beginning his infamous occupation.

While it would not have felt this way to the men fighting and dying, casualties were incredibly low by the day's standards—200 or so on each side. Confederate naval losses are hard to pin down, as well as the various small Confederate garrisons that eventually surrendered.[9]

Even if their casualties were light, what did the loss of New Orleans really cost the Confederacy?

Owing in large part to its location near the mouth of the Mississippi River, the city was the heart of commerce and trade in the South, and the fourth-largest commercial port in the world. Historian Amanda Foreman describes it as "the epicenter of the slave trade and the gateway not only for the majority of the South's cotton crop, but also for its tobacco and sugar."[10]

Access to outside trade was important because, throughout the war, the Confederacy was badly outmatched in a manufacturing capacity. Without the arms industry needed to equip tens of thousands of soldiers, they relied on European imports smuggled through a tightening blockade and arms captured from the enemy. However, that problem grew after losing New Orleans as an industrial base. In the 1860 census, New Orleans had ranked second in value of manufactured goods among cities that seceded, behind only Richmond, Virginia.[11]

---

7 United States. War Records Office, et al. The War of the Rebellion: a Compilation of the Official Records of the Union And Confederate Armies, Series I, Volume VI, Chapter XVI. 1880, 515, 841.

8 Ibid, 511.

9 Dufour, 283-284.

10 Amanda Foreman, *A World on Fire*. Random House, 2010, 110.

11 *Statistics of the United States Census (Including Mortality, Property, &c.) in 1860*, Washington Government Printing Office, 1866, XVII-XX.

After the war, Lt. Col. J.W. Mallet of the Confederate Ordnance Bureau wrote that in the entire Confederacy, "There were but two first class foundries and machine shops—the Tredegar Works at Richmond and the Leeds Foundry at New Orleans; the loss of the latter was one of the sorest consequences of the fall of that city."[12]

As a center of ocean commerce and manufacturing, New Orleans could have become a hub of Confederate naval shipbuilding, something they sorely lacked throughout the war. What naval defenses the city actually mounted against Farragut's fleet were largely converted commercial vessels, such as the small ironclad ram *Manassas*. When the city fell, both the *Louisiana* and *Mississippi* were massive and powerful ironclad warships that were supposedly near completion, though accounts vary. Instead, when Farragut ran the forts, the *Louisiana* functioned as a floating battery before being blown up to avoid capture. The *Mississippi* was torched without ever firing a shot.

Confederate Secretary of the Navy Stephen Mallory optimistically believed that both could have posed a significant threat to Farragut's wooden fleet, and eventually to the Union blockade. In particular, he was convinced that the *Mississippi* alone would have raised the entire blockade across the South in a matter of days. That was wishful thinking—however advanced, one or two ships would always have limitations. But they may well have reopened New Orleans to badly-needed foreign trade, at least temporarily, delaying future Union efforts to capture the city, allowing more time to spin up badly needed naval shipbuilding.[13]

The possibilities do not end there. New Orleans served as a staging point for Banks's 1863 campaign against Port Hudson and a supply source for Grant's Vicksburg campaign. However, neither of those cities would have been as critically important if the Confederacy still held New Orleans. As it was, Vicksburg presented an immense challenge that took Grant a year to crack. How much longer would it have taken him to restore Union control of the "Father of Waters," as Lincoln called the Mississippi River, if he had

---

12 Lt. Col. J.W. Mallet, "Work of the Ordnance Bureau of the War Department of the Confederate States, 1861-5," *Battles and Leaders of the Civil War*, Vol. 37, accessed via Tufts University Perseus Digital Library.

13 Dufour, 336.

to campaign down the river through Port Hudson, Baton Rouge, and finally, New Orleans?

Like any counterfactual, it is impossible to answer the question of what would have happened if New Orleans had been held. No single city in the South would have offset the North's considerable advantages in manpower, arms, or financing. But the scale of the defeat—and the accompanying lost opportunities for the Confederacy—help us understand why these reactions were not hyperbolic:

- Mary Chestnut wrote in her diary, "New Orleans gone and with it the Confederacy."[14]

- The *Richmond Examiner* wrote, "The extent of the loss is not to be disguised. It annihilated us in Louisiana . . . led to our virtual abandonment of the great and fruitful Valley of the Mississippi, and cost the Confederacy ... the commercial capital of the South . . . and . . . the largest exporting city in the world."[15]

- Gustavus Fox, assistant aecretary of the Navy, called capturing New Orleans the "great event second only to the final surrender of Lee."[16]

14 Mary Boykin Miller Chesnut, *A Diary From Dixie*, Appleton and Company, 1905, accessed via University of North Carolina, 158-159.

15 Donald L. Miller, *Vicksburg* (New York: Simon & Schuster, 2019), 118.

16 Dufour, 136.

1. The Battle of Memphis and Its Fallen Federal Leader

by Chris Mackowski

*Originally published as a blog post at Emerging Civil War
on June 6, 2022*

One of the most consequential battles of the war—and one of the shortest—took place on June 6, 1862: the battle of Memphis.[1] Federals suffered only a single casualty, Col. Charles Ellet, Jr., the man most responsible for the victory in the first place. Although he would not die immediately, Ellet would not live long enough to see the incredible fruits of the victory he helped make possible.

A Pennsylvania native, Ellet was an engineer by trade. He designed and oversaw the construction of the first cable-suspension bridge in the U.S., a 358-foot span over the Schuylkill River north of Philadelphia. (He'd originally pitched one for the Potomac River but was denied). His bridge-building got bigger. Subsequent bridges in Wheeling, Virginia (now West Virginia) and Niagara Falls, New York, measured more than 1,000 feet and 750 feet, respectively.

---

1 The author would like to offer his thanks to historian Curt Fields for taking him to the banks of the Mississippi in Memphis to show him the scene of the battle.

Ellet also worked on flood control studies along the Mississippi, whose long-term impact would make him a one-man Tennessee Valley Authority. Early biographer Gene D. Lewis says, "Ellet's interest thus ranged broadly from bridge-building, canal and railroad construction, and the economics of transportation to the improvement of western rivers, and to projects for defeating the Confederacy."[2]

A fluke accident led to his most important impact on the Civil War. While traveling overseas in the mid-1850s, Ellet heard news of a paddle steamer, the USS *Arctic*, that was accidentally sunk by a much smaller ship, the propeller-driven USS *Vesta*, which had run into the *Arctic*. The *Arctic* was 11 times bigger than the *Vesta*. The incident convinced Ellet that a steam-powered ship like the *Vesta* could, with enough momentum, effectively serve as a ram that could batter opposing ships into sinking.

Ellet came from deep Revolutionary stock: both grandfathers served in the American Revolution. Although his father was a Quaker, a sect known for pacifism, Ellet felt compelled to do his part when war broke out in 1861. He tried to get anyone in the army or navy to listen to his ideas about rams. Finally, in early 1862, he found a receptive audience in Secretary of War Edwin Stanton.

On March 20, 1862, Stanton summoned Ellet to a meeting of Stanton's top army advisers to make his pitch. After, Quartermaster Montgomery Meigs admitted Ellet "might be usefully employed by the government in gunboat construction in the west." Stanton did Meigs one better. "Perhaps he would be as good a man as we could get for that purpose," the secretary replied, adding:

> He has more ingenuity, more personal courage, and more enterprise than anybody else I have ever seen. . . . He is a clear, forcible, controversial writer. He can beat anybody at figures. He would cipher anybody to death. If I had a proposition that I desired to work out to some definite result, I do not know of any one to whom I would intrust it so soon as Ellet. His fancy and will are predominant points, and once having taken a notion he will not allow it to be questioned.

2 Gene D. Lewis, Charles Ellet Jr., *The Engineer and Individualist, 1810-1862* (Urbana, IL: University of Illinois Press, 1968), 3.

"Is there any better person to whom I could commit that duty?" Stanton concluded.[3]

When informed of his new assignment, Ellet was delighted. He asked if it would be possible to be placed outside the chain of command, ostensibly because of his lack of military experience. Another factor may have been that he did not want to serve under Secretary of the Navy Gideon Welles, who'd spurned his suggestions for a year and a half before Stanton had taken notice. However, as Stanton pointed out, Ellet as a civilian, would be legally ineligible to command any of the ships. Therefore, the secretary countered with an offer to make Ellet a colonel with a direct report to the secretary of war. Furthermore, Ellet would command the ram fleet directly. However, when it finally took to the water, the overall fleet would fall under the operational command of Flag Officer Charles H. Davis, and Ellet's rams were expected to operate in conjunction. This unconventional command structure seemed to suit Ellet, who anticipated action "not in accordance with naval usage."[4]

Stanton instructed Ellet to start work in three places— Pittsburgh, Cincinnati, and New Albany—to "bring out the whole mechanical energy of the Ohio Valley."[5] The plan was "to take the largest and most powerful river boats, remove the upper works, fill the bows with timber, and furnish such protection as can be afforded. . . ." One of Stanton's advisers suggested iron plating for the rams, but Stanton nixed the idea. "We do not want to wait for iron armor," he said. "Ellet calculates upon destroying a boat right off by running into her."

Work on the ram fleet progressed smoothly and quickly. Meanwhile, Maj. Gen. Henry Halleck, just then setting his sights on the Confederate supply base at Corinth, Mississippi, expressed anxiousness about threats to his supply line, in particular, "ironclad boats now being built at New Orleans, to be sent up the river for the purpose of interfering with our flotilla." What was "the proper way to meet these boats?" Halleck inquired.[6]

---

3 George Congdon Gorham, *Life and Public Services of Edwin M. Stanton* (Boston: Houghton, Mifflin, and Company, 1899), 290, 292.

4 *Official Records of the Union and Confederate Navies in the War of the Rebellion*, Series 1, Volume XXIII, 74.

5 Quoted in Gorham, 295.

6 Gorham, 291.

The answer was the ram fleet. Ellet envisioned a fast, decisive strike down the Mississippi. "What we do with these rams will probably be accomplished within a month after striking the first boat . . ." he wrote. "I think if I can get the boats safely below Memphis I can command the river." He did worry about the river batteries at Memphis and believed he'd have to run the rams past them; once below the city, they would be unable to return and must either "go down the Mississippi or be sunk or taken."[7]

Ellet's boats rendezvoused and, with Ellet in command of *The Queen of the West*, they began their

Enthusiastic or rash? Tragic irony or just desserts? The fate of Charles Ellet, Jr., remains controversial. *Lives and Works of Civil and Military Engineers of America*

movement downriver—even as word arrived of the Confederate fleet moving northward to meet them. The forces, when they clashed, would be closely matched: Federals had nine vessels; Confederates eight.

The two forces met around 5:30 a.m. on June 6, 1862, on the edge of Memphis, Tennessee. "Rebel gunboats made a stand early this morning opposite Memphis, and opened a vigorous fire upon our gunboats, which was returned with equal spirit," Ellet wrote.[8]

Davis ordered the Federal armada to approach with caution (and backwards so as to not pick up too much speed), but the ram fleet darted ahead in the lead. "[A]ll of them opened fire, and continued the same from the time they got within good range, until the end of the battle," reported Union naval officer Henry Walke.[9]

7 *OR*, Vol. X, Pt. 2, 112.

8 *OR*, Vol. X, Pt. 1, 907.

9 Henry Walke, *Naval scenes and reminiscences of the Civil War in the United States, on the southern and western waters during the years 1861, 1862 and 1863, with the history of that period compared and corrected from authentic sources, by Rear-Admiral H. Walke* (New York, F. R. Reed, 1877), 278.

Ellet's *Queen of the West* opened the battle by ramming the Confederate flagship, *Colonel Lovell*.[10] "My speed was high, time was short," Ellet said, picking the *Lovell* as the easiest of three targets that had, in the midst of turning around, presented their broadsides to the rams. The *Queen* hit just forward of the *Lovell*'s wheelhouse. "The crash was terrific," Ellet said. "Everything loose about the *Queen*—some tables, pantry ware, and a half-eaten breakfast—where overthrown and broken by the shock. The hull of the rebel steamer was crushed in, her chimneys surged over as if they were going to fall over on the bow of the Queen."[11] Ellet recalled "the surface of the Mississippi strewn with the fragments of the rebel vessel."[12]

Less than half a minute later, though, the *Queen* herself was struck. A double-team by the *Sumter,* and the *Beauregard* disabled her with a blow directly to the wheelhouse. "The blow broke her tiller rope, crushed in her wheel and a portion of her hull, and left her nearly helpless," Ellet reported.[13] His ram drifted to the Arkansas shore with only one wheel and without a rudder and there it grounded.

Shortly thereafter, another Federal ram—the USS *Monarch*, captained by Ellet's brother, Alfred—disabled the *General Price*, which ran aground not far from Ellet's *Queen*. Ellet could not resist and sent a boarding party to the disabled Confederate ship. A flagship, after all, would make a fine spoil of war.

Confederates resisted the Federal attempt to board, though, and in the ensuing gunfight, a bullet clipped Ellet in the knee. The "pistol-shot wound in the leg deprived me of the power to witness the remainder of the fight."[14]

There were plenty of other witnesses to the fight, though: nearly the entire population of Memphis gathered on the bluffs overlooking the river to watch the spectacle unfold—"some of them apparently as gay and cheerful as a bright May morning, and others watching with silent awe the impending struggle," wrote Walke:

10 ECW naval historian Neil Chatelain points out, "the Confederate River Defense Fleet vessels were civilian contracted vessels of the CS army, not navy, and technically thus would not have a CSS designation." The same was true for Ellet's boats. However, it does help to use them for clarity.

11 Ibid., 926.

12 Ibid.

13 Ibid.

14 Ibid., 907.

The roar of cannon and shell soon shook the earth on either shore for many miles; first, wild yells, shrieks, and clamors, then loud, despairing murmurs, filled the affrighted city. The screaming, plunging shell crashed into the boats, blowing them and their crews into fragments; and the rams rushed upon each other like wild beasts in deadly conflict. Amidst all this confusion and horror, the air was filled with the coal and sulphurous blinding smoke; and, as the battle progressed, all the cheering voices on shore were silenced, every voice became tremulous and disheartened, as it became evident that their fleet was faltering, and one after another of their vessels sank or became disabled.[15]

Ellet crowed about a last-ditch Confederate effort at escape: "The rebel rams endeavored to back downstream and then to turn and run, but the movement was fatal to them."[16]

Within ninety minutes, the battle was over. "The enemy's rams did most of the execution, and were handled more adroitly than ours," said Confederate Gen. M. Jeff Thompson, among the crowd watching from the bluffs. "[A]nd I am sorry to say that in my opinion many of our boats were handled badly or the plan of battle was very faulty."[17]

Memphis surrendered that afternoon. Ellet sent his son, Medical Cadet Charles R. Ellet, into the city with a pair of U.S. flags, one to fly over the customs house and the other to fly over the post office "as evidence of the return of your city to the care and protection of the Constitution."[18] Ellet the Younger was accompanied by members of the 59th Illinois Infantry. A good thing, too: an "excited crowd, using angry and threatening language," fired upon the party and threw stones. Strong Federal patrols went into the city that evening to quell the public disquiet.

Stanton received news of the victory at Memphis on the evening of June 8th. His elation was "dampened only by your personal injury," he wrote to Ellet. The secretary personally assumed the duty of telling Ellet's wife,

15 Walke, 281.

16 Ellet, 907.

17 Quoted in Gorham, 299.

18 O.R., Vol X, Pt. 1, 910.

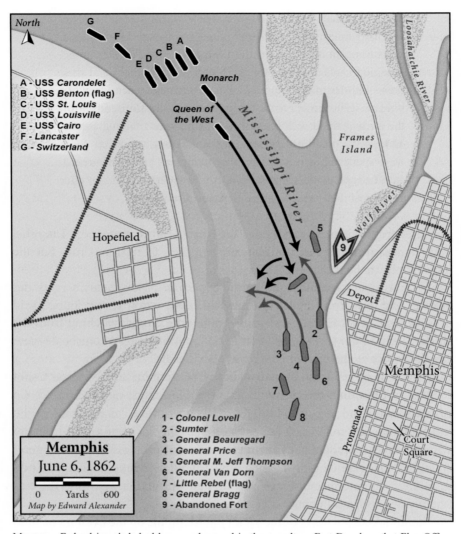

MEMPHIS—Federal ironclads had been so damaged in the assault on Fort Donelson that Flag Officer Charles H. Davis backed them down the river to better protect and control them in the current. Charles Ellet, in a lack of coordination with Davis, sped past the naval vessels with two of his rams and engaged the hastily assembled Confederate fleet. Spectators on the bluffs watched as, one by one, the over-matched Confederate vessels were knocked out of the fight.

Elvira (called "Ellie"), about Ellet's injury. "She was, of course, deeply affected, but bore the information with as much spirit and courage as could be expected," Stanton reported. "It is her design to proceed immediately to join you." Stanton furnished her with a pass for free passage for her and the

Ellets' daughter, Mary. "You will keep me advised of your state of health and everything you want," Stanton added.[19]

What Ellet wanted was to continue his mission downriver. On June 8, as Stanton was penning his congratulations, Ellet was hoping to start southward with the ram fleet the next day. Davis even offered to send a gunboat along with the rams. "Of course I will not decline," Ellet said, "though I fear the slowness of the gunboat will impede the progress of my expedition."[20]

Ellet was not looking a gift horse in the mouth. He had been pleased with how Davis's ships supported the ram fleet. "Of the gunboats I can only say that they bore themselves as our Navy always does—bravely and well," he wrote.[21] Davis, meanwhile, noted Ellet "was conspicuous for his gallantry" and believed Ellet's wound serious but not dangerous.[22]

However, the wound was more serious than anyone first imagined. Complicating matters, Ellet contracted measles during his convalescence. On June 11th, as he wrote a follow-up report to the battle, he stopped midway through. The Official Records note Ellet's report was discontinued "on account of Colonel Ellet's exhaustion" and never resumed.[23]

On May 15th, Ellie and Mary arrived from Philadelphia. Writing to Stanton on June 16th, Ellet thanked him for sending them along. He also petitioned Stanton to place his brother, Alfred Ellet, in charge of the ram fleet in his stead. "The great prostration of my system points, I fear, to slow recovery," the wounded colonel admitted. "I can do nothing here but lie in my bed and suffer."[24]

Stanton, who received the letter on the 18th, complied with Ellet's request two days later. Writing to Alfred, he said, "I regret that your brother's illness deprives the Government of his skillful and gallant services, but have

19 Quoted in Gorham, 299.

20 O.R., Vol. X, Pt. 1, 907.

21 Ibid., 908.

22 Ibid., 907.

23 Ibid., 927.

24 O.R. LII, 257.

confidence that you will supply his place better than anyone else."[25] The fleet started south the next day.

One of the fleet's boats did not go southward. The USS *Switzerland* was tasked with transporting Ellet and his family northward to the army hospital in Cairo, Illinois. Ellet died as the ship reached port around 4 p.m. on June 21, 1862. Quartermaster James Brooks informed Stanton of the news by telegraph.[26]

Ellet's body was shipped east, where it lay in state in Independence Hall under the Liberty Bell. The Philadelphia City Council, grateful for Ellet's role in the fall of Memphis, appropriated $500 to help defer funeral expenses, and Ellet was buried in the city's Laurel Hill Cemetery. Unfortunately, Ellie, exhausted and overcome with grief, died within a fortnight and was buried with her husband.[27]

Ellet would not see the incredible impact his victory would have. Coupled with Grant's victory on the Tennessee River at Pittsburg Landing and Halleck's move from there toward Corinth, the fall of Memphis allowed Federal forces to advance against the Deep South. Memphis, in particular, would serve as the staging area for all future operations against Vicksburg. By some accounts, more than a million soldiers would move back and forth through the city as part of those operations, swelling the city's population and bringing economic prosperity.

Early Ellet biographer George Gorham credited the victory at Memphis to "the zeal and energy of two civilians": "Stanton's confidence in Ellet and the latter's confidence in himself. . . ."[28] Indeed, Stanton said in March when he had approved Ellet's plan for the ram fleet: "Mr. Ellet himself is willing to risk it." Ultimately, Ellet risked it all. The verdict of history has been, in the words of one historian who captured the sentiments of many, that "few Northern triumphs in the Civil War were more complete or one-sided than the Battle of Memphis."[29]

25 Ibid., 258.

26 Ibid., 258.

27 Lewis, 207.

28 Gorham, 299.

29 Quoted in Lewis, 207.

What If...
Vicksburg Had Fallen in July '62?

by Dwight Hughes

Originally published as a blog post at Emerging Civil War
on August 15, 2022

In his memoirs, Admiral David D. Porter recollected a November 1861 meeting with President Lincoln and navy secretary Gideon Welles in which—he says—he suggested the plan to seize New Orleans from the sea.

Lincoln liked the idea and added: "while we are about it, we can push on to Vicksburg and open the river all the way along." Porter's foster brother, Capt. David G. Farragut, would command the expedition while then-Commander Porter led the assisting mortar-boat squadron.[1]

January 20, 1862: Secretary Welles promoted Farragut to flag officer and command of the West Gulf Blockading Squadron. His first order was to "take possession of [New Orleans] under the guns of your squadron, and hoist the American flag thereon." But that was not the only objective: "If the Mississippi expedition from Cairo shall not have descended the river, you

---

1 Admiral Porter, *Incidents and Anecdotes of the Civil War* (New York: D. Appleton and Company, 1885), 69.

OPPOSITE: "WHAT IF" VICKSBURG—If General Halleck had chosen to assist Admiral Farragut as requested, he could have dispatched columns down the railroad to Jackson and then west and/or down the river by steam transport, closing a giant joint pincer movement on Vicksburg. Grant and Sherman undoubtedly would have jumped at the chance. Halleck's lack of coordination with Farragut underscores how visionary Grant's own attitudes were when it came to cooperating with the Navy.

will take advantage of the panic to push a strong force up the river to take all their defenses in the rear."[2]

From the base at Cairo, Illinois, the navy was assisting the army in assembling a squadron of ironclad and wooden river gunboats with supply and transport vessels to descend the Mississippi and split the Confederacy. In early February, under Flag Officer Andrew H. Foote, the Western Gunboat Flotilla facilitated Brig. Gen. U. S. Grant's conquest of Forts Henry and Donelson, Tennessee. Foote then proceeded downriver to take Island No. 10 near New Madrid, Missouri, on April 7th, the second day of the battle of Shiloh.

April 24: Farragut blasted his big warships past Forts Jackson and St. Philip, brushed aside Rebel river forces, and secured the city; Maj. Gen. Benjamin Butler and 5,000 troops took possession on May 1st.

After several days of repairing battle damage, the Gulf Squadron surged northward. Baton Rouge and Natchez—nearly defenseless—surrendered, but powerful Vicksburg batteries absorbed concentrated bombardment and returned blistering fire. The flag officer assessed the fortress as unassailable from the river while water levels were falling, threatening to strand his deep-draft vessels.

May 16, Fox to Farragut: Assistant Secretary of the Navy, Gustavus V. Fox, read in New York papers that the squadron had retreated south rather than continuing upriver past Vicksburg to Memphis. He dispatched a letter in triplicate by the fastest three ships he could find: "This information may not be true," the letter said, "but the probability of it has distressed the President." First, he telegraphed Farragut at New Orleans: "Carry out your instructions of January 20 about ascending the Mississippi River, as it is of the utmost importance."

2 Welles to Farragut, January 20, 1862, in *Official Records of the Union and Confederate Navies in the War of the Rebellion*, 2 series, 29 vols. (Washington, D.C., 1894-1922), series 1, vol. 18, 7. Hereafter cited as *ORN*. All references are to Series 1, vol. 18.

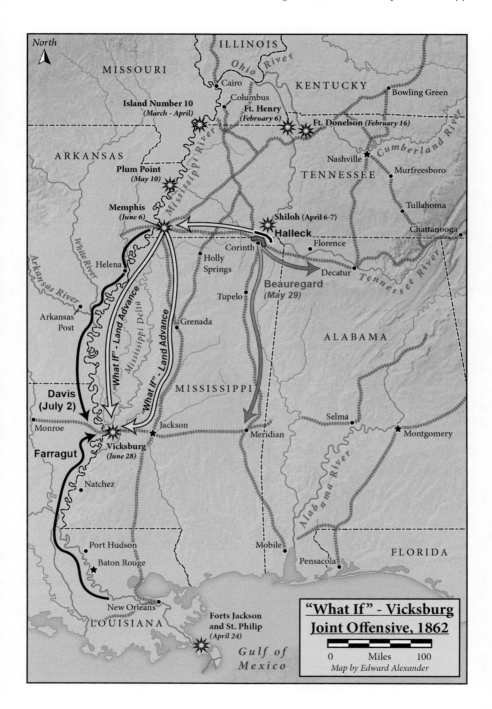

North

ILLINOIS

MISSOURI

Ohio River

Cairo

Columbus

KENTUCKY

Bowling Green

Island Number 10
(March - April)

Ft. Henry
(February 6)

Ft. Donelson *(February 16)*

Cumberland River

ARKANSAS

Plum Point
(May 10)

Nashville

TENNESSEE

Murfreesboro

Mississippi River

Tullahoma

Memphis
(June 6)

Shiloh *(April 6-7)*

Halleck

Chattanooga

Corinth

Florence

Helena

White River

Holly
Springs

"What If" Land Advance

Beauregard
(May 29)

Tennessee River

Arkansas River

Tupelo

Decatur

Arkansas
Post

"What If" Land Advance

Grenada

ALABAMA

Mississippi Delta

MISSISSIPPI

Selma

Davis
(July 2)

Jackson

Meridian

Montgomery

Monroe

Vicksburg
(June 28)

Farragut

Natchez

Alabama River

Port Hudson

Mobile

FLORIDA

Baton Rouge

Pensacola

New Orleans

LOUISIANA

Forts Jackson
and St. Philip
(April 24)

Gulf of
Mexico

**"What If" - Vicksburg
Joint Offensive, 1862**

0   Miles   100

Map by Edward Alexander

After the bloodbath and near disaster at Shiloh, Maj. Gen. Henry W. Halleck sidelined General Grant and conducted a month-long, tedious siege of Corinth, Mississippi, where Gen. P. G. T. Beauregard holed up with his army.

Fox's letter to Farragut continued: "So soon as we heard of the fall of New Orleans, we notified Foote and Halleck that you would be in Beauregard's rear at once." They had learned "with great pleasure" of his progress toward Vicksburg. Now, "this retreat may be a fatal step as regards our western movements."

The Gulf Squadron's presence at Memphis would flank Corinth, blockade the river, and force Beauregard to fight or retreat, besides capturing the enemy's gunboats, "which have already made one attack upon our Western Flotilla, and are preparing for another."

Meanwhile, Flag Officer Charles H. Davis had relived Foote and led the Western Gunboat Flotilla downriver. At Plum Point above Memphis on May 10th, Rebel gunboats rammed and sank two of his ironclads, although they were quickly raised and returned to service.

Fox informed Farragut that the Gulf Squadron's initial ascent had caught Confederates by surprise, but now they were rapidly fortifying the river. "Still it is of paramount importance that you go up and clear the river with the utmost expedition. Mobile, Pensacola, and, in fact, the whole coast sinks into insignificance compared with this."

Farragut's complete execution of his orders would be "the most glorious consummation in history." Fox had hardly slept, he wrote, "especially as three weeks have passed and nothing except a return [to New Orleans] is rumored. . . . At any rate there is not a moment to be lost in the Mississippi."[3]

May 19, Welles to Farragut: "SIR: The President of the United States requires you to use your utmost exertions (without a moment's delay, and before any other naval operations shall be permitted to interfere) to open the river Mississippi and effect a junction with Flag-Officer Davis."[4]

Farragut struggled back upriver, where Porter joined him with the mortar boats. At the same time, Davis, on June 6th, destroyed what was left of the Confederate river defense fleet at Memphis and continued toward

---

3 Fox to Farragut, May 16, 1862, *ORN*, 498-499.

4 Welles to Farragut, May 19, 1862, *ORN*, 502.

Vicksburg with his gunboats, now redesignated the Mississippi River Squadron. Confederates abandoned Corinth on May 29th.

June 28, Farragut to Davis: "We have been shelling [the city] with the mortar fleet two days and made the attack with the fleet proper this morning at 4 o'clock." Vicksburg lay in the outside curve of a tight horseshoe bend with fortifications mounting 30 or 40 guns. As the warships steamed up channel straight at Rebel muzzles—not yet within the arc of fire of their broadside guns—the enemy blasted away at the unprotected bows. The Confederates took cover while the ships rounded the corner with sailors returning their best shots on the way by, and then opened up again on fragile sterns after the vessels passed.

Despite heavy fire in both directions, neither side inflicted much damage. One fired up at the bluffs while steaming, and the other shot down at moving targets on the river below, with many rounds passing harmlessly over. Farragut's flagship, USS *Hartford*, took several 50-pound rifle rounds and 8-inch solid shots to the hull; the nine ships lost four killed and thirteen wounded.

Farragut explained to Davis that the 3,000 soldiers with the Gulf Squadron could not land on the east bank against Maj. Gen. Earl Van Dorn's division of some eight or ten thousand men ensconced there. And he would need to get back below the city soon to reconnect with their river supply line.

"I think, therefore, that so long as [Confederates] have the military force to hold the back country it will be impossible for me to reduce the place without your assistance and that of the army. . . . My orders are so peremptory that I must do all in my power to free the river of all impediments; that I must attack them, although I know it is useless, the river will soon be so low that we will not be able to get our ships down, so you see my position."[5]

June 28, Farragut to Welles: "SIR: I passed up the river this morning, but to no purpose. . . . I am satisfied that it is not possible for us to take Vicksburg without an army force of twelve or fifteen thousand men. . . . The water is too low for me to go over 12 or 15 miles above Vicksburg."[6]

---

5 Farragut to Davis, June 28, 1862, *ORN*, 589.

6 Farragut to Welles, June 28, 1862, *ORN*, 588.

<u>June 28, Farragut to Halleck at Corinth</u>: "SIR: I have the honor to inform you that I have passed the batteries and am now above Vicksburg with the greater part of my fleet. . . . My orders, general, are to clear the river. This I find impossible without your assistance. Can you aid me in this matter to carry out the peremptory order of the President? I am satisfied that you will act for the best advantage of our Government in this matter, and shall therefore await with great anxiety your reply."

Flag Officer Davis and the River Squadron joined the Gulf Squadron on July 2. The largest U.S. Navy armada ever assembled on a river continued bombarding the city.[7]

<u>July 3, Halleck to Farragut from Corinth</u>: "The scattered and weakened condition of my forces renders it impossible for me at the present to detach any troops to cooperate with you on Vicksburg. Probably I shall be able to do so as soon as I can get my troops more concentrated. This may delay the clearing of the river, but its accomplishment will be certain in a few weeks. Allow me to congratulate you on your great success."[8]

The general would explain to Secretary of War Stanton: "I can not at present give Commodore Farragut any aid against Vicksburg. I am sending reinforcements to General Curtis in Arkansas and to General Buell in Tennessee and Kentucky."[9]

<u>July 10, Farragut to Welles</u>: "SIR: It is not perhaps my province to take the liberty to say to the Department where my services may be most needed, but . . . under existing circumstances the services of my squadron would be much more essential to the interests of the country on the coast than in this river. Why?"

Because, he continued, the River Squadron had destroyed waterborne resistance and possesses sufficient naval force to keep the river clear. "I can do nothing here but blockade the port until the army arrives, which can be done as well by Flag-Officer Davis as by [us] both." The city must be

7 Farragut to Halleck, June 28, 1862, *ORN*, 590.

8 Halleck to Farragut, July 3, 1862, *ORN*, 593.

9 Halleck to Stanton, July 16, 1862, *ORN*, 636.

reduced by "the army getting in the rear" and holding it. "My services are required outside to look after my squadron from Pensacola to Brazos."[10]

July 14, Welles to Farragut: "SIR: The evacuation of Corinth has much lessened the importance of your continuing your operations on the Mississippi. The Army has failed to furnish the necessary troops for the capture of Vicksburg, and has not at present, it is represented, an available force to send there to cooperate with you in its capture." He should return to the Gulf and operate, "at such point or points on the Southern coast as you may deem advisable, leaving Flag-Officer Davis in possession and control of the Mississippi as far down as may be expedient."[11]

"It was a fatal mistake," recalled William T. Sherman in his memoirs, "that halted General Halleck at Corinth, and led him to disperse and scatter the best materials for a fighting army that, up to that date, had been assembled in the West."[12]

Secretary Welles groused in his diary in January 1863: "Had the army seconded Farragut and the Navy months ago, Vicksburg would have been in our possession. Halleck was good for nothing then, nor is he now."[13] Porter, Grant, and Sherman, would return to finish the job in July 1863.

What if?

---

10 Farragut to Welles, July 10, 1862, *ORN*, 675.

11 Welles to Farragut, July 14, 1862, *ORN*, 595.

12 William T. Sherman, *Memoirs of Gen. William T. Sherman — Volume 1* (Kindle Edition) 179.

13 Gideon Welles, *Diary of Gideon Welles, Secretary of the Navy under Lincoln and Johnson*, Howard K. Beale, ed., 3 vols. (New York, 1960), vol. 1, 218.

I. The Great March from Cumberland Gap

by Chris Kolakowski

*Originally published as a blog post at Emerging Civil War
on October 3, 2016*

October 3, 1862, ended one of the epic marches in American military history, the evacuation of the Union garrison at Cumberland Gap to the Ohio River.[1] The men—7,000 under Brig. Gen. George W. Morgan—endured a test not often found in the annals of the United States Army. What they achieved is on par with other great movements like Benedict Arnold's march to Quebec in 1775, Stephen Kearny's march to California in 1846, and Joseph Stilwell's walkout from Burma in 1942. Yet, it is largely forgotten outside of Kentucky.

Here is that story.

When the Confederates invaded Kentucky in August 1862, a 9,000-member division under Carter Stevenson diverted to besiege George Morgan's garrison at Cumberland Gap. Cut off from the outside, the men from East Tennessee and Eastern Kentucky, could only watch their rations

---

1 The material in this post is taken from Christopher L. Kolakowski, *The Civil War at Perryville: Battling for the Bluegrass* (Charleston, SC: The History Press 2009), 57-68.

Cumberland Gap, viewed from the north side. *Author's collection*

dwindle and wonder what was happening elsewhere. No word came as August turned into September.

On September 6, the garrison's bread ran out. Six days later, the post quartermaster reported that feed for the horses and mules was almost exhausted. If these animals starved to death, the garrison would lose its mobility and could never leave the Gap.

George Morgan now faced a critical decision. On September 14, he met with his staff and senior commanders. After considering the situation carefully, all agreed that the Gap needed to be evacuated. Having decided to leave Cumberland Gap, the next question was where to go. A march on the Old Wilderness Road toward Lexington or Central Kentucky would mean a likely encounter with Confederates, not something George Morgan was willing to risk with his half-starved men. Win or lose, a major fight might so cripple his force that it would be unable to get to Union lines.

The only alternative was going through the mountains to the Ohio River, 200 miles to the north. However, this option meant a major move into a wild region using narrow roads and defiles that an intrepid opponent could easily block. George Morgan marked a possible route on a map, and showed it to some officers familiar with Eastern Kentucky's mountains. Everyone agreed it would be a tough road, with little forage or water. One officer, the former Kentucky State Geologist, said that the Federals could "possibly" get through, but only "by abandoning the artillery and wagons." Despite the risks, George Morgan decided to try bringing his whole force through the mountains.

After days of preparations, George Morgan's men left Cumberland Gap at 8:00 p.m. on September 17th. They burned everything not movable and blocked the road to delay pursuit. Turning northeast past Manchester, the Federals moved into the mountains while Confederates under John Hunt

Because of their remarkable march, perhaps George Morgan's men might have been designated "foot cavalry."
Author's collection

Morgan and Humphrey Marshall exerted every effort to block their progress. While the wagons moved through defiles, East Tennessee infantry covered from the ridges above.

George Morgan later summarized the hunt in the Eastern Kentucky mountains: "Frequent skirmishes took place, and it several times happened that while the one Morgan was clearing out the obstructions at the entrance to a defile, the other Morgan was blocking the exit from the same defile with enormous rocks and felled trees. In the work of clearing away these obstructions, one thousand men, wielding axes, saws, picks, spades, and block and tackle, under the general direction of Captain William F. Patterson, commanding his company of engineer-mechanics, and of Captain Sidney S. Lyon, labored with skill and courage. In one instance they were forced to cut a new road through the forest for a distance of four miles in order to turn a blockade of one mile." The Confederates finally broke off the pursuit on October 1.

On October 3, 1862, George Morgan's command crossed the Ohio River at Greenupsburg. After 219 miles and 16 days on the road, they had made it despite limited water, dwindling rations, and Confederate efforts. Federal losses totaled 80 men killed, wounded, and missing/deserted. Despite all odds, George Morgan had brought his men, wagons, and artillery to safety in the Buckeye State.

1. Whiskey and War:
The Case of Joseph Mower at the Battle of Corinth

by Daniel T. Davis

*Originally published as a blog post at Emerging Civil War
on June 2, 2015*

As I worked on *Calamaity in Carolina: The Battles of Averasboro and Bentonville*, one of the officers who grabbed my attention was Maj. Gen. Joseph Mower. After serving in the Mexican War, Mower compiled an impressive combat record during the Civil War, fighting at Island Number 10, Iuka, and Vicksburg. He participated in the Red River Campaign and the March to the Sea. He probably had his finest hour at Bentonville, where he turned Gen. Joseph Johnston's left flank, coming within a hair of cutting the Confederate line of retreat. Even more extraordinary is that Mower began the war as a captain of a company in the 1st U.S. Infantry and ended as the commander of the XX Corps in the Army of Georgia, all without a West Point education. Like many of his contemporaries, however, Mower does have question marks on his record. A recent visit to Corinth left me to contemplate them and their possible answers further.

On October 4, 1862, Mower, then a colonel and brigade commander, executed a reconnaissance of the enemy lines. The night before, Mower imbibed heavily and became intoxicated. Despite his condition, he led his men out on horseback. While positioning his skirmishers, Mower encountered the Confederates. They unleashed a volley, striking Mower in the neck and killing his horse. Pinned beneath the animal, he was captured. During the Confederate withdrawal, Mower took advantage of the confusion and returned to the Union lines. Mower convinced the Union commander, Maj. Gen. William Rosecrans, that he was not drunk (writing after the war, Rosecrans indicated that he believed Mower). Several months after Corinth, Mower received a promotion to brigadier general. Rather than a roadblock, Corinth became a steppingstone.

At the battle of Iuka, Joseph Mower earned the nickname "the Wolf." At Bentonville, he earned the nickname "the Swamp Lizard." *Library of Congress*

There is, however, one more piece to consider: Mower's health.

After the Mexican War, Mower was discharged from the U.S. Engineers for disability. Despite his health or overall physical condition, he was commissioned a second lieutenant in 1855. At the culmination of the Vicksburg Campaign, Mower went home on furlough. During this time, he received a medical examination. The surgeons found he suffered from "general debility" and deemed him "unfit for duty," although he would return to active military service. At the Carolinas Campaign began, Mower's infantry led the advance of Maj. Gen. William T. Sherman's Army Group into the South Carolina swamps. The weather was bitterly cold, and Mower spent his time on the skirmish line. One staff officer lamented that his exposure to the elements during the campaign contributed to his health problems that took his life in 1870.

There is ample evidence that Mower was not in top health during the war. His near-constant time in the field took its toll. The question remains as to why. Certainly, Mower was devoted to the Union cause. At the same time, despite the eventual promotion and continued rise, did the stain of Corinth linger in his mind? Was it to the point that he would jeopardize his own life to restore his honor? I am only left to wonder.

Finding Miss Susie

by Sheritta Bitikofer

*Original published as a blog post at Emerging Civil War
on August 27, 2021*

Studying history has taught me that everything is connected. Places, people, and events that shaped the nation did not occur in a vacuum. The generals and civilians we read about did not exist in just one place at a certain time. They lived on—mostly—to travel, have relationships, and pursue happiness. Like us, they made connections, leaving an impact on the world that echoes through time. One such connection hit me proverbially in the face quite unexpectedly during some of my travels.

The Reconstruction Era National Historical Park was established in 2017. Located in Beaufort, South Carolina, the rangers and historians of the park are dedicated to telling the story of Reconstruction during and following the Civil War. Beaufort became ground zero for the Reconstruction experiment after its capture in November 1861. Most of the white population fled after the arrival of the Federals, fearing execution for treason. This left the enslaved population in the hands of a United States Army that did not know what to do with them.

Numerous charitable projects popped up through Beaufort and the islands, namely in education for those now considered "contraband." The collective endeavors of philanthropists from New York City, Boston, and Philadelphia became known as the "Port Royal Experiment." They made tremendous headway in establishing political, social, and economic reform in the Beaufort area.

The Militia Act of 1862 allowed formerly enslaved men to enlist in the cause that paved the way for their freedom. A training camp was established in the Fall of 1862 on the grounds of John Joyner Smith Plantation. Camp Saxton, named after Gen. Rufus Saxton, governor of the Department of the South from 1862 to 1865, served as a hub for black recruitment. Charged by Secretary of War Edwin M. Stanton, Saxton was to "arm, uniform, equip, and receive into service . . . such number of volunteers of African descent . . . not exceeding 5,000." Soon, the 1st South Carolina Infantry formed and received training at the site between November 1862 and January 1863 before mustering into service.

Perhaps the most famous of the events at Camp Saxton was the reading of the Emancipation Proclamation on New Year's Day, 1863. A crowd of 5,000 assembled at Camp Saxton to listen to the words of freedom. During the ceremonies, an unknown elder began singing "My Country Tis of Thee," and the free men and women joined in. One woman in attendance was Susie King Taylor, a laundress who had arrived at the camp the previous October. She wrote later that she had several uncles and cousins in the 1st South Carolina Infantry, as well as a husband in Company E.[1]

Before she arrived, Susie had taught illiterate children and adults on St. Simon's Island, having learned to read as a young, enslaved girl in Savannah, Georgia. Under the care of her free grandmother, she and her brother wrapped their books in paper. They went to Mrs. Woodhouse for their lessons.[2] This illegal education afforded her opportunities to help her family and community, including writing passes for her grandmother, allowing her to be on the streets after 9:00 p.m.[3] After the capture of Fort Pulaski in April 1862, Susie, aged 13, and her family journeyed to St. Catherine Island with her uncle, then to St. Simon's Island where "to my unbounding joy, I saw the 'Yankee'" for the first time. There, she impressed officers with her ability

---

1 Susie King Taylor, ed. Patricia W. Romero, *Reminiscence of my Life in Camp with the 33rd U.S. Colored Troops, Late 1st South Carolina Volunteers. A Black Woman's Civil War memoirs*, (New York: Markus Wiener Publishing, 2007), 42.

2 Ibid. 29.

3 Ibid. 31.

to read and write and was given charge of over forty students before she followed future enlistees under Capt. C. T. Trowbridge to Camp Saxton. She worked as a teacher, laundress, and nurse for the men of the 1st South Carolina Infantry—later designated the 33rd U.S. Colored Infantry.

Susie remembered Emancipation Day with fondness and pride:

> It was a glorious day for us all, and we enjoyed every minute of it, and as fitting close and the crowning event of this occasion we had a grand barbeque. A number of oxen were roasted whole, and we had a fine feast. Although not served as tastily or correctly as it would have been at home, yet it was enjoyed with keen appetites and relish. The soldiers had a good time. They sang or shouted 'Hurrah!' all through the camp, and seemed overflowing with fun and frolic until taps were sounded, when men, no doubt, dreamt of this memorable day.[4]

Today, a visitor can stand where Susie stood as the promise for a free and hopeful future was read aloud to the spectators that January 1863.

After the war, Susie and her husband Edward returned to Savannah, Georgia, where she opened a school for black children on Oglethorpe Avenue. She kept twenty students and received a dollar for each pupil every month.[5] Edward struggled to find work, despite his carpentry proficiency, and took a job unloading shipping vessels. Susie taught for almost a year before a free school, the Beach Institute, opened its doors and took several of her students. That September, she lost her husband while expecting their first child. With her brother-in-law's assistance, she opened a night school to teach adults, until the Beach Institute offered night classes as well, and she lost her pupils again.

In 1872, Susie received a $100 claim for her husband's bounty from the Army. In the fall, she began work as a laundress, an occupation she knew just as well as teaching. Mrs. Charles Green of Savannah employed her.[6]

4 Ibid., 49-50.

5 Ibid., 124.

6 Ibid., 127.

History buffs may recognize this name, but not instantly connect it with Susie's story. Charles Green was an Englishman who arrived in Savannah in 1833, quickly making his fortune as a successful cotton merchant and ship owner. He built his home in 1853 in the iconic Gothic Revival style—a major departure from the customary Greek Revival style of Southern mansions of the era. At $93,000, the home was designed for luxury and opulence and filled with furniture from all across Europe. Even today, the home's interior impresses its visitors with its ornamental crown moldings and decadent patterned wallpaper. Green spared no expense while creating a grand and elegant home that epitomized his family's wealth and elitist lifestyle.

The Green House's claim to fame is not for Susie's employment, but for Gen. William T. Sherman's arrival in December 1864. Having completed

Susie King Taylor is widely regarded as the first Black nurse during the Civil War, and the first Black woman to publish her memoirs. *Library of Congress*

his March to the Sea from Atlanta, Sherman captured Savannah. Mr. Green invited Sherman to establish his headquarters in his home adjacent to Madison Square. In the upstairs study, Sherman penned the well-known telegram to President Lincoln reading, "I beg to present you as a Christmas gift the city of Savannah with 150 heavy guns and plenty of ammunition and also about 25,000 bales of cotton."[7]

---

7 Telegram from Maj. Gen. William Tecumseh Sherman to President Abraham Lincoln, presenting the city of Savannah as a Christmas gift, December 22, 1864.(National Archives Identifier: 301637); Series: Telegrams Sent by the Field Office of the Military Telegraph and Collected by the Office of the Secretary of War., 1860 - 1870; Records of the Office of the Secretary of War; Record Group 107; National Archives.

The home is maintained by the St. John's Episcopal Church, located next door, and remains a National Historic Landmark, open for tours to the public. Today, visitors can stand in the room where the telegram was written, and walk the halls Susie King Taylor once walked. They can climb the stairs she might have climbed daily and peer out the windows she might have gazed through between her chores. One must wonder if she knew where she was working, its significance, and what she thought about standing in the same space Gen. Sherman once occupied.

Not much is known about the two years Susie worked for the Green family, apart from her memoirs, which only chronicle a trip she took with the Greens to Rye Beach when she took the place of their cook and also won a prize at a fair. In 1874, she moved to Boston, Massachusetts, and continued domestic employment. She died in Boston on October 6, 1912, and is buried in Mount Hope Cemetery. Before she died, she penned a lasting legacy in her memoirs, *Reminiscences of My Life in Camp with the 33d United States Colored Troops Late 1st S. C. Volunteers,* published in 1902. It remains one of the few narratives written by a formerly enslaved African American woman and gives readers a look into her life and the history she endured. Her candid reflections on the times and events she lived through have become a valuable primary source for historians.

Very few places Susie King Taylor touched can be easily found today. However, thanks to the preservation efforts at the Reconstruction Era National Historical Park and the caretakers of the Green-Meldrim House in Savannah, we can walk in the footsteps of a courageous woman who made a difference to history in her humble way.

A bench at Reconstruction Era National Historical Park offers a place to sit—and much to sit and think about. *Sheritta Bitikofer*

True Courage:
The 44th Mississippi at Stones River

by Robert M. Dunkerly

Originally published as a blog post at Emerging Civil War on January 1, 2020

In 1861, men from the far reaches of Mississippi organized into the 1st Mississippi Infantry Battalion, or Blythe's Battalion. These volunteers came from Calhoun, Clay, and De Soto counties in the north, and from Amite County in the state's far southern corner. The following year the unit was reorganized as the 44th Mississippi Infantry. Their first taste of combat came at Shiloh, Tennessee, in April 1862. The unit also fought at Munfordville, Kentucky, in September. At the time of Stones River in December, it was part of Gen. James Chalmers's brigade.[1]

Before the battle, smallpox broke out. While quarantined from the rest of the brigade, their rifles were taken and given to other commands. When the battle of Stones River began, they were still largely unarmed. The Mississippians moved into position on December 28th and waited in the cold. As they formed for battle along the Nashville Pike on December 31, 1862, they lined up with the rest of their brigade, "guns or no guns."[2]

---

1 www.nps.gov/civilwar/search-battle-units-detail.htm?battleUnitCode=CMS0044RI.

2 J. N. Thompson. "The Gallant Old Forty-Fourth Mississippi," *Confederate Veteran* (1920), Vol. 10, 406.

The Confederate attack at Stones River began at dawn on December 31st with a devastating surprise assault on the Union Army. Quickly, the Confederates overran the Federal camps and pushed back the routed troops.

Anchoring the Union line on its left flank, not far from Stones River, was a wooded area known as the Round Forest. Several Union units defended it, including a brigade led by Gen. William B. Hazen. Throughout the day, Confederate assaults, all piecemeal, struck at the Round Forest.

The first assault saw Gen. James Chalmers lead his Mississippi troops forward at around 9:00 a.m. During the attack, Chalmers fell, struck in the head by a shell fragment. The furious Confederate assault closed in on Hazen's defenders. During the din, his division commander called out to Gen. Hazen, saying, "Hazen, you'll have to fall back." In reply he shouted, "I'd like to know where in hell I'll fall back to?"[3]

The Confederates had to attack across 1,000 yards of open ground, and past the ruins of the burned out Cowan home. Union infantry and artillery had them in range the whole way. About fifty cannons were deployed with the defenders.

Chalmers attacked twice, the second time coming to within 50 yards of the Union line. The two sides blazed away for thirty minutes, and the Confederates finally fell back. Hazen's 41st Ohio ran out of ammunition, and he ordered the unit to fix bayonets and club their muskets if another attack came, but was able to replace them with the 9th Indiana before those desperate measures were needed.[4]

C.P. Ball of the 41st Ohio recalled, "I will never forget the splendid appearance of the rebel line of battle as it advanced to engage our brigade . . . they came at us with a yell, as if to gobble us up."[5]

Perhaps few units were as ill-prepared to attack as the 44th Mississippi, on the right of Chalmers's line. Five days earlier, they had been re-issued weapons as they prepared for the assault, but most were inoperable. All the regiment's rifles had been gathered five days earlier for redistribution among the brigades' other units. Two days later, several wagons arrived with what Maj. Thompson called "refuse guns." Thompson was horrified to find

---

3   William B. Hazen, *A Narrative of Military Service* (Boston: Ticknor and Co., 1885), 80.

4   *Official Records of the War of the Rebellion,* Vol. 20, 544.

5   C. P. Ball, "Friend Converse," *Jeffersonian Democrat*, January 22, 1863.

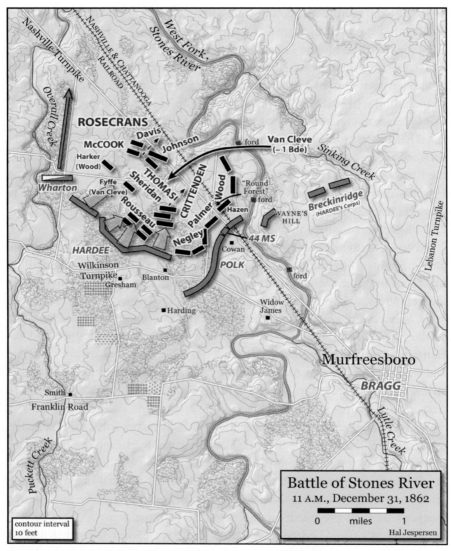

BATTLE OF STONES RIVER—The battle positions at 11 a.m. The Round Forest is in the very center of the map, at Hazen's position. The Confederates attacked past the Round Forest. The 44th Mississippi attacked near the railroad as part of Polk's corps. *Courtesy of Bert Dunkerly*

that "Many of these guns were worthless—some being bent, some cocked could not be pulled down, some whose hammers had to be carried in the men's pockets until time to commence firing, others so foul as to render it impossible to ram home the cartridge, many without ramrods and only one bayonet in the lot." He continues, "one half of the regiment moved out with no other resemblance to a gun than such sticks as they could gather."[6] Some men were still without weapons as they stepped off. If officers told the men that rifles would be available soon, the reason was not reassuring.

Picture the troops lined up for their assault, already under enemy fire, and imagine the courage of those who lined up with broken rifles, sticks, or nothing at all. The regiment lost four killed, 31 wounded, and 17 missing in their attack. Chalmers was badly wounded, carried off the field, and did not file a report on the battle. Nor did any other officers of the other regiments. A report might have mentioned the stick charge if Chalmers or the others knew about it. The survivors of the attack emerged with captured Enfield rifles. The Mississippians were undoubtedly very motivated to capture weapons from the Federals, which is a testimony to the fact that they closed in and fought hand-to-hand with the defenders. However, details about the stick charge are sketchy and difficult to verify. According to Confederate veteran John C. Stiles, who investigated the incident, "it will have to be proved or disproved by some one who was there."[7]

Company D from Desoto County lost several men in the attack. Pvt. William H. Burton was wounded in the right hand. Pvt. John Collins of Corinth was wounded and captured, dying in a Union hospital eleven days later. Pvt. Ephraim R. Haynes was also wounded and captured, but survived and was exchanged in April. Pvt. Solomon Payne fell mortally wounded, shot through the left side, and died the next day on January 1st. Pvt. Valincourt A. Spencer went down, wounded below the knee, but returned to service. Lastly, Pvt. William D. Young of Tupelo was wounded slightly in the right hand. Did these particular men carry functioning weapons, unserviceable rifles, or were they unarmed, looking for the chance to pick up a working weapon? We will never know.

6 Stephen D. Lutz, "Stick Charge at Stone's River, *Civil War Times*, Vol. XLI, No. 6, pp. 68, 70, 72.

7 John C. Stiles, "Forty-Fourth Mississippi at Murfreesboro," Confederate Veteran, Vol XXVII, No. 2 (Feb. 1920), 26.

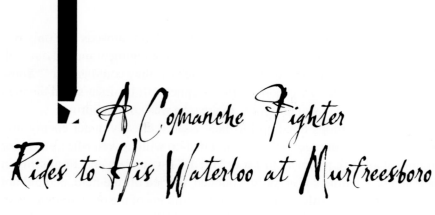

7. A Comanche Fighter Rides to His Waterloo at Murfreesboro

by Brian Swartz

Adapted from a blog post at Maine at War, *an ECW partner,*
originally published on February 21, 2013

What Comanche warriors could not accomplish with a regular Army officer in Texas, Confederates did at Murfreesboro.

Married circa 1812, Maine natives Col. Joshua Carpenter and his wife, Susannah (Heald) Carpenter, had five sons and three daughters. The colonel had a penchant for naming his boys after American legends; he named his second son (and third child) after Navy hero Stephen Decatur, his fourth son after Benjamin Franklin, and his fifth son after Thomas Jefferson.

Born in rural Foxcroft on May 14, 1818, Stephen Decatur Carpenter graduated from West Point on July 1, 1840, and immediately joined the 1st Infantry Regiment as a shave-tail lieutenant. He fought Seminoles, Mexicans, and Comanches, in that order.

While traipsing from post to post in the Upper Midwest, Carpenter married Margaret Ann Gear at Fort Snelling in Minnesota. The newlyweds had a daughter, Alice, but Margaret Ann later died giving birth to another child at Fort Terrett in Texas.

Now a widow, Carpenter met Laura Clark, 25 years old when she left her home in Hampden, Maine, to teach a planter's children and their cousins at a plantation in Brazoria, Texas. Carpenter and Clark fell in love, and he married her in Bangor, Maine, in October 1856. Alice traveled with them to Maine and then to her father's new duty post at Fort Lancaster in Texas. The Carpenters soon had a daughter, Sara Elvira.

One day Carpenter, the post surgeon, and five enlisted men rode out to find a tree suitable for a flagpole. Far from the fort, 20 Comanche warriors ambushed "the little party," which "was saved only by the coolness and intrepidity of its leader," reported Bangor historian Charles P. Roberts.[1]

With Comanche arrows dropping around him, Carpenter concealed his men in the tall grass. Encircling the soldiers, the Comanches charged. Carpenter ordered his men to shoot. He killed two warriors with his revolver, and the Comanches fled while abandoning five dead warriors. One soldier was slightly wounded, and an arrow stuck in Carpenter's hand.

Life at the remote fort was difficult, but "Alice loved her mother [Laura] dearly and was dearly loved in return," Carpenter noted. Sadness engulfed the family when Laura died while giving birth to a son, John, in December 1860.[2]

Before Carpenter could figure out what to do with an infant son and two young daughters, Texas seceded from the Union, and U.S. Army Brig. Gen. David Twiggs betrayed the Federal troops under his command by surrendering them and every fort in Texas to Confederate militia.

Carpenter then commanded Camp Cooper on the road to California. Confederates arrived, their senior officer demanded that Carpenter surrender, and "he . . . declared that rather than surrender as demanded, the bones of himself and his men should bleach on the prairie. His subordinate officers, in council, shared the noble and heroic resolution," according to Roberts.

The Confederate commander negotiated with Carpenter. He and his men could march "with their arms and their country's untarnished flag, to Indianola, the nearest place on the coast, seven hundred and fifty miles" away on Matagorda Bay, Roberts indicated.

Twiggs, of course, joined the Confederacy, and he imprisoned most Federal soldiers stationed in Texas. Not Carpenter and his men and his children; for several weeks, they trekked across central Texas to the Gulf

---

1 "The Funeral of Col. Carpenter," *Daily Whig & Courier*, Thursday, February 12, 1863.

2 Fort Lancaster State Historic Site, Facebook; *Daily Whig & Courier*, Thursday, February 12, 1863.

Coast, where as "the last U.S. troops which quitted Texas, they embarked for Key West," Roberts stated.

As for his children, Carpenter must have brought at least John to Bangor, where he died at age 9-and-a half months on July 7, 1861. The toddler was buried in Bangor's Mount Hope Cemetery.[3]

The 19th U.S. Infantry Regiment organized in spring 1861 in Indianapolis, with the colonelcy going to Edward R. S. Canby. Issued on June 18, General Order No. 33 transferred Carpenter and other officers to the regiment; assigned as its senior major, he arrived on August 7 and took charge of the recruits coming from twelve recruiting offices, including eleven in Indiana and one in Cincinnati.

In February 1862 the War Department organized eight companies as the First Battalion, put Carpenter in charge, and soon sent him with two companies to join Maj. Gen. Don Carlos Buell in Louisville. The First Battalion comprised five companies (A through E) and belonged to the 4th Brigade (Brig. Gen. Lovell H. Rousseau), 2nd Division (Brig. Gen. Alexander McD. McCook) when Buell march south to join Ulysses S. Grant and his Army of the Tennessee at Pittsburg Landing in early spring 1862.[4]

The April 6 surprise attack launched by Albert Sidney Johnston backed Grant's troops to the landing, but Buell arrived and started sending men across the Tennessee River. Carpenter's regulars "huddled, during the night, on board a steamboat, without room to lie down, exposed to a drenching rain," Roberts stated.

"Without breakfast or even a mug of coffee," Carpenter and his men "went into the work of retrieving the waning fortunes of the preceding day. Major Carpenter's battalion occupied" the center of the Union line, "which was hardest pushed by the enemy."

During the afternoon Confederate troops formed to take "our left directly in flank," Carpenter reported. "I immediately changed my front forward on the left company" and asked Rousseau for help. He sent the 6th Indiana Infantry.

---

3 *Daily Whig & Courier*, Thursday, February 12, 1863.

4 *The Army of the US Historical Sketches of Staff and Line with Portraits of Generals-in-Chief*, Theophilus Francis Rodenbough and William L. Haskin, editors, (New York, NY, 1896), 657-658.

"We were engaged hotly by the enemy in front . . . after hard fighting, in which our own and the enemy's forces nearly came together, he finally gave way and fled," Carpenter said. Losing five men killed and 30 men wounded, his regulars recaptured a Union artillery battery lost the previous day.[5]

War, sickness, and deployments elsewhere depleted the First Battalion, only 150 men strong when it headed with Maj. Gen. William Rosecrans and his Army of the Cumberland toward Murfreesboro in Tennessee on December 26, 1862. Facing off near the Stones River on December 31, Rosecrans and his Confederate counterpart, Maj. Gen. Braxton Bragg, each envisioned delivering a thundering left hook against his opponent.

Screaming the Rebel yell, Confederate infantrymen struck first and struck hard on December 31. In action by 9:30 a.m., Carpenter's battalion initially supported Battery H, 5th U.S. Artillery. Both units were "ordered into the cedars" around 10 a.m., said Capt. James B. Mulligan; advancing Confederates soon ejected the Yankees "under a most destructive fire."

With its brigade, the First Battalion deployed "on the hill near the railroad," but was ordered "with the remainder of the brigade, to advance in line of battle into the cedars" around noon, Mulligan said. "We there engaged an overwhelming force of the enemy for full twenty minutes."[6]

The attacking 8th Tennessee Infantry Regiment shifted to the west near the Cowan House ruins and ran squarely into the 19th Infantry. The regiments shot each other apart on terrain later called "Hell's Half Acre." The 8th Tennessee's Col. W. L. Moore died there, but his troops pressed Carpenter's men backwards. "It was evident that if the flanks were weakened, the enemy could very easily surround us almost completely and so have us wholly at their mercy," recalled Pvt. Joseph R. Prentice, Co. E.

"To defeat this plan, Major Carpenter ordered us to retreat in good order and after we had about faced, he fell behind and proceeded to follow us in the rear. No sooner did the enemy see us retreating than they opened fire on us again," Prentice said.

---

5 *Daily Whig & Courier*, Thursday, February 12, 1863; Maj. Stephen D. Carpenter, in *The War of the Rebellion: A Compilation of the Official Records of the Union and Confederate Armies*, 128 vols. (Washington, DC, U.S. Government Printing Office, 1880-1901), Series 1, vol. 10, pt. 1, 314.

6 Capt. James B. Mulligan, *OR* 10, pt. 1, 405-406.

Standing amidst unharvested hay at Stones River National Battlefield, a 12-pounder bronze Napoleon marks where a Union artillery battery was deployed during the December 31, 1862–January 2, 1863, battle of Murfreesboro. *Brian F. Swartz*

"Scatter and run, boys!" Carpenter shouted. The Tennesseans fired another volley, and six bullets struck Carpenter: two in the head and four in the body. He pitched dead from his wounded horse, which bolted past Prentice.

He "rushed after the boys to tell them" what happened to Carpenter. Granted "permission to return and look for him," Prentice "rushed to the spot." As "bullets ploughed up little puffs of dust at my feet and whistled around my head," he found the major "lying face downward upon the dust" and then carried the dead Carpenter into Union lines.[7]

His comrades quickly buried Carpenter, but once Bragg withdrew from Murfreesboro, the 19th Infantry's surviving officers paid to retrieve the body and have it embalmed and shipped to Bangor. Carpenter's lieutenant colonel's commission arrived soon after his death.

The city held a hero's funeral for the slain Carpenter on Wednesday, February 11, 1863. He was buried beside his son, John, at Mount Hope Cemetery. His elderly father was among the mourners.

In mid-June 1864, Bangoreans gathered by the graves to dedicate the Soldiers' Monument, the second Civil War monument funded by Northern

7 dan-masters-civil-war.blogspot.com.

civilians. The Carpenters lay next to the monument, but 17 years later relatives paid to relocate father and son to a quieter plot overlooking the Penobscot River. They lie there side by side today.[8]

Yet Stephen Decatur Carpenter lives on. While marching toward Murfreesboro in late 1862, he brought along his school-age daughter, Sara Elvira. She survived her father, married, and had children—and her descendants live into the 21st century. Her older half-sister, Alice, became a ward of Iowa resident John Gear (likely a relative of her mother's) after her father died at Murfreesboro. She married Gear's son and had children, but died at age 29.

Joseph R. Prentice later received the Medal of Honor for recovering Carpenter's body at Murfreesboro.

Joseph Prentice's Medal of Honor is on display at the Stones River National Battlefield Visitor Center. "Voluntarily rescued the body of his commanding officer, who had fallen mortally wounded," the citation reads. "He brought off the field his mortally wounded leader under direct and constant rifle fire." *Chris Mackowski*

8 *Daily Whig & Courier*, Thursday, February 12, 1863; *Daily Whig & Courier,* Saturday, June 18, 1864.

Boomerang Bragg

by Robert M. Dunkerly

*Originally published as a blog post at Emerging Civil War
on January 11, 2022*

Following the end of the regular football season, we see losing college and NFL coaches get the ax and many other administrative changes in our favorite teams—which leads me to this comparison, so please bear with me.

The Confederate Army of Tennessee is well known for its internal command issues, mostly centered around Gen. Braxton Bragg. Nearly anytime you read about this army, dissent looms in the background, and Bragg was replaced. When did this problem start? In early January 1863, following the battle of Stones River.

For the better part of three days from December 31, 1862, to January 2, 1863, the two primary western armies of the Union and Confederacy struggled in the fields and woods west of Murfreesboro, Tennessee. Neither force could drive the other off, as was typical of Civil War battles. The cost was 13,249 Union and 10,266 Confederates, for a total of 23,515 killed, wounded, missing, and captured—eleven times the population of nearby Murfreesboro. The Federals also lost 28 guns.[1]

Both armies remained after the fighting ended on January 2nd. Around noon on the 3rd, Bragg met with his key commanders: Generals Leonidas

---

1 *Official Records of the War of the Rebellion,* Vol. 20, 215, 674.

Polk, William Hardee, and Patrick Cleburne at his headquarters along the Nashville Pike. All agreed that a retreat was necessary. The army was not strong enough to drive away the Federal troops and was not strong enough to remain. The Federals were getting reinforcements and supplies. The rest of the afternoon, baggage and ordinance wagons began moving south along the roads to Shelbyville and Manchester. Gen. John C. Breckinridge's division covered the rear and was the last Confederate force to leave.[2]

The Army of Tennessee retreated south with its cavalry covering the infantry. Hardee's Corps followed along the muddy road to Wartrace, while Polk's men trudged toward Shelbyville. Bragg halted behind the Duck River, making his new headquarters in the public square in the center of Tullahoma.

Though the indecisive battle at Stones River was frustrating and the men were exhausted, Bragg put a positive spin on it in his speech to the troops on the 8th:

> Soldiers of the Army of Tennessee! Your gallant deeds have won the admiration of your general, your Government, and your country. For myself, I thank you and am proud of you; for them, I tender you the gratitude and praise you have so nobly won . . . In retreating to a stronger position, without molestation from a superior force, you have left him a barren field . . .[3]

Few men in the ranks shared the general's assessment. The inconclusive battle at Perryville in October, withdrawal from Kentucky, and now supreme effort at Murfreesboro that had come up short had sapped the troop's morale. Newspapers, both local and as far away as Virginia, Georgia, and Alabama, criticized Bragg's retreat.

This was Bragg's second major battle as commander. He faced scrutiny for the failed Kentucky Campaign; the Stones River Campaign ruined his reputation, setting the stage for future controversy and tension in the army's high command. Retreat from Murfreesboro was not unreasonable given the

2 Ibid., 682.

3 Ibid., 675.

situation: his army had limited supplies and no reinforcements on the way, while the opposing force had both. Yet the withdrawal cast a negative light on Bragg's army.[4]

Additionally, there was great dissatisfaction and tension among the army commanders, and perhaps the most disastrous infighting to plague any Civil War army unfolded over the next few weeks. On January 10th, Bragg held a staff meeting with Generals Patrick Cleburne, Leonidas Polk, William Hardee, Frank Cheatham, and John C. Breckinridge, asking if he held the army's confidence, and stated if the answer was no, he would resign.[5]

It was a two-part question: Bragg asked if the other officers agreed with the decision to retreat after the battle, and secondly, Bragg asked if they thought him fit to command. "I shall retire without regret if I find that I have lost the good opinion of my generals . . ." Bragg stated. Can you imagine an NFL or college head coach doing this after a tough loss?[6]

Bragg reminded the officers that many advised retreat, concurred with the decision at the time, and asked them to publicly state it to quell the outcry in the newspapers. All the officers agreed that withdrawing from Murfreesboro was the right decision, but surprisingly, several commanders also said he should resign. Bragg felt stunned and insulted, refusing to step down, sparking a bout of infighting not seen elsewhere during the war.

Hardee noted that his subordinates agreed "that a change of command of this army is necessary." Gen. Patrick Cleburne responded quite diplomatically on the topic, writing to Bragg, "I have consulted with all my brigade commanders at this place, as you request, showing them your letter and inclosuers, and they unite with me in personal regard for yourself, in a high appreciation of your patriotism and gallantry, and in a conviction of your great capacity for organization, but at the same time they see with regret, and it has also met my observation that you do not possess the confidence of the army in other respects in that degree necessary to secure success." Brigade commander Gen. William Preston wrote privately of "Boomerang

---

4 Earl J. Hess, *Braxton Bragg: The Most Hated Man in the Confederacy* (Chapel Hill: University of North Carolina Press, 2016), 113.

5 Ibid., 115-121.

6 Peter Cozzens, *No Better Place to Die* (Urbana: University of Illinois Press, 1990), 209.

Bragg" with a "heart of ice and a head of wood," criticizing him to many contacts, including some in leadership in Richmond.[7]

It's easy to understand why Bragg was offended: he had been an equal of Polk and Hardee: all were corps commanders just six months earlier at Shiloh. Some big names and egos were involved, raising the stakes. Leonidas Polk was the Episcopal Bishop of Louisiana. New Orleans was the largest city in the Confederacy, and Polk's prestige extended well beyond the pulpit and Crescent City. William Hardee was well respected for writing the U.S. Army's manual on infantry tactics before the war. Then there was John C. Breckinridge, a former Vice President, and one-time presidential candidate. His status would eventually elevate him to Confederate Secretary of War. Bragg tangled with some well-connected and powerful men.

The result created a poisonous atmosphere among the army's high command, and as time went on, it became clear that the infighting and finger-pointing would undermine the army's effectiveness. Bitterness developed between Bragg and three officers in particular: Frank Cheatham, Samuel McGowan, and Breckinridge.[8]

Bragg wrote to President Jefferson Davis on January 17th that only a few officers were dissatisfied, many were new to the army and their opinions should not be counted. He also again justified the decision to retreat from Stones River. Davis sent Gen. Joseph E. Johnston to investigate. Although he heard of the dissatisfaction firsthand, the troops seemed recovered from Stones River, and he recommended not replacing Bragg. Writers theorize that Johnston likely did not want to take command from a fellow officer.

Eventually, Hardee, frustrated by the situation, got a transfer to another department. Polk and Cheatham grudgingly continued to serve under Bragg. The army would fight at Chickamauga and Chattanooga while enduring these internal divisions until Bragg's eventual resignation after Chattanooga. For two years—half the war—the army endured this infighting. We can trace the roots of the no-confidence in Bragg sentiment to the immediate aftermath of Stones River.

7 *Official Records*, 684; Hardee to Bragg, Jan. 12, 1863, Hardee Papers, Alabama Department of Archives and History.

8 *Official Records*, 684; Hardee to Bragg, Jan. 12, 1863, Hardee Papers, Alabama Department of Archives and History.

1. The Purge of the Second Louisiana Native Guards

by Neil P. Chatelain

Originally published as a blog post at Emerging Civil War
on September 3, 2021

Sometimes, courage and leadership among military officers lie not in leading a battlefield charge, but in challenging injustice directly. Such leadership occurred by the line officers of the Louisiana Native Guards, the largest concentration of African American military officers in the Civil War, who encountered trials on battlefields and in camp while facing a determined and thorough purge of their ranks by senior commanders who did not trust them with the responsibility of command.

The Louisiana Native Guards often get attention because of their origins. In 1861, many wealthy and elite freedmen of New Orleans organized an African American militia. Provided uniforms but not entrusted with weapons, the Native Guards famously marched in Confederate parades through the crescent city's streets. When David Farragut's naval squadron ascended the Mississippi River, however, the Native Guards were left behind in the Confederate evacuation.[1]

---

1 "The Parade This Morning", *The Daily Picayune*, New Orleans, LA, November 23, 1861; "The Louisiana Native Guards", *Daily Crescent*, New Orleans, LA, December 9, 1861.

Major General Benjamin Butler, desperate for reinforcements to expand control of southeast Louisiana, renewed the idea. He organized three regiments of Native Guards in late 1862. They spent that year's latter months garrisoning areas between New Orleans and Brashear City (modern-day Morgan City) on the Atchafalaya River. What made Butler's Louisiana Native Guards unique was its officer corps. While the senior field officers were white, the regiments had African American, mixed-race, and creole company line officers.

As 1863 dawned, the 1st and 3rd Native Guards remained in Louisiana, guarding the approaches to New Orleans and the rail lines connecting it to Brashear City. Colonel Nathaniel W. Daniels's 2nd Louisiana Native Guards were reassigned to guard the Louisiana and Mississippi coastline. Seven companies of the Second landed at Ship Island in January 1863. Daniels found a "good Headquarters," but "no barracks for my soldiers." The men immediately began adding to the island's fortifications and constructing shelters. Within a month, they had enlarged its defenses to include "rifle pits, barricades, and two large magazines."[2] The regiment's remaining three companies went to Fort Pike, guarding Lake Pontchartrain and Lake Borgne.

Racial tensions quickly heated up at Ship Island. Elements of the 13th Maine and 8th Vermont Infantry Regiments were also at the barrier island. These white soldiers resented working alongside the Native Guards, and many were arrested for insubordination against the Second's African American and creole officers. Tensions escalated so quickly that the white soldiers were transferred off Ship Island in February 1863.[3]

The insubordination convinced Maj. Gen. Nathaniel Banks, who replaced Butler at the end of 1862, that the African American officers had to go. Banks commenced a systemic purge of these officers by convening competency boards to evaluate the fitness of all African American officers. Captain Samuel W. Ringgold highlighted the discriminatory issues of these boards in a letter to Banks, protesting that "a Board of Examination has been formed to investigate the Military Capacity of the <u>Colored Officers</u> of this Regiment and

---

2   January 12, January 21, and February 16, 1863, *Nathan W. Daniels Diary; Volume I, 1861, Dec.-1864, May*, mss84934, Box 1, Manuscript Division, Library of Congress.

3   Theresa Arnold-Scriber and Terry G. Scriber, *Ship Island, Mississippi: Rosters and History of the Civil War Prison*, (Jefferson, NC: McFarland & Company, 2008), 55-56; Edward T. Cotham Jr., Ed., *The Southern Journey of a Civil War Marine: The Illustrated Note-Book of Henry O. Gusley*, (Austin, TX: University of Texas Press, 2006), 134.

that the officers detailed to compose said board are in the majority of inferior rank . . . whose promotion would be effected by our dismissal."[4]

The purge began when three officers of the Second failed their competency boards in February 1863 and were relieved for incompetence. In response, the remaining African American officers at Ship Island and Fort Pike sent a letter to General Banks protesting the competency boards. "From the many rumors that have reached us," the officers noted, "we are led to believe that it is the intention of the General to relieve us."[5]

The regiment's African American officers faced the competency boards one by one. Those who passed the examination faced continuous prejudiced treatment to the point that many began resigning their commissions in protest. Captain Arnold Bertonneau initially volunteered, hoping that "the success of my country would suffice to alter a prejudice which had long existed." Instead, after surviving his competency board, he resigned in March 1863, after his "five months experiences proved the contrary."[6] Captain Samuel W. Ringgold, who complained to Banks of the contradictions among the examination boards, resigned in July 1863 as a protest after passing his examination. Joining him in resigning that month was Maj. Francis E. Dumas, a wealthy creole officer who, after inheriting numerous enslaved persons just before the war, freed them to allow them to enlist with the Native Guards as well.[7]

One of the last African American officers of the 2nd Louisiana Native Guards was arguably its most famous member, Capt. P. B. S. Pinchback. Serving as the "only Colored officer" at Fort Pike, Pinchback tendered

---

4 S.W. Ringgold to Nathaniel Banks, July 7, 1863, Ringgold, Samuel W., Compiled Military Service Records of Volunteer Union Soldiers Who Served the United States Colored Troops: 56th-138th USCT Infantry, 1864-1866 (hereafter CMSR), 300398, RG 94, National Archives, Washington, DC; Edwin C. Bearss, *Gulf Islands: Ship Island*, Historic Resource Study, (United States Department of the Interior, National Park Service, Denver Service Center, July 1984), 215.

5 PBS Pinchback to Nathaniel Banks, March 2, 1863, Ira Berlin, Joseph P. Reidy, and Leslie S. Rowland, ed., *Freedom: A Documentary History of Emancipation, 1861-1867*, (Cambridge, United Kingdom: Cambridge University Press, 1982), Series 2, 321-323; James G. Hollandsworth Jr., *The Louisiana Native Guards: The Black Military Experience During the Civil War*, (Baton Rouge, LA: LSU Press, 1995), 73.

6 Arnold Bertonneau to Wickham Hoffman, March 2, 1863, Bertonneau Arnold, CMSR.

7 Francis Dumas to A.G. Hall, July 31, 1863, Dumas, Francis E, CMSR.

The Second Louisiana Native Guards spent much of their service standing watch on Ship Island, Mississippi, to support the staging base and blockade repair station there. When organized, the regiment's line officers were all African American, as shown in this photograph of Company C, but by the end of the war, only one remained. *Library of Congress*

his resignation in September 1863, noting the regiment's white officers constantly acted "inimical" and would produce nothing "but dissatisfaction and discontent."[8] Nine years later, while serving as Louisiana's lieutenant governor, Pinchback took the oath of office as the state's—and nation's—first African American state governor, when he stepped in after Governor Henry C. Warmoth was impeached in 1872.

Only one African American officer, First Lieutenant Charles S. Sauvinet, retained his commission to the war's conclusion within the 2nd Louisiana Native Guards. It was reclassified in the summer of 1863 as the Second Regiment Corps D'Afrique, and in 1864, as the 74th United States Colored Infantry. The other two regiments of Native Guards underwent a similar

8 Eliot Bridgman to G. Norman Luibes, September 9, 1863, and P.B. Pinchback to N.P. Banks, September 10, 1863, Pinchback, Pinckney, CMSR.

purge of African American officers, even as they participated in the siege of Port Hudson. Their fighting spirit undeterred, at least ten of these resigned or dismissed officers sought to recruit more regiments where they might regain their commissions and prove themselves in battle, but Banks refused.[9]

The 2nd Louisiana Native Guards spent the rest of the war guarding coastal Louisiana and Mississippi. Because of this, it became a footnote in the Civil War's landscape, especially compared to its brother regiments who fought at Port Hudson. Though it did not participate in significant battles, the regiment served as a proving ground for African American soldiers and officers. These officers, however, faced Nathaniel Banks' competency boards, highlighting the many challenges African American soldiers encountered elsewhere, including discrimination and lower pay, throughout the war and the follow-on reconstruction process. Ultimately, their resistance to this purge through resignation and protest highlighted the spirit of the African American community to fight for equality while contributing to the United States' victory in the Civil War, and the desire to shape the postwar nation.

---

9 Charles S. Sauvinet Service Record, CMSR; Adolph J. Gla et al. to N. P. Banks, 7 Apr. 1863, Letters Received, series 1920, Civil Affairs, Department of the Gulf, U.S. Army Continental Commands, Record Group 393 Pt. 1, National Archives.

1. The Bangor Connections to Grierson's Raid

by Brian Swartz

Inspired by a three-part blog series originally published
January 6, 13, and 20, 2016, at Maine at War

Two army officers affiliated with Bangor, Maine, bookended Grierson's Raid—the famed Federal cavalry raid through the Mississippi interior in the spring of 1863.

The first bookend was born to Nathaniel and Elizabeth (Scott) Hatch in Bangor on December 22, 1832. Edward Hatch had deep New England roots, both parents being born in Maine and his paternal grandfather, Isaac Hatch, hailing from Falmouth, Massachusetts. Educated at Norwich Military Academy in eastern Vermont, the young Edward joined the out-migration of Mainers seeking better soil, longer growing seasons, and tall trees in the Midwest.

Circa 1852 Hatch arrived at Muscatine, Iowa, on the Mississippi River below Moline, Illinois. Within seven years he and W. H. Fullerton co-owned Hatch & Fullerton, a lumberyard with locations at Mulberry and 6th streets in Muscatine and on Muscatine Island.[1]

---

1 *William's Muscatine Directory City Guide and Business Mirror, Volume 1, 1859-1860* (Muscatine, IA, 1859).

Soon after the Civil War erupted, Hatch raised Co. A, 2nd Iowa Cavalry, and initially enlisted as its captain. "He was by nature a military genius of the first magnitude," recalled Sgt. Lyman B. Pierce. Commissioned a lieutenant colonel before the 2nd Iowa mustered on August 25, 1861, Hatch "soon became the pride and idol of the regiment," which was commanded by Washington L. Elliott.[2]

The second bookend was born in Bangor on June 23, 1839, to Judge John Edwards and Elizabeth Angela (Stackpole) Godfrey. John Franklin Godfrey, too, hailed from solid New England stock; both Maine-born, his parents also traced their heritage to Massachusetts. They objected vigorously and futilely when 15-year-old "Frank" left Bangor High School and went to sea aboard the Liverpool-bound *Young Eagle*. He wound up sheepherding in Argentina.[3]

Then 22, Godfrey heard about the war by early summer 1861, sailed home to Bangor, and joined the 1st Maine Cavalry as Pvt. Frank Godfrey on September 21. Listing his occupation as "merchant," he stood 5-10 with hazel eyes, dark hair, and a dark complexion.

He transferred to the 1st Maine Battery as a junior second lieutenant on January 1, 1862. The battery reached New Orleans in early May. By early August, Maj. Gen. Ben Butler ordered Godfrey to recruit a cavalry company. He raised Co. C, 1st Louisiana Cavalry Regiment (U.S.), and Butler promoted him to captain. Often skirmishing with Confederate cavalry operating in the Louisiana swamps, Co. C camped near Baton Rouge by April 7, 1863.[4]

The 2nd Iowa Cavalry participated in the capture of New Madrid and "first discovered that the rebels had evacuated 'Island No. 10,'" according to Pierce. The regiment constantly patrolled and picketed and occasionally raided behind Confederate lines during Henry Halleck's creeping advance toward Corinth, Mississippi. When Elliott got brigade command, Hatch took over the 2nd Iowa.[5]

---

2 Lyman B. Pierce, *History of the Second Iowa Cavalry* (Burlington, IA, 1865), 10.

3 John Franklin "Frank" Godfrey, Find A Grave.

4 Frank Godfrey soldiers' files, Maine State Archives; Candace Sawyer and Laura Orcutt, *The Civil Letters of Capt. John Franklin Godfrey* (Portland, ME, 1993), 14-15, 46.

5 Pierce, *History of the Second Iowa* Cavalry, 14-19.

LEFT: Colonel Edward Hatch commanded the 2nd Iowa Cavalry Regiment during the opening phase of Grierson's Raid. He skillfully maneuvered his regiment to draw Southern cavalry away from Col. Benjamin H. Grierson and his raiders. *Library of Congress*

RIGHT: Captain John Franklin "Frank" Godfrey commanded Co. C, 1st Louisiana Cavalry (U.S.) in spring 1863. He was camped near Baton Rouge when a 7th Illinois Cavalry trooper suddenly appeared in his tent on Saturday, May 2, 1863. *Bangor Public Library*

In April 1863, Maj. Gen. Ulysses S. Grant ordered a cavalry raid organized to penetrate south through central Mississippi. The troopers would destroy railroad lines, war-related manufacturing facilities and supplies, and bridges while drawing Confederate attention away from the Mississippi River, which Grant would cross with his Vicksburg-bound army.

Assigned to the raid were the 6th and 7th Illinois cavalry regiments, the 2nd Iowa, and Battery K, 1st Illinois Artillery. Grant picked Col. Benjamin H. Grierson of the 6th Illinois to command the raid, which would originate at La Grange, Tennessee.[6]

Leaving La Grange on a splendid April 17, 1863, Grierson rode south with 1,700 troopers, unsure as to where they were going. The colonel

6 Timothy B. Smith, *The Real Horse Soldiers: Benjamin Grierson's Epic 1863 Civil War Raid Through Mississippi* (El Dorado Hills, CA, 2020), 62-63, 67, 70.

intended to conduct the raid with the Illinois regiments and battery; the 2nd Iowa would mess with Confederate minds elsewhere.

Hatch and his troopers left Grierson on April 18 "and moved through Ripley and Molino," skirmished "with Smith's regiment of Partisan Rangers," and rejoined the main column "five miles below Pontotoc" on April 19, Pierce noted. A 2nd Iowa detachment turned north for La Grange, and Grierson headed south. At "the junction of the roads leading to Louisville, West Point and Columbus," Hatch and his remaining troopers left the column (this time for good).

He planned to ride to West Point, destroy "the railroad bridge over the Oktibbeha River," then "move rapidly southward to Macon" and destroy "the railroad and Government stores" there. He would "then ... find my way north to La Grange by the most practicable route."

The Iowans repulsed pursuing Confederate cavalrymen at Palo Alto. Upon learning that "an Alabama regiment . . . with artillery" was between him and West Point, Hatch "moved slowly northward" and drew the Southerners away from Grierson.

At 4 p.m. on April 22, the Iowans charged into Okolona and "burned thirty barracks filled with Confederate British stamped cotton," Pierce said; Hatch remembered "burning the barracks for 5,000 men." After riding hither and yon to confuse the enemy, he and the 2nd Iowa returned to La Grange on April 26. Pierce reported only one trooper killed and none wounded.[7]

"Grierson's Raid," as history dubbed the expedition, proved incredibly successful. Hatch's gyrations and multiple Union incursions elsewhere in Alabama and Mississippi confused senior Confederate officers as to where the real danger lay, and Grierson wreaked havoc through Mississippi. Ultimately, he decided to head for Union-held Baton Rouge.

Sunrise on Saturday, May 2 found Frank Godfrey resting in his tent. Suddenly "I was surprised by a young man appearing at my tent, and saying that he belonged to the 7th Illinois Cavalry, and that he had come all the way through the Confederacy from Legrange (*sic*), Tenn. and that about eight hundred of the 6th and 7th Illinois Cavalry were about seven miles off,"

---

7 "Gen. Grierson's Great Raid," *New York Times*, Aug. 30, 1863; Pierce, *History of the Second Iowa Cavalry*, 48-55; Col. Edward Hatch, in *The War of the Rebellion: A Compilation of the Official Records of the Union and Confederate Armies*, 128 vols. (Washington, D.C., U.S. Government Printing Office, 1880-1901), Series 1, vol. 24, pt. 1, 530-531.

Godfrey told his parents in a May 4 letter. "I immediately saddled up and went out to meet them."

The young man possibly was a Grierson orderly asleep in the saddle when the colonel "halted to feed with 4 miles of the town." The sleeping trooper rode up to wide-awake Union pickets who doubted his story about Grierson being nearby. Baton Rouge's commander, Maj. Gen. Christopher C. Augur, "sent two companies of cavalry, under Captain [J. Franklin] Godfrey, to meet us," Grierson said.

Warned that enemy cavalry approached from Baton Rouge, he doubted their identity and "rode out alone to meet the troops, without waking my command." Seeing a solitary cavalryman approach, Godfrey ordered his men to dismount and take firing positions. Concealed behind a fence, he spoke with Grierson, but doubted "we were really and truly 'bona fide' Illinois troops from Tennessee," the colonel recalled. He finally convinced Godfrey as to the truth, and Grierson's men "marched into the town about 3 p.m., and we were most heartily welcomed by the United States forces at this point."[8]

"I saw the commanding officer Col. Grearson (sic), and Col. Prince, the Col. of one of the Regts. He was acquainted with Eugene Godfrey [a relative] and came from the same place," Godfrey wrote. "This little command have marched over five hundred miles through the heart of the enemy's country, and have outwitted every thing that has been sent to capture them.

"It was one of the most brilliant exploits of history, and all honor should be accorded to the heroes who accomplished it," Godfrey wrote. "The officers are as modest as they are brave. Col. Grearson said when I spoke to him about it, that he had been very fortunate, he had the good fortune to be the commander of some brave men, and had done some service [with the raid], and his soul was in the cause, and he was glad for his country's sake that he had been so successful.

"You will probably hear all the particulars of this great raid in the newspapers," Godfrey told his parents, "and all you may read will be no exaggeration."[9]

---

8 Smith, *The Real Horse Soldiers*, 283-285; Col. Benjamin H. Grierson, *OR* 24, pt. 1, 528.

9 Candace Sawyer and Laura Orcutt, *The Civil Letters of Capt. John Franklin Godfrey* (Portland, ME, 1993), 49-50.

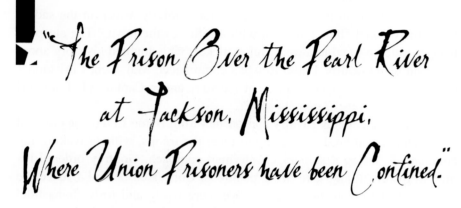

"The Prison Over the Pearl River at Jackson, Mississippi, Where Union Prisoners have been Confined."

by Chris Mackowski

Originally published as a blog post at Emerging Civil War
on May 14, 2022

In researching my book on the battle of Jackson, Mississippi—which took place in 1863 as part of Grant's campaign through Mississippi to take Vicksburg—I stumbled on a little bit of a mystery, although I didn't know it at the time. My friend Jim Woodrick, a longtime historian for the Mississippi Department of History and Archives, picked up on it as he reviewed my manuscript, and we've both been scratching our heads over it since. It deals with a "prison bridge" over the Pearl River.

"Have you ever heard of such a thing?" Jim asked me.

"Aside from the one in Jackson, no," I replied.

Neither had Jim—nor has he been able to run down any real info on it.

I first stumbled upon the bridge in the June 6, 1863, issue of *Harper's Weekly* as I searched for images I could use in the book. I found a sketch

The Pearl River prison bridge showed up in accounts but not on maps. *Harper's Weekly*

captioned "The prison over the Pearl River at Jackson, Mississippi, where Union prisoners have been confined."

I knew there was a state prison in Jackson. In my research, I found accounts where Confederate authorities released prisoners before the arrival of the Federal Army, and the freed convicts promptly set fire to all the prison's buildings. I'd also found accounts of Federal prisoners being moved through Jackson a few days before the battle but no one who'd actually been kept there.

Ultimately, I wasn't sure what to make of the prison bridge, so I skirted around it. I used the image and captioned it with a good quote from one of Sherman's men in the aftermath of the battle: "Pearl river bridge having been burnt by the enemy, its abutments were battered down by our artillery," wrote Charles A. Willison of the 76th Ohio.

But were the Pearl River bridge and the prison bridge the same thing or different? Jim wasn't sure what to make of it, particularly because he knew of only one account of the prison bridge. It appeared in the old silver Time-Life book *War on the Mississippi:*

When Federal troops took Jackson, Mississippi, on May 14, 1863, they liberated fellow soldiers held captive in an unusual Confederate prison—the ruin of a covered bridge on the Pearl River.

One of the prisoners was Colonel Thomas Clement Fletcher, who sketched in pencil on ruled paper—the only materials available. Colonel Fletcher, commander of the 31st Missouri Wide Awake Zouaves, had been wounded and captured that previous December during General Sherman's ill-fated offensive at Chickasaw Bluffs.

Conditions for Fletcher and the 19 other officers and 380 enlisted men crowded within the rickety structure were miserable. During the winter of 1862-1863, the prisoners had to endure the cold without beds or blankets. Afraid the bridge might burn, the Confederates allowed no fires, or even candles, inside. Exposure and disease caused frequent deaths among the inmates. According to an account published in *Harper's Weekly*, almost every day, two or three were carried out dead, and sometimes the dead lay at the bridge entrance unburied for four days.

According to the Museum of Fine Arts in Boston, which has the original sketch by Fletcher, "The artist was confined here by the Confederates, February 1863. Reproduced in wood engraving in *Harper's Weekly*, June 6, 1863."
Fletcher's account in *Harper's Weekly* reads thus:

The Prison at Jackson, Mississippi

We illustrate on page 364 the Prison at Jackson, Mississippi, where many good Union men have been confined since the war broke out, and which lately was destroyed by General Grant. The gentleman who sends us the sketch adds the following account:

"On the 29th December last, at the gallant charge of Blair's brigade upon the works of the rebels at Chickasaw Bluffs near Vicksburg, Colonel Thomas C. Fletcher, of the Missouri Wide Awake Zouaves, who was wounded and captured by the rebels, was with twenty other officers put in the jail at Vicksburg, where they were kept in the loathsome cells and fed upon the worst fare ever meted out to the vilest criminals for one month. They were then removed to Jackson, Mississippi, and thrust into the old rickety ruin of the bridge which was yet standing above water, the remaining part having fallen down. Here they were kept for another month in the coldest season of the year, without beds or bedding; no fire or lights were allowed them. Three hundred and eighty privates, also prisoners, were put into the bridge with them. Almost every day two or three were carried out dead, and sometimes the dead lay at the entrance of the bridge unburied for four days. The above is a sketch of the bridge made by Colonel Fletcher himself, and we have from his assurances of the correctedness of the statement of a cruelty and barbarity of treatment shown to him while wounded, and to his fellow-prisoners and brother officers, unequaled even by the rebels in the cruelty to our soldiers heretofore while in their hands."

Colonel Fletcher appends the following certificate:

"The within statement is in all respects correct, but does not fully represent the barbarity of our treatment by the rebels."

Thomas C. Fletcher,
Colonel, 31st Missouri Volunteers
Annapolis, MD, May 7, 1863[1]

The author of the Time-Life piece assumed that Grant's arriving army on May 14th freed the Union captives from the prison bridge, as suggested by the *Harper's Weekly* article. However, I found no mention of that by anyone. Surely it would have shown up in official reports somewhere. On closer reading, though, *Harper's Weekly* only says the bridge "lately was destroyed by General Grant," with no mention of prisoners. Fletcher's

---

1 *Harper's Weekly*, June 6, 1863: https://archive.org/details/harpersweeklyv7bonn/page/362/mode/2up.

letter, dated from Annapolis on May 7th—a full week before Grant arrived in Jackson—suggests the prisoners were released before Grant's arrival and that Grant did the honors of dispatching the deserted prison.

By May 19, Fletcher had traveled from Annapolis to DeSoto, Missouri, south of St. Louis. Asked to give a speech, Fletcher again described conditions at the prison bridge:

> At Jackson, they were driven, like so many mules or cattle, into the ruins of an old bridge standing over the Pearl river, without blankets, straw or fire in the most inclement season of the year. They suffered there indescribable torture. A rebel officer, an old friend and clever fellow, brought him a blanket and give him some medicine while he was sick. His fellow prisoners suffered greatly, and several died from the exposure. A Confederate General … had the officers removed from the bridge to a house where they were comparatively comfortable. The men, poor fellows, were left there and died in great numbers.[2]

I did some further digging, which turned up an account from George Ady published in the *Chicago Tribune* on January 12, 1891, that confirmed the prisoners were exchanged. Ady's account is interesting enough that I'll include the bulk of it although he doesn't get to the prison bridge until the second half:

> The writer, who had received a severe wound, was placed in the Jackson (Miss.) hospital for treatment. He says that he had nothing to complain of in his personal experiences there, but he writes the following narrative of the cruel treatment inflicted on the Union prisoners collected there in the winter of 1862-'63. Finally in the spring all of the Union soldiers who remained alive and were able to stand the journey to New Orleans were exchanged. Mr. Ady gives this description of their arrival in New Orleans:
>
> All old soldiers of the war can remember that January, February, March, and April, 1863, were the darkest days of the war. In

2 *Daily Missouri Democrat*, May 20, 1863, St. Louis, MO—thanks to Kristen Trout for running down this source for me.

December, '62, Sherman had been defeated at Vicksburg and
Burnside at Fredericksburg, while Rosecrans' battle at Stones
River was a draw, or at least a victory barren of results. Nothing
our side had done had shown any results yet. Grant's army was
in the mud and swamps, on a campaign that was confidently
expected by the Confederates to end in failure. Rosecrans was
doing nothing apparently at that time, and the Army of the
Potomac was stuck in the mud. Traitors at home were making
as much capital as possible out of our failures, and urging the
abandonment of the war, and the Confederates thought everything
was going their way.

At this time, when there seemed nothing to keep up our faith in
the ultimate success of the Union, R— and I had it intimated
to us that if we would come over to the side of the South and
take the oath of allegiance we could both have commissions in
the Confederate army and meet with success among new friends.
Of course we only laughed at such a proposition. I presume it
was meant in earnest, but I do not remember that it made any
impression on my mind at the time except that it was offered
as a compliment by some who had formed a friendly feeling
and some admiration for us. It never struck me at the time that
any one would suppose us capable of doing such a thing as turn
traitor to our country, but since studying the situation, thinking
over the events and feelings of the times, I am led to think it was
something of an astonishment to them that we should so lightly
decline so much honor.

The Southern people at that time thought their independence
already sure, and that everyone would, in a short time, recognize
their power and want to be in favor with them.

Bad Quarters and Worse Food.

The winter passed along, slowly enough to us in the hospital, but
more slowly still to the poor fellows who were kept prisoners in
the old covered bridge over the Pearl River. There were about

350 prisoners in Jackson that winter who had been gathered up from various fights and skirmishes and forwarded there for safe keeping. Soon after R— and I came to Jackson the bridge over Pearl River had broken down under the weight of a battery of artillery, letting men, horses, and guns into the river. Some of the men were badly hurt and were brought to the hospital, and from them and other sources we learned at the time we were moving towards Coffeeville there had been a scare at Jackson, and the military commander had ordered the timbers of the bridge sawed, so that in case of a cavalry dash on the town they would break down and let men and horses into the river. It seemed that in the change of commander, or forces, this had been forgotten, and that the first heavy weight broke down the bridge under their own men.

The bridges was of wood, roofed over with shingles, but with nothing on the sides except the timbers. Into this bridge our prisoners were put, and kept there the balance of the winter. They were more easily guarded than in the empty store buildings, where they had been kept, and then it cost the Confederate Government no rent. Besides the advantages, it kept the men exposed but with little clothing all through the worst part of the winter to the cold, damp, miasmatic atmosphere arising from the sluggish muddy stream so that, in proportion to the ease and cheapness with which there were kept in the bridge, the number to guard and feed was decreased by the ravages of disease. The food, too, was of the poorest quality, very scant, and the medical attendance could scarcely be called by that name. Many of the prisoners were soon sick, and some in their delirium threw themselves into the river and were drowned. I did not know much about this at the time, but learned it afterwards when we were exchanged. None of the sick or wounded were ever brought from the bridge to the hospital. When they were sick, they fared no better, as to quarters, than when well. There were plenty of empty houses at the time in Jackson in which these brave men could have been sheltered.[3]

---

3 "History of Pearl River Bridge from Witness," *Chicago Tribune*, January 12, 1891, Chicago, IL: https://chicagotribune.newspapers.com/clip/63805957/history-of-pearl-river-bridge-from/.

The rest of Ady's account talks about the trip to New Orleans for exchange, which he dates as "that 13th day of March, 1863. . . ."

These accounts provide enough clues to follow for additional research. For instance, I suspect the artillery crashing through the bridge, destroying half of it, would be something Jackson's three newspapers would've covered. Perhaps they might have written about converting the bridge ruins into a prison.

I haven't had the chance to confirm info on the writer, George Ady, Esq., but the *Tribune* says his piece was first published in the Denver *Commonwealth* Magazine. There was a George Ady in Co. G of the 2nd Iowa Cavalry who lived in Denver after the war. His record says he was wounded on December 5, 1862, in Coffeeville, Mississippi, (he mentions in his account that he was there). He was taken as a POW there and later paroled. I'll have to spend some time trying to follow up.

Along similar lines, nearly every bio of Thomas Fletcher says he was captured at Chickasaw Bayou and taken to Libby Prison, with no mention of his infernal time on Jackson's prison bridge, despite Fletcher's published account otherwise. I need to run that down more, too.

In any event, this still doesn't let Jim or I know where the prison bridge was located, but now we at least have some breadcrumbs to follow.

Capt. Samuel Jones Ridley at the Battle of Champion Hill

by Kevin Pawlak

*Originally published as a blog post at Emerging Civil War
on May 16, 2019*

Just after noon on May 16, 1863, Federals of John Logan's and Alvin Hovey's divisions smashed into the left flank of John Pemberton's Army of Vicksburg on the Champion Hill battlefield. Pemberton's left threatened to buckle under the pressure. If the field was lost, Ulysses S. Grant could cut Pemberton off from Vicksburg, making capturing that city easy.

Major General Carter Stevenson, Pemberton's division commander holding the left of the Confederate line at Champion Hill, immediately rushed reinforcements from the right end of his line to the threatened left. There, John Stevenson's Federal troops threatened to overlap the Army of Vicksburg's left flank. Seth Barton's Georgians moved quickly to that exposed sector and pitched into the Union soldiers opposing them. But still, the enemy outflanked the Confederate position. Barton pushed the four guns of the Cherokee Georgia Artillery to hold his left against the onslaught. Those four guns faced four regiments of Union infantry.

Soon, more help arrived for the Georgia artillerists. Admittedly, it was not much, just two guns under Capt. Samuel Ridley's command. The captain's gunners rushed into the fray, posting their two guns to the left of the four already there. Carter Stevenson's artillery chief, Maj. Joseph W. Anderson was spurred towards the left to personally oversee the artillery's critical stand against the oncoming Yankees.

Samuel Ridley's gunners traveled from near Pemberton's headquarters to reach their new position. Ridley himself journeyed much further to reach this moment. He was 41-years-old in May 1863, and many of his years were spent as a planter in Mississippi. The captain was tall and carried himself well, receiving the unanimous vote of his battery to be its leader in March 1862. Ridley stood six feet, three inches tall. "He was a splendid specimen of manhood," wrote his orderly sergeant, who continued, saying Ridley was "a typical Southern planter and gentleman."[1]

Ridley shouted orders, ordering the guns to deploy in the face of the advancing enemy. While the cannoneers moved into position, Col. Charles D. Phillips's 52nd Georgia Infantry arrived to support the six guns holding Pemberton's extreme left.

Suddenly, John Stevenson's Illinoisans and Ohioans burst from a strip of timber and came in full view of the Confederate gunners posted on a hill above them. The six guns unleashed shot and shell into the exposed Federals. However, they could only do so much. Stevenson's Federals overlapped the pieced-together line, scattering the supporting Georgia infantry. With their infantry support gone, the gunners didn't stand a chance.

Samuel Ridley continued to exhort his men to load and fire the pieces. Despite the heroic efforts of Ridley's Mississippians, the Federals continued gaining ground. They leveled their rifles, pouring destructive volleys into the two batteries, killing men and horses alike. In one volley, Maj. Joseph Anderson went down. Above the fire, Ridley instructed his orderly sergeant "to get the men away if possible."[2] Ridley, incredibly still mounted, jerked at his horse's reins to turn the horse away from the blue tide engulfing his guns when he was struck, killed by six bullets.

Inspired by their captain, Ridley's gunners fought until the very end. Some continued to fight even as Stevenson's men closed in. "It was the

1 "The Brave and True Capt. S.J. Ridley," *Confederate Veteran*, vol. 2, 343.

2 Ibid.

most deadly fight I ever saw," recalled one survivor.[3] He was a lucky one. Ridley's section of guns entered the action with 82 men and left with eight.

Overall, the heroics of the men who stood beside Capt. Ridley on that hillside did not halt the Federal assault. However, it did not diminish his performance in the eyes of those who witnessed it. Indeed, even some Union soldiers admired the captain's bravery until the end. Despite his battery's horses falling all around him, Ridley remained mounted to inspire his men on the ground. He paid for it with his life. "His name and his memory will be cherished by every member of the old battery until they shall be ordered to meet him on the camping grounds of life eternal," eulogized one of his men.[4]

3 Timothy B. Smith, *Champion Hill: Decisive Battle for Vicksburg* (El Dorado Hills, CA: Savas Beatie, 2006), 229.

4 "The Brave and True Capt. S.J. Ridley," *Confederate Veteran*, vol. 2, 343.

1. Arkansas's Role in the Vicksburg Campaign

by Carson Butler

Originally published as a two-part blog post at Emerging Civil War on April 8-9, 2021

The Mississippi River is one of the most defining features of the North American continent. During the Civil War, it proved vital in dictating who would win the conflict. President Abraham Lincoln and President Jefferson Davis commented that controlling the Mississippi River was critical for the war effort. The river served as a route to transport military supplies to different armies during the war, and divided the states of Texas, Louisiana, Arkansas, and Missouri from the rest of the south. With the fall of New Orleans and other Confederate strongholds along the Mississippi during 1862, the Federal Army was set on controlling the entire river. By 1863, the Confederacy controlled only a small portion, beginning with the fortified position at Port Hudson, Louisiana, and ending with the Confederate stronghold at Vicksburg, Mississippi. This led Union Gen. Ulysses S. Grant to launch a campaign to capture Vicksburg and the fortifications at Port Hudson, effectively cutting the Confederacy in two.

The state of Arkansas sent several regiments to aid with the defense of Vicksburg and Port Hudson. The regiments sent to Confederate Gen. John Pemberton's army defending the stronghold at Vicksburg were placed in a

The Arkansas Memorial at Vicksburg was erected in 1954 at a cost of $50,000. *Chris Mackowski*

single brigade commanded by Gen. Martin Edwin Green. These Arkansans quickly became known as Pemberton's shock troops in the Confederate Army of Mississippi, as they were hard-fighting soldiers who bore the brunt of the combat during the Vicksburg Campaign. At Port Hudson, the Arkansan regiments were placed under Confederate Gen. Franklin Gardner's command. They would defend the fortifications until forced to surrender after a 48-day siege.

To the soldiers from Arkansas, keeping the Mississippi River in Confederate hands was personal for them. They did not want their state to be cut off from the rest of the Confederacy. To stop the Federal invasions into Arkansas, the state needed the flow of supplies and manpower from other southern states east of the Mississippi River to thwart the Federal campaigns. However, with the Mississippi River in the hands of the Federal Army, there would be no help or support from the rest of the Confederacy. Arkansas and the Trans-Mississippi region would be isolated, forced to deal with the advancing Federals on their own.

With these thoughts in mind, the Arkansans embarked upon the Vicksburg Campaign steadfastly determination not to yield Vicksburg, Port Hudson, and the Mississippi River to the Federals. By trying to achieve this goal, the soldiers from Arkansas found themselves in almost every major campaign engagement, and as a result, they suffered horrendous casualties.

The opening battle of the Vicksburg campaign began on May 1, 1863, at a place called Port Gibson, south of Vicksburg. After multiple failed attempts to bypass the strong Confederate river batteries and fortifications at Vicksburg, Gen. Grant decided the best way to attack the city would be by marching down the Louisiana side of the Mississippi and crossing the river south of the city. To stop the Federals from achieving a beachhead or foothold on the Mississippi side of the river, Pemberton sent Gen. John Bowen's Division to prevent the crossing. General Martin Green's Arkansas Brigade was a part of Bowen's Division. They were ordered to dig in at Magnolia Church, a mile west of Port Gibson, to await the advancing Federal columns.

At midnight on May 1, 1863, the 12th Arkansas Sharpshooter Battalion rifled muskets fired the Vicksburg campaign's first shots. Lieutenant John S. Bell of the 1st Battalion wrote about this tense moment before chaos erupted on the battlefield. "We could hear the enemy forming," he stated, "and it was so still we could hear every command given. Our men had orders not to fire until word was given. Soon we could see their line of skirmishers coming down the road and could hear them say there was no one here. . . . When they were within 50 yards, the word 'fire' was given."[1]

For the next three hours, under cover of darkness, the Arkansans defended their position at Magnolia Church, despite multiple Federal attacks. When the fighting resumed in the morning, and more Federal reinforcements arrived, Bowen realized his hopeless situation and ordered a withdrawal through the town of Port Gibson back to the fortifications around Vicksburg. At the battle of Port Gibson, the Arkansans alone suffered 13 men killed, 51 wounded, and 86 missing.[2]

---

1 Edwin C. Bearss, *The Vicksburg Campaign: Grant Strikes a Fatal Blow*, vol. 2 (Dayton, Ohio: Morningside Press, 1986), 355.

2 Bearss, *The Vicksburg Campaign*, vol. 2, 402.

Following the victory at Port Gibson, Grant pushed his forces north-eastward, and ultimately marched his army toward Jackson, the capital of Mississippi. After defeating a Confederate force under Gen. John Gregg at Raymond on May 12, 1863, his pathway to Jackson was uncontested. Despite some resistance, Jackson fell on May 14, 1863. Pemberton realized he had to do something about Grant's army and launched a surprise attack on the Federal forces. The Confederate and Federal forces ran into each other on May 16, 1863, at a place between Vicksburg and Jackson called Champion Hill.

After initial success atop Champion Hill, the Confederates defending the hill retreated after numerous Federal attacks on their position. The retirement of these Confederates put Pemberton in an awkward position, as Federal forces cut off his escape route back to Vicksburg. Pemberton then ordered Bowen's Division to counterattack the Federals to reopen his retreat route, and Green's Arkansas Brigade was ordered to charge. Private A. H. Reynolds of the 19th Arkansas Infantry described the scene:

> With a forward march we passed those troops that were falling back, and then we were ordered to charge. We had caught the enemy with empty guns, and they gave way easily. We were charging up the long slope from the negro quarters to the highest peak of Champion Hill and almost parallel with the public road to Bolton. At the top of the hill we met another long line of blues climbing the steep hill. They were within eighty feet of us when we gained the top of the hill, and without orders it seemed as if every man in our ranks fired at once. Never before nor since have I ever witnessed such a sight. The whole line seemed to fall and tumble head-long to the bottom of the hill. In a moment they came again, and we were ready and again repulsed them.[3]

Colonel Thomas P. Dockery, also of the 19th, wrote:

> The formation of the country was such that the troops could scarcely advance faster than a walk, and many of the hills were

---

3 A. H. Reynolds, "Vivid Experiences at Champion Hill, Miss.," *Confederate Veteran* 18 (January 1910), 21.

ascended with great difficulty; notwithstanding, the command pushed impetuously forward, driving back in confusion the many fresh lines formed to meet our gallant troops. The enemy had been driven over a mile, all the artillery captured from Major-General Stevenson's division recaptured, and several pieces taken from the enemy. I notified General Green, commanding brigade, that my ammunition was about exhausted. He replied that the ordnance train had been ordered from the field, and it would be impossible to refill the cartridge-boxes; that the men must use the ammunition of our and the enemy's killed and wounded; that the enemy must be driven as long as it were possible to advance the lines, [even] if it had to be done with empty guns. . . .[4]

While sustaining heavy losses, the Arkansans held their position for as long as possible. However, after multiple Federal attacks, the Arkansas Brigade fled from the battlefield toward the defenses at Vicksburg.

The battle of Champion's Hill, or Baker's Creek, would not be the final engagement the Arkansans participated in during the Vicksburg campaign, as a day later, Green's Brigade manned earthworks east of the Big Black River to cover the retreat of the rest of the Army of Mississippi. On the morning of May 17th, the Federals attacked the Confederate positions. After three minutes, the Confederate line broke. Since the Arkansans' backs were to the river, there was no opportunity for the entire brigade to make it safely back to the fortifications at Vicksburg. As a result, part of Green's Brigade was captured at the battle of the Big Black River. Many other Arkansans had to swim across the river to safety, leaving those who could not swim to be captured by the enemy or drowning in the escape attempt.

Despite heavy casualties at the battles of Port Gibson, Champion's Hill/ Baker's Creek, and Big Black River, the Arkansans continued to fight on. They played an essential role in plugging the holes in the defensive lines that had been damaged by artillery or infantry attacks during the two Federal attempts to take Vicksburg on May 19th and 22nd, respectively.

---

4 United States War Department, *The War of the Rebellion: A Compilation of the Official Records of the Union and Confederate Armies,* 70 vols. in 128 parts (Washington D.C.: Government Printing Office, 1880-1901), Series I, volume 24, part 2, p. 116 (hereafter cited as *O.R.,* I, 24, pt. 2, 116).

With these attacks unsuccessful, Grant ordered his army to besiege the city. Similarly, 150 miles to the south, the Federal Army under Gen. Nathaniel Banks began to besiege the Confederates at Port Hudson under Franklin Gardner. For the remainder of both sieges, Arkansans stabilized weak sections of the Confederate works, helping to drive off the Federals.

However, by July 4, 1863, the starving Confederates at Vicksburg had had enough, and Pemberton surrendered the city to Grant. As a result, the Arkansans of Green's Brigade, as well as the other 30,000 soldiers at Vicksburg, were paroled and allowed to go home until they were exchanged. A few days later, on July 9th, Gardner surrendered Port Hudson to Banks, and the 6,500 men under his command were paroled and allowed to go home.

Colonel Thomas P. Dockery's bas relief monument at Vicksburg. *Chris Mackowski*

In December 1863, the Arkansans who served in the Vicksburg campaign either at Vicksburg or Port Hudson were exchanged and reorganized to serve in the Trans-Mississippi theatre of operations. With the loss of the Mississippi River, Arkansas suffered from being cut off. With the defeat of Confederate forces at the battle of Helena, Arkansas, on July 4, 1863, there were no major campaigns to retake the Confederate territory lost to the Federal forces in Arkansas other than Confederate Gen. Sterling Price's campaign on Missouri in 1864. While some Arkansans continued to fight until the war's end, when the Confederate Trans-Mississippi Department surrendered on May 10, 1865, others deserted the Confederate Army and returned home to try to pick up their civilian lives again.

When thinking about the grandeur of the Vicksburg campaign, the courage and bravery of the Arkansas soldiers should not be forgotten. By remembering them, we can assure their personal sacrifices will not be lost to history.

Enslaved During a Siege

by Sarah Kay Bierle

George. Was that the name his enslaved mother had given him? It was the name Mary Ann Loughborough called him in her reminiscence of the siege of Vicksburg. Through the writings of this white civilian woman who published her experiences during the siege of Vicksburg, there are glimpses of the life of an enslaved young man and what he survived and endured in the dangerous weeks of 1863. The pieces of his story are badly fragmented in Loughborough's writings, and he tends to appear on her pages only when it serves to record something about his "faithfulness" or some way that he made her life easier or safer.

As I read Loughborough's writings, I kept track of each time she mentioned George, the only enslaved servant that she regularly mentions. I wondered what his story would look like from this primary source if her self-focused commentary, mild justifications for slavery, and occasional degrading language were stripped away. What are the facts of George's experience through the siege of Vicksburg, and could it serve as a start for exploring his story?

George was enslaved. No one asked if he wanted to stay in Vicksburg. No one gave him a choice. Major and Mrs. Loughborough were staying, and since they said they owned him, he would stay. It raises an interesting question: when did the Loughborough's buy George? Where had he lived? Mary Ann Webster Loughborough was born and raised in New York. She married James Moore Loughborough of Kentucky in 1857, and the couple resided in St. Louis, Missouri. Siding with the Confederacy when the Civil War broke out, the Loughboroughs headed south, where James Loughborough was promoted to major and served on staff for several generals. Without a permanent home, Mrs. Loughborough followed her husband, and stayed with civilian friends when possible. She traveled with a small entourage of servants, and tried to keep her young daughter, Jean, safe. She entered the city of Vicksburg on April 15, 1863, thinking it would be a place of safety.

George does not appear on the 1860 Slave Schedule (Census) with Mr. James M. Loughborough's name in Missouri. Only one enslaved person is listed on that record which matches the Loughborough's pre-war residence. That person is a woman, perhaps one of the other servants not mentioned by name in the written account.[1] Most likely, George was purchased after the Loughborough's went into the Confederacy, a reminder that the slave trade happened in Confederate territory throughout the Civil War. His age is not specified, but from descriptions of his brisk activity, swift movements, and hints that he was young, I would guess he was in his teens or early twenties.

Mrs. Loughborough moved from the house to a cave to take shelter from the artillery projectiles falling into the city. She also took her servants and recorded with apparent delight, "it would have been an amusing sight to a spectator to witness the domestic scenes presented without by the number of servants preparing the meals under the high bank containing the caves."[2] Whether George felt safer in the subterranean dugout is questionable. He frequently ran errands, cooked outside, and did other semi-dangerous activities when directed by Mrs. Loughborough, who preferred to stay inside.

He did not like the "rush and explosion of the shells," and one afternoon, when loud, feminine screams echoed outside, he hesitated several times before going out into the exploding world to bring back word. The discovery must have been horrifying; a nearby cave had been hit, and a black man had been buried alive. "Workmen were instantly set to deliver him, if possible,"

1 Ancestry.com. *1860 U.S. Federal Census - Slave Schedules* [database online]. Lehi, UT, USA: Ancestry.com Operations Inc, 2010. Original data: United States of America, Bureau of the Census. Eighth Census of the United States, 1860. Washington, D.C.: National Archives and Records Administration, 1860. M653, 1,438 rolls.

2 Mary Ann Webster Loughborough, *My Cave Life in Vicksburg, With Letters of Trial and Travel* (New York: D. Appleton & Company, 1864), 60. Digitized by Google Books.

Cave life during the Vicksburg siege offered some level of protection but also its own unique miseries. *Library of Congress*

and perhaps George joined in. However, the poor man had been killed, and his family gathered, weeping over his sudden, unexpected death.[3]

Despite witnessing this, George's courage did not fail, frequently "cross[ing] the street for water at any time" it was needed or ordered by the white inhabitants. Mrs. Loughborough gave George a pistol, and at night, he slept across the cave's entrance, assuring her that she should not be afraid.

On many occasions, George "never refused to carry any article" to Major Loughborough on the battle-trench lines. However, I wonder if he would have refused to constantly go into danger if he had been allowed to make his own decisions. George knew how to ride and planned to "ride out to the battlefield . . . to a dangerous locality, where the shells were flying thickly" until the mule obstinately refused to cooperate.[4]

George had several additional, recorded close brushes with death. On one evening, he said he would keep watch at the entrance of the cave to say if any shells where landing near their position. He stood on a "hillock of loose earth . . . look[ing] intently upward" and he called out his observations, "'Here she comes! going over!' then again, 'Coming—falling—falling right

3 Ibid., 63.

4 Ibid., 65.

dis way!'" Sometime later that night, George fell asleep outside the cave and away from his usual post at the entrance. Mrs. Loughborough saw "many fragments of shell falling around him" and called, waking him, and telling him to seek shelter. Startled, he hastened toward the cave . . . just as a "huge piece of shell came whizzing along . . . and it fell in the very spot where he had so lately slept."[5]

In another brush with death, George saved the occupants of the cave. It happened on a "Wednesday evening" at "about four o'clock" when a new Federal battery opened with Parrot shells. George seems to have been outside doing chores when Mrs. Loughborough "call[ed] the servants in." Everyone crouched in the cave, frightened by the new barrage. Then "a Parrott shell came whirling in at the entrance, and fell in the centre of the cave before us all, lying there smoking. Our eyes were fastened upon it, while we expected every moment the terrific explosion would ensue." Mrs. Loughborough was frozen with terror and clutched her young daughter. Suddenly, George "rushed forward, seized the shell, and threw it into the street, running swiftly in the opposite direction. Fortunately, the fuse had become nearly extinguished, and the shell fell harmless—remaining near the mouth of the cave." Over the next few days, George displayed his powers for captivating storytelling to the rest of the enslaved population in the caves and reenacted his heroism, pantomiming the lack of courage among the white people to the great delight of his audience.[6]

In the day-to-day life of surviving a siege, George demonstrated creative resourcefulness. When helping with the cooking, he had "a continual warfare" with the stray dogs roaming the area. He had to devise ways to chase them off.[7] After moving the Loughborough family to a new cave, closer to the battle area (which somewhat reduced the shelling effects, but put them closer to flying bullets), he found a large patch of sassafras roots, using them to make tea.[8] As food grew scarce, George must have faced the shortages with trepidation. Would he be guaranteed sustenance if the

---

5 Ibid., 69-70.

6 Ibid., 73-76.

7 Ibid., 78.

8 Ibid., 103-104.

situation worsened? When a cow was killed nearby, "George and some of the boys in the camp cut the meat in strips" and hung it in the cave to dry as jerky.[9]

When a summer storm darkened the skies, George was ordered to go out "with a spade to slope the earth about the roof of our home, and widen the water ditch around it." After the heavy rain began falling, he was sent out several times to pack the earth and work on the ditch, in efforts to keep the sheltering cave from collapsing on its inhabitants. Water did flood the back of the shelter, but—thanks to George's efforts—the roof held. As the storm passed and the women sat in puddles, Major Loughborough ordered George to dig a new firepit and prepare breakfast. George laughed at Mrs. Loughborough and assured her that the roof was secure while he mixed the morning meal. He "set the breakfast on the table" and witnessed the Loughborough's cheerfulness, mostly due to his efforts in the storm and preparing fire and food.[10]

George's first recorded meeting with "Yankees" after Vicksburg's surrender on July 4, 1863, did not go well, according to Mrs. Loughborough. He "rode into the city on his mule" and with Major Loughborough's "handsome, silver-mounted dragoon saddle." There, a Yankee ordered him to give up the fine saddle, and when George refused, threatened him with a pistol. He gave up the expensive tack, returned with a wooden, common saddle, and told the tale "with a sorry face."[11]

Later, an African American in Federal uniform approached the cave and seemed to threaten Mrs. Loughborough. George came from the sassafras patch, "carving knife in hand, with which he was digging some of the root." Placing himself between Mrs. Loughborough and the soldier, George demanded, "Where are you gwin', old man?" "None your business," he returned, pausing a moment. George threatened the man with the knife, and he left. Just a little later, George ran off another "Yankee soldier" who was trying to steal the tent fly lying over the cave's entrance.[12]

9 Ibid., 117-118.

10 Ibid., 109-113.

11 Ibid., 140-141.

12 Ibid., 144-145.

George's final act recorded in the reminiscences was an attempt to follow Major Loughborough, who was a prisoner. He found a pair of blue pants and tried to follow the column, acting as a Federal soldier. Someone realized his ruse and sent him back. George begged Mrs. Loughborough to help him secure a military pass and departed. Mrs. Loughborough claimed, "to this day I do not know whether he ever reached M[ajor] or not."[13] It is a sudden and disappointing ending to George's story. Surely his experiences did not end with his disappearance.

Since George's experiences during the Siege of Vicksburg exist through the eyes of another, many details linger unanswered. How did he feel about his situation? Did he take some pride in keeping Mrs. Loughborough and her daughter safe, or was that what the lady wanted to believe? Did he know about the Emancipation Proclamation and the promise of freedom when Union troops took Vicksburg? Would his experience of being on the receiving end of the Federal bombardment or his encounters with thieving soldiers have lessened his enthusiasm for interactions with "Yankees"? Or did he portray a clever act that ended in his escape to freedom through mysterious disappearance?

I wish I knew the answers. Peeling back Mrs. Loughborough's interpretation of submissive loyalty and looking at the bare, recorded facts about George's life offers new ways to see his reactions. Boldly, he met dangers, struggled through difficulties to find solutions, and laughed at the fears or cowardice of the white people around him. Creative, insightful, courageous, and industrious, George lived through the Siege of Vicksburg and probably found freedom later in 1863. Perhaps additional research can match his first name with other existing records to help build the rest of his life story before and after the siege. His appearances in Mrs. Loughborough's writing served her purposes as she crafted the remembrance of her experiences. However, a closer look reveals a young man in bondage, fighting for his survival, and displaying courage and character through the incidents of war.

13 Ibid., 145.

The Fall of Vicksburg: Breaking the Backbone of the Rebellion

by JoAnna M. McDonald

*Originally published as a blog post at Emerging Civil War
on July 4, 2022*

On July 4, 1863, Maj. Gen. Ulysses S. Grant's army captured Vicksburg, Mississippi. The fall of the river fortress culminated in a complicated, joint Army-Navy campaign over many months of maneuvering, fighting, and working. However, this campaign often gets hastily passed over in historical conversations. Gettysburg and Fourth of July festivities take precedence. I am at fault for neglecting this event as well. Still, the fall of this small town played a pivotal role in the destruction of the Confederacy around 21 months later.[1]

Why was Vicksburg so important? Think of the town as the hub of a wagon wheel. That is how significant its location was. It occupied the first high ground south of Memphis, overlooking the Mississippi River—the most crucial highway in the nation. On land, two railroad lines traversed through the region. One line ran east and connected with other roads "leading to all

---

1 Many thanks to Bill Jayne for his editorial comments. Bill is a lifelong student of military history. He is president of the Cape Fear Civil War Roundtable. He served in the 26th Marines at Khe Sanh. After Vietnam, he attended Berkeley, where he earned an English degree.

points of the Southern States.[2] The other railroad line started from the opposite side of the river and extended "west as far as Shreveport, Louisiana."[3]

Vicksburg was the last stronghold guarding the Mississippi River. The side that held this town thus commanded the tons of supplies moving to and fro. The Confederacy could only challenge the Federal Navy's river control using the land-based artillery at Vicksburg. Furthermore, Port Hudson, Louisiana, and other forts south of the city would become untenable if Vicksburg fell. By 1863, Vicksburg stood as the last remaining junction connecting the communication lines across the breadth of the Confederacy. Arkansas, Texas, and Louisiana lay to the west. Mississippi, Alabama, Tennessee, Georgia, Florida, South Carolina, North Carolina, and Virginia lay to the east.[4]

From the beginning, President Abraham Lincoln understood the strategic situation. He aptly referred to the mighty Mississippi River back in 1862 as "the backbone of the Rebellion [and the] key to the whole situation." If the Confederates held it, they could "obtain supplies of all kinds, and it [was] a barrier against our forces."[5] Taking the strongholds along the Mississippi had to be done in order to bring all the southern states back into the union.

The Confederacy, on the other hand, had Gen. Robert E. Lee. He looked at the situation through a narrow lens. On April 10, 1862, he wrote to Maj. Gen. John C. Pemberton, commanding general in the western theater: "If [the] Mississippi Valley [was] lost [the] Atlantic States [would] be ruined."[6] Herein lay the problem for the Confederacy. Despite his admission, Lee only had one strategy: win the war in Virginia.

Lee saw the Vicksburg and Mississippi Valley dilemma as "a question between Virginia and the Mississippi."[7] This was a crucial point. Would the

2 U. S. Grant, *Personal Memoirs*, vol. 1, 250.

3 Ibid.

4 Ibid.

5 David Porter, "The Opening of the Lower Mississippi," *Battles and Leaders*, vol. 2, 24. For more on Vicksburg, see Shea and Winshel, *Vicksburg is the Key*, and Terrence J. Winshel, *Triumph and Defeat: The Vicksburg Campaign* (New York: Savas Beatie, 2004), and Dr. C. Gabel, *Staff Ride Handbook for the Vicksburg Campaign, December 1862–July 1863* (Pickle Partners Publishing, ebook).

6 R. E. Lee to Major General John C. Pemberton, Richmond, VA, April 10, 1862, *O.R.*, Ser. 1, vol. 6, 432.

7 R. E. Lee to James Seddon, Fredericksburg, May 10, 1863, *O.R.* Ser. 1, vol. 25, pt. 2, 790.

entire Confederacy collapse if Richmond was captured, or would it fail if the government moved elsewhere, such as Atlanta? Lee refused to consider these and many more questions.[8] By early spring 1863, he refused to transfer any divisions out west. At that point, there was still time to try and relieve pressure out west, but no relief came.[9]

Instead, Grant's army gobbled up the Mississippi Valley. The Naval expedition to subdue Vicksburg began May-June 1862. The siege lasted May-July 1863.[10] It was exceptionally brutal. Civilians were trapped and starving in the city, and much of Vicksburg lay in ruins. The Confederates finally surrendered. The Union forces captured a foundry, 60,000 rifled muskets, 172 cannons, a substantial amount of ammunition, and 31,600 Confederate soldiers.[11]

The surrender of Vicksburg was like a domino effect. Shortly, Union troops walked into an abandoned Jackson, Mississippi, as most of Mississippi fell into Union hands.[12] Six days after Vicksburg fell, the

---

8 Edward Porter Alexander, *Fighting for the Confederacy*, criticizes Lee several times for his Virginia-centric view of the strategic problem. The 1907 edition of this book is on Google Books for free.

9 On March 11, Lee attended a council of war in Richmond to discuss the strategic situation. For meeting and date, see Archer Jones, "The Gettysburg Decision," *Virginia Magazine of History and Biography* 68, no. 3 (July 1960): 332. On April 6, Secretary of War Seddon wrote to Lee and again asked him if he could send just two brigades to Bragg. See James Seddon to R. E. Lee, Richmond, VA, April 6, 1863, *O.R.*, Ser. 1, vol. 25, pt. 2, 708–09. Then, on April 14, Adjutant and Inspector Samuel Cooper, on behalf of President Davis, beseeched Lee to relinquish two divisions for Middle Tennessee. See Adjutant and Inspector General S. Cooper, Richmond, VA, April 14, 1863, *O.R.*, Ser. 1, vol. 25, pt. 2, 720. Davis had seen the dire situation was in Tennessee and Mississippi as he had traveled to these states in December 1862, see Joseph Johnston, "Jefferson Davis and the Mississippi Campaign," *Battles and Leaders*, vol. 3, 474–75.

10 Grant, *Personal Memoirs*, vol. 1, 250.

11 *Battles and Leaders*, vol. 3, 537.

12 General Johnston had two choices at Jackson, Mississippi: he could prepare for a siege that would trap his army or evacuate his army, see J. E. Johnston to Davis, Jackson, July 16, 1863, and Brandon, July 16, 1863, found in Johnston, *Narrative*, 567. For Vicksburg, see *O.R.*, Ser. 1, vol. 24, pts., 1–3 and vol. 26 pts., 1–2, and U. S. Grant, *Personal Memoirs*, vol. 1, 422–570. For quote, see David Porter, "The Opening of the Lower Mississippi," *Battles and Leaders*, vol. 2, 24.

Confederate garrison at Port Hudson surrendered.[13] The entire Mississippi River and Valley was gone from the Confederacy. The Union armies and navy had severed the "backbone of the Rebellion." Louisiana, Texas, and Arkansas lay isolated, while the southern states to the east were exposed to invasion from the north and west. It was just a matter of time before the Confederacy capitulated.[14]

---

13 The South lost another 5,500 soldiers as prisoners, including one major general and one brigadier general, "20 pieces of heavy artillery, 5 complete batteries, numbering 31 pieces of field artillery, a good supply of projectiles for small-arms, [and] 150,000 rounds of small-arms ammunition." See Major General Nathaniel P. Banks to Major General Henry W. Halleck, General-in-Chief, Headquarters, Port Hudson, LA, July 10, 1863, *O.R.*, Ser. 1, vol. 26, pt. 1, 55.

14 Illustration 1: Strategic Significance of Vicksburg, map taken from *R. E. Lee's Grand Strategy and Leadership* by JoAnna McDonald. Savas and Beatie Publications, El Dorado Hills, CA. Date: TBD. Illustration 2: Steamboat, https://shiphistory.org/2021/02/26/steamboats-enslavement-and-freedom/. Illustration 3: Mississippi: Backbone of the Rebellion, https://www.nps.gov/articles/the-siege-of-port-hudson-forty-days-and-nights-in-the-wilderness-of-death-teaching-with-historic-places.htm. Illustration 4: Vicksburg, http://npshistory.com/publications/civil_war_series/24/sec9.htm. Illustration 5: Captured cannon, https://mississippiconfederates.wordpress.com/2014/05/14/artillery-during-the-siege-of-vicksburg.

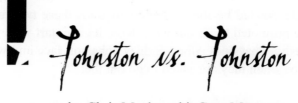

I. Johnston vs. Johnston

by Chris Mackowski, Greg Mertz,
Angela M. Riotto, and Kristopher D. White

*This is an edited transcript of an Emerging Civil War Podcast episode
that dropped on January 21, 2021. It has been edited for brevity and clarity.*

Historians Greg Mertz, Angela Riotto, and Kris White joined Chris Mackowski on
the Emerging Civil War Podcast to talk about two "Johnstons" who commanded
in the Western Theater: Albert Sidney Johnston and Joseph E. Johnston.

Albert Sidney, the second-highest ranking officer in the Confederacy, was
placed in command of the Western Theater early in the war and charged with
defending the entire Confederate border between the Appalachian Mountains
and the Mississippi River. After a challenging first few months that included
the falls of Fort Henry and Donelson, as well as the Tennessee capital of
Nashville, he was killed on the first day of the battle of Shiloh, April 6, 1862.

Joseph E., the fourth-highest ranking officer in the Confederacy, was sent to
the Western Theater in later November 1862 to oversee the army in Middle
Tennessee under Braxton Bragg and the army in Vicksburg, Mississippi, under
John Pemberton. He made his headquarters with Bragg's army for the first
several months but was ordered to Mississippi in early May 1863 in response
to Ulysses S. Grant's inland campaign against Vicksburg. He would eventually
be placed in field command of Bragg's army after the Union army broke out
of the siege of Chattanooga in November 1863. Removed from command in
July 1864 after giving up most of northern Georgia, he was reinstated in early
1865 to contest Sherman's advance through the Carolinas.

*   *   *

Chris M.:   I'm fascinated by the strategic situations these two men faced when they were promoted to go out west. Kris, let me start with you. Can you outline briefly: what does Albert Sidney Johnston face and what does Joe Johnston face when they are asked to go out there?

Kris W.:   They absolutely face two thankless and, really, insurmountable tasks. Albert Sidney Johnson, a Kentucky native, is going to be challenged with basically defending the Confederacy from what is today West Virginia all the way out to Mississippi and basically almost Arkansas. He has about 40,000 men to do so, and he has to make a lot of people happy. Remember, the Confederacy is a loosely based organization where nobody wants to play with anyone else. They don't want a strong central government. They don't want to have a lot of governmental oversight. So Johnston, like Jefferson Davis, the president of the Confederacy, has to play to many masters. He's out there, trying to defend a lot of territory with ill-trained troops—and too few of them.

Throw in there that you have Kentucky, which is neutral at this point of the war—and you don't want to trip up Kentucky's neutrality, because that could really sway things out west. Both Jefferson Davis and Abraham Lincoln would strongly prefer having Kentucky on their respective sides of the war. They thought that could be the tipping point. And in some ways that will be out west.

Johnston is a West Point graduate of the class of '28. He has risen to the rank of colonel in the old army and then brevet brigadier general, so he is going to be one of the ranking generals in the army.

Joe Johnston, who is going to come out West in late '62 to help defend that part of the Confederacy after a series of setbacks: the fall of New Orleans, the falls of Forts Henry and Donaldson, defeats at Shiloh and Corinth—you name it, it's not going well out west. And he's facing the potential sieges of Vicksburg and Port Hudson. He's going to be dealing with the best of the Union coming at him, Ulysses S. Grant, and he'll have a pair of B-listers under him with Brxton Bragg and John Pemberton. The greatest line about Braxton Bragg is that Jefferson Davis tried to do what God himself could not do, and that was make a general officer out of Braxton Bragg. And people don't know where Pemberton's loyalties lie because he's a Pennsylvanian who's thrown in with the South.

Finally, Joe Johnston is thrust into this job after losing command of what became known as the Army of Northern Virginia to someone who was his friend, Robert E. Lee.

A lot of problems manifest in the Western Theater, and neither Johnston has the resources or the skills to overcome everything that's thrown at them.

Chris M.:   Greg, let me shift over to you. Albert Sidney gets sent west first. Put me in his shoes for a second. Put me in his mindset. How is he feeling about this assignment to go west?

Greg M.:   Well, one aspect of Albert Sidney Johnston to look at, to understand how he might feel about this, is his relationship with Jefferson Davis. The two are basically lifelong friends at a time when it was not unusual for younger people to go to college. Even though they are six years apart in age, they will both attend Transylvania University and later both attend West Point two years apart. They would both fight in the Black Hawk War, and both serve in the Mexican War in the battle of Monterey.

Johnston will find that Davis has a great deal of confidence in him, and that gives us an opportunity later on to contrast that with Joseph E. Johnston. That's an important part of Sidney Johnston's eventual mindset going out there. He knows he has the confidence of his president, even after he makes his greatest mistake out there—the loss of Fort Donaldson—and has to abandon virtually all of Tennessee, and Nashville becomes the first Confederate state capital to fall into Union hands. All but one member of the Tennessee delegation in Richmond calls for Johnston's resignation, but Jefferson Davis says, "If Sidney Johnston is not a general, then we have no general." So that's one of the important things to look at.

The other to touch on, which Kris mentioned, is this aspect of dealing with Kentucky. Johnston is a former Secretary of War for the Republic of Texas. He also will eventually put on his staff governors in exile from Kentucky. He'll have Tennessee Governor Isham Harris on his staff. He understands the political aspect of things, and he will send some troops into Kentucky shortly after Leonidas Polk violates the state's neutrality [in September 1861]. Johnston will send a proclamation saying, basically, "I'm here for the people of Kentucky to help you decide whether you're going to be neutral, or side with the Confederacy, or side with the Union, but just know that if you do stay with the Union that the Confederate army will go wherever and whenever it needs to defend its territory."

So those are two things that struck me the most as I look at his mindset.

Chris M.:   We'll come back and unpack some of that, but Angela, I want to turn to you and have you put me in Joe Johnston's shoes as he gets sent out west.

Angela R.: Well, it's very different from Albert Sidney. He does not have the confidence of Jefferson Davis. If anything, they have a very strained relationship. In fact, Johnston has a tumultuous relationship with the entire Confederate high command. He already had issues in the Eastern Theater as head of the Army of Northern Virginia, and then once he's wounded at the battle of Fair Oaks in late May 1862, he has to take a six-month leave to recover. And in that time, Lee, as we know, makes some brazen attacks to shift the momentum of the war in the east. So when Johnson comes back to the field and is then sent out west, he kind of has to deal with this cloud over his head of what Lee is doing in the East.

Also, as we mentioned, it's not looking good in the West when he takes command. At this point, we've had the losses of Shiloh and Corinth. He goes to Mississippi and has to fight against Grant for Vicksburg, and he has to abandon the Mississippi capital, Jackson. It does not look good. So that already-strained relationship with the Confederate high command becomes even more strained, and it's only going to get worse. We know as Confederates are pushed back across to the East, he is eventually removed from command and then reinstated. But it's just going to get worse for Joe. The West is such a huge area.

Chris M.: And I think that that's one of the problems. Kris, Albert Sidney is told defend this whole frontier. And that's a different charge than Joe Johnson is given when he eventually gets sent west. Tell me, how does Jefferson Davis factor into the missions he gives each of these guys?

Kris W.:   Well, good old Jeff Davis, who's a West Point graduate himself and thinks he is the next coming of Napoleon at times, is going to be a hindrance because Sidney Johnston is charged with putting together a cordon defense and pretty much has to defend any avenues of Union advance into the western Confederacy from the Cumberland pass out to the Mississippi. How's he going to do this? He'll do this with small covering forces.

Now, Joe Johnston, on the other hand, believes you should keep your main armies together as much as possible. You can spread out a little and have them within supporting distance—for instance, a corps is supposed to be able to fight on its own for about a day, but then you bring back the rest of the army together.

But so many Southern politicians, as well as civilians, think that every place on the map is important, so what you have to do is defend all these small places. That's what Albert Sidney Johnston ends up doing, and it creates a weak picket line that's very porous, and the Union army is *still* able to come. Nashville falls in February of 1862 because Tennessee is untenable. Sidney Johnston had his headquarters, at that point, in Bowling Green, Kentucky. He had to fall back out of Kentucky and farther to the south. This is something that Davis doesn't like, nor does Robert E. Lee. They only want to give up territory whenever necessary.

On the other side, you have Joe Johnston. All he can do is give up territory. That guy is excellent at falling back, in some ways. It's just that he doesn't bring everything with him like he's supposed to. He'll never tell you that he's retreating, but he's going to do it. One Confederate said he could fall back from the Centerville line all the way to the Gulf of Mexico and wouldn't be happy.

So that's what you start to deal with with Joe Johnson. He thinks you should have a centralized defense where you can move your men to meet the enemy, whereas Albert Sidney Johnson is forced, especially early in the war, to spread out his men.

So what you're seeing are two different commands styles. Jefferson Davis wants to defend everything. Albert Sidney Johnson tries to make Davis happy. Joe Johnson doesn't care what Davis says, and he won't talk to him. It gets so cantankerous between them that, on two different dispatches, Davis—in his own hand—actually puts the word "insubordinate" whenever he's talking about Joe Johnston.

Angela R.: You bring up a good point, and it shows kind of a shift in the strategic situation. Albert Sidney Johnston has to maintain control, right? He has to maintain the lines of communication, the rail lines, the water lines. It's a huge area. But that's his goal: to maintain control.

By the time Joe Johnston takes command, maintaining control is no longer an option because they no longer have control of the main transportation centers or the hubs of communication. So, their strategic shift becomes more like denying enemy access to these areas. It's so porous that, now, they're just trying to maybe delay the enemy from getting access to these places and hold off as long as possible.

Chris M.: And I think Jefferson Davis has the very front-forward mindset to be on the attack, be aggressive. That's not Joe Johnston's mindset, with his famous Fabian defenses: "I don't have to win. I just have to survive and not lose." That might have had its place, but it's not politically tenable for Davis, who looks at Albert Sidney as being that take-it-to-them aggressor. Greg, is that the right person to have in place to defend this huge frontier with 40,000 guys?

Greg M.:   I think it is. Sidney Johnston had a reputation for encouraging aggressive action, whether that was against the Mexicans or Indians or even in the Mormon Expedition. That was part of his personality, and I think perhaps the reason why he was able—with the lack of resources out in that line along southern Kentucky and northern Tennessee—to maintain things for so long, because he at least put up a good front. He's a good person at bluffing. He would advance, and some of his opponents were fearful that he was going to attack. Johnston would instruct his cavalry: when you go out and approach the enemy, I want you to give them the impression that you are in the advance of something coming, not just some lightning raid to strike and head out. Make it look like there's something behind you, and you're the precursor to what is to come.

The person in charge of the Union forces in Kentucky when Albert Sidney took command was Robert Anderson of Fort Sumter fame, who was a native of Kentucky. Anderson would leave, and William T. Sherman took his place, and Sherman made a proclamation that 200,000 soldiers were needed to defend the area and basically suffered a nervous breakdown. He was in command of Kentucky, I think, just a little over a month or so. I'm sure most people have heard that Sherman had a nervous breakdown, but many not may not realize it's because of some of the aggressive actions that Johnston took.

Even on the eve of the battle of Shiloh, there is a prominent meeting, and a lot of things have gone wrong, and the advance to Shiloh took longer than anyone thought it would. And so the night before the battle, P. G. T. Beauregard, the second in command of the Confederate Army, and Braxton Bragg, in command of the largest corps, both argue that the army should go back to Corinth. Abandon the attack. And Johnston decided they would go forward. Not only is he just showing resolve and aggressiveness, but he actually has some reason behind it. Most people have heard his phrase, "I would fight them if they were a million," but what follows that is instructive. The Union army is between two creeks, and Albert Sidney says, "They can present no greater front between these creeks than we can." And he's seen no evidence from the Union Army that they have changed their position or improved their position.

So I do think he proved to be the right man for the job and did have a degree of aggressiveness that maybe not a lot of people see.

Kris W.:   I also think that Albert Sidney Johnson probably had a little easier task, even though he's spreading out over such a large area, because everyone is so new to this war. At this point, everyone's seeing hundreds of thousands of soldiers gathering here, gathering there. Unless it's George McClellan—then it's, like, six million. But, you know, you see all of these men learning the ways of warfare.

By the time Joe Johnston comes into command, now you're dealing with a veteran opponent whose morale is soaring in the West. Let's forget about the Eastern Theater for a second, and Robert E. Lee and everything going well there. In the Western Theater, everything's coming up roses for the Union forces at this point. By the time Joe Johnston takes over, it's been victory after victory after victory, and now you're dealing with a more veteran opponent—not to make excuses for Joe Johnson, but that is something to consider.

Chris M.:   At some point after Donelson falls, Albert Sidney has kind of a "come to Jesus" moment where he realizes what he's been doing is not working. Greg, let me let me ask you about that because that sets up what becomes the battle of Shiloh, as he reevaluates how he's approaching his defense.

Greg M.:   One important aspect of that is that Jefferson Davis freed him from this idea of holding the cordon defense and allowed him to bring his forces together to form an army, which he had not really not been permitted to do. So, he is able to, for a variety of reasons, form an army around Corinth and get some 44,000 troops to attack at Shiloh.

By the way, he doesn't draw everybody there. One of the twin battles, if you will, of Shiloh that gets very little attention is the battle of Island Number 10 on the Mississippi, which has General John Pope as the victor. This is a complete victory similar to Grant capturing some 12,000 soldiers or more at Donelson. There are something like seven-thousand Confederates captured at Island Number 10, so Union commander Maj. Gen. John Pope is probably a little upset that Shiloh is taking all the press because he's actually accomplished something pretty significant there. And that, of course, will lead to him eventually take over the Army of Virginia in the summer of 1862. So, let's give him a little bit of credit that helps us understand why Lincoln put him in such an important position later on.

Chris M.:   And that's a great point. I don't think people realize that, as Grant is having success at Shiloh, Pope is out there having success at Island Number 10.

Of course, Shiloh brings an abrupt end to Albert Sidney Johnston's career. I want to come back to that in a few minutes. But things in the West hang in limbo for a little while as the Army of Tennessee figures out its leadership situation, which becomes tumultuous and that's why Joe Johnston gets called from the bullpen in November of '62 to try to sort things out.

Angela, tell me: Joe Johnston comes out west and he's told, "Go see the Army of Tennessee," but he's also put in charge of the army out in Vicksburg. That's a pretty disparate charge, isn't it?

Angela R.: For sure. The idea that he has a headquarters in southern Tennessee, and he's supposed to have command of this entire area in Mississippi, as well. And at this point, the lines of communications are becoming more tenuous, so trying to keep in contact with his various units is becoming incredibly difficult.

Also, the relationships are kind of tenuous. Are Braxton Bragg and John Pembertson willing and even questionably able to take commands from Joe Johnston? Who is this guy who has been sent to us to take command when we've been in this area this entire time?

And there's kind of this push and pull in the correspondence of what the main plan for the defenses of Vicksburg are, and then for northern Mississippi, and that's going to become an issue when Grant pushes up from the south and comes up to Jackson. That strained relationship between Johnston and Pemberton, and Johnston's realization that he doesn't have the resources, doesn't have the men, and telling Pemberton to pull back to the defense of the Vicksburg—and Pemberton pushes back—that's going to become an issue. That sort of thing is going to become an issue for Joe Johnston with many of his subordinate commanders. We can see that in correspondence. He doesn't have a good relationship with many of his corps commanders. He doesn't have a good relationship with Jefferson Davis.

Chris M.:   And Joe Johnston doesn't want this gig to begin with.

Angela R.: He doesn't want to be out there. He kind of sees it as being tossed aside—being relegated to the Western Theater.

Chris M.:   In his correspondence with Senator Wigfall from Texas, he says he's being set up for failure, like. I'm being sent out there because Davis is trying to embarrass me in an untenable situation.

Kris W.:   And Wigfall is using Johnston, as well, as a pawn to get at Davis, because they're political rivals and he knows that [Secretary of State] Judah Benjamin and others do not have a good relationship with Johnston. Johnston doesn't like Benjamin at all, and he doesn't like Davis, which goes back to the fact that he writes a 2,000-plus-word response to not becoming the highest-ranking general in the Confederacy.

Johnston's always so worried—and he admitted to it in the pre-war years—that he's always focused on rank. They nicknamed him "The Colonel" at West Point, and it wasn't because he was this great officer. He was kind of a snooty guy who was always stern and strict and kind of a jerk about rank.

And he ends up becoming the fourth-ranking general in the Confederate armies, which doesn't sit well with him. . . .

That's where you start with Johnston: this massive ego. And this is true for a lot of the generals on both sides, but especially the Confederacy: these egos that you couldn't fit inside the Confederacy are just going up loggerheads against each other.

Angela R.: We can look at Johnston's relationship with Beauregard, right? The idea that a more junior Beauregard is having these wonderful campaigns, and it's going to weigh heavily on Joe Johnston that a more junior general is having more excitement, more action, getting more attention in the press than he is.

Chris M.: And Beauregard, of course, just has this natural aura about him. He has the claim of being the hero of Fort Sumter, and he's a major contributing factor to the victory at First Manassas, so Joe Johnston has to share his coattails there. So, there's no real clear delineation that helps Johnston distinguish himself from Beauregard, so I can see how that would certainly gnaw at him.

Angela R.: But Albert Sidney doesn't have that type of relationship with Beauregard, right?

Chris M.: Greg, you can probably speak to this: Beauregard is sent out to basically hang out with Albert Sidney as part of the Shiloh campaign.

Greg M.: Well, just as Joseph Johnston felt that being sent west was kind of an insult, the same thing was true with Beauregard. Beauregard quarreled with Davis and so is sent out to serve under Sidney Johnston. It's clear that he doesn't want to be there. He also thinks he should be rated higher than Sidney Johnston. Now, regarding the five full generals, as just a little background: We have Samuel Cooper as the adjutant general, who was first. We then have Albert Sidney Johnston, who was second. Robert E. Lee is third, and then we have Joseph Johnston coming fourth and Beauregard last. So, in both Joseph Johnston and Beauregard, you've got the victors of First Manassas. You've got Beauregard as the victor of Fort Sumter. And what has Albert Sidney Johnston done at this point?

Beauregard waltzes in there, and he has a plan he devised when he was in Virginia of what Johnston should do. It's early February of '62 at this point, and Grant is moving in the area of Henry and Donelson. So Beauregard's idea is, "Let's concentrate forces, take care of Grant, and then we'll turn on the other army—the one that had been under Anderson and Sherman and is now under Don Carlos Buell. And as soon as Sidney Johnston explains to Beauregard just what kind of forces they have, he realizes that part of the reason they haven't done certain things is because they don't have the troops to do them. Beauregard threatened to go back to Virginia, and Johnston talked him into staying. So one aspect of their relationship we see: I think we see the same Beauregard we find everywhere else in the war, the one who thinks his ideas are the important ones. It's not much of an exaggeration to say, as you read Beauregard's accounts of his service with Johnston—especially since Johnston will never have a chance to give his version of things—almost everything that happens is something that Beauregard came up with the idea for or has urged Johnston to do or has had to kind of twist his arm.

One of the things I find particularly interesting about their relationship is how Beauregard criticizes virtually everything that Johnston does, even if Beauregard shows some inconsistency at it. For example, when the word comes that Buell was approaching a merger with Grant and that Confederates should launch an attack on Grant before Buell arrived—which is the battle of Shiloh—and as soon as the intelligence comes, Beauregard notes that Sidney Johnston goes over to Bragg's headquarters to consult with him, which gives Beauregard the impression that Johnston doesn't know what to do. He's always asking other people what they think. Yet the night before the battle, when both Bragg and Beauregard say that they want to turn around and go back, one of Beauregard's comments is that Sidney Johnston did not seek the opinions of the other corps commanders. So, he criticizes Johnston when he seeks advice, and he criticizes Johnson when he doesn't seek advice. It's a wonder that that Johnston seems to put up with him.

Even when the battle starts and Johnston makes the decision that he is going to the front and Beauregard will stay to the rear direct reinforcements, Johnston will say to him, "Now if *I* call for reinforcements, you still need to weigh the information that's brought to you." Just because Sidney Johnson tells Beauregard "I need troops" doesn't mean he automatically has to send troops there if he feels there's a greater need elsewhere.

So constantly throughout the last correspondence that Sidney Johnson has with Beauregard, he treats him with respect, seems to value his opinion. Yet Beauregard, particularly in his postwar writings, is *very* critical of virtually everything that Johnston does.

Chris M.: I really think about how Sidney Johnson, in that particular moment, has some "rock star egos" to deal with, as I call them. Leonidas Polk is a corps commander but also an influential Bishop. John Breckinridge, another corps commander, is a former vice president of the United States. Beauregard is the hero of Fort Sumter and all that stuff. It seems like Albert Sidney navigates those personalities fairly successfully, but contrasting that to Joe Johnson when he comes out to the West later, it's almost like he tries to dance around and avoid dealing with personalities. Angela, how does Joe Johnston navigate that kind of ego landscape?

Angela R.: He doesn't do it well at all. He's very directive in a lot of the correspondence. He doesn't really ask for feedback. The idea of having councils of war and sitting down and getting feedback from his generals is not something we see Joe Johnston doing. He thinks he has the right approach to defend against Grant, and he's telling his commanders what to do—and they're going to push back. And he's very focused on being right, being in command. He doesn't want to be there, but if he's going to be there, he's the one everyone has to answer to, which, we'll see, is going to cause some delays because we have this pushback from his corps and division commanders.

Kris W.:   With Joe Johnson, he's another one of these egotistical guys who is going to deal with a bunch of egotists himself. Robert E. Lee has a volcanic temper on him, but he can hide that temper, and he can work with other people—and he can work with some real strange ones, like Stonewall Jackson, who is not easy to work with.

When you start looking at Joe Johnston, there's none of that there. Though a lot of the soldiers still love him, his subordinate commanders aren't so much in love with him. He has a core of officers who really respect him, and that's Jeb Stewart, James Longstreet, and a few others who are not directly serving under him anymore. Anyone serving directly under him doesn't seem to have that same affinity. They got to know this guy in the field and they're, like, "We've had enough of this." John Bell Hood in '64 obviously has his eye on an army command at that point, but he has nothing really glowing to say about Joe Johnston.

Joe Johnston, to his defense, whenever he's asked if he should relieve Braxton Bragg, he doesn't relieve Braxton Bragg immediately. He's actually not going to undermine him, even though Johnston wants a field command.

At that point, what you're seeing with Joe Johnson, especially, is that he is always right. Jefferson Davis: he's always right. P. G. T. Beauregard: always right. And when you start putting these three together in the Thunderdome, as it were, it doesn't go well.

Angela R.: Yeah, I think one of the terms that keeps coming up when you research Joe Johnston is the idea of a feud. He's feuding with Jeff Davis. He's feuding with Beauregard. He's feuding with Hood. If you are commanding such a large area like the Western Theater, you probably shouldn't be feuding with your second and third and fourth in command.

Chris M.:   It also seems like he's spending an awful lot of time trying to cover his ass. When he gets sent out to Jackson, Mississippi, and he starts out by saying, "I'm not fit for this, but I'm going to go." And then everything he starts writing and communicating is basically trying to excuse, ahead of time, the fact that he's about to fail so that he's got some sort of justification that he can point to and say, "See, I told you," even though it becomes a lot of self-fulfilling prophecy.

Kris W.:   He does the same thing at Harpers Ferry in '61. He's writing to Benjamin and Davis and Lee and anyone who will listen: "Man, we've got to get out of here." Yeah, Harpers Ferry is a *terrible* defensive position, but at that point, you're going up against Robert Patterson. We're not talking about an A-list general here.

And whenever he does make one of his famous retrograde movements, he leaves everything he can behind—after being told not to do so. And he does it without telling Davis. In March 1862, he's like, "Whoops, gotta get out of Centerville! I don't know where I'm going, but I'm out of here." And he leaves behind the stores. They need thsse large-caliber guns. They need those small arms. They need those supplies. And he just leaves them. That's the ironic thing about Joe Johnson: He's probably known for his Fabian tactics, but when he does retreat, he's still not even good at it. But he does it so much. It's just ironic.

Angela R.: Usually, when commanders assess the battlefield, they have certain variables they discuss. When Joe Johnson discusses these variables—such as the supplies, the men, the environment, the weather—it's always in the negative. It's not like, "This is how many troops I have, and this is what I'm going to do with this offensive." Even his assessments before battle are negative and overly cautious. So it's not surprising that then it does not go well because he's already approaching it from the perspective of what he's lacking.

Chris M.:   The first thing he writes when he gets to Jackson, Mississippi, on May 13, 1863, is, "I'm too late." And then starts putting together plans for withdrawal rather than trying to consolidate forces and get ready to respond to Grant. He just runs away.

Angela R.: Yeah, he starts talking about how he's so undermanned. How he doesn't have the supplies. He's like, "Pemberton is too far away."

Kris W.:   Yeah, he has no offensive mindset, it seems. He will only go on the offensive when his back is completely against the wall. And there are times in his in his retreats, especially during the Atlanta campaign, when he does establish a defensive line at Kennesaw and Sherman finally takes the bait, he can't even take advantage of that. It's partially the terrain, and it's partially the army group that's coming against him, but he can't even take advantage of that. But that's the purpose of these movements: At some point, you have to fight.

They have very aggressive opponents coming down at them—a Ulysses S. Grant or William T. Sherman or others. But Johnston didn't understand that, even when you're giving up these places, you can't always give up the most strategic spots. He was ready to give up Atlanta. At that point, where do you go? I mean, you can back yourself up to Savannah, Mobile, or Pensacola. Yeah, they have great defenses, but you're up against the Gulf or you're up against the Atlantic.

So at some point you have to stand and fight. And I think that's where Albert Sidney Johnston comes in. When he's finally given an opportunity, he strikes out. But when Joe Johnston is given these *multiple* opportunities like Robert E. Lee is—Lee takes the ball and run with it—Joe Johnston just takes his ball and goes home.

Angela R.: He's ready to give up Atlanta. He gives up Jackson. He gives up Meridian. He has a history of giving up places. And maybe it's like he's denying access to the enemy, but his time denying them access isn't very long at all.

Kris W.:   No, no. He's already always two steps ahead of his enemy, and that first step is, "Oh, I gotta get out of here." And the second step is "Bye."

Johnston is going to complain during the Atlanta Campaign that, when he's falling back, he is not getting the same good press that Robert E. Lee is as he fell back towards Richmond in the spring of 1864 during the Overland Campaign. The difference was Robert E. Lee was doing what the people of the Southern Confederacy wanted, and that was at least putting up some sort of a fight.

And that's the other thing that Joe Johnson never understood: this was a democratic republic, whose presidency and government told him what to do. It wasn't the reverse. The military worked for the Confederacy, not the other way around. And he never understood that. And he never understood the public will and sentiment of the Southern people.

A lot of people think Southerners had given up by 1864. That's not the case. I mean, the morale of both North and South is like a roller coaster. It goes up; it goes down. It's just like it is today whenever you see something in the newspaper: "Hey, that's great; hey, that's bad." But Johnston never understood the public sentiment, nor the government's role. It was the Joe Johnston Show, he thought, and that's just not the way the war could be executed.

Angela R.: I kind of feel bad. I feel like we're beating up on Joe Johnston a whole bunch. He does have his weaknesses, for sure, but when we get to the Atlanta campaign, something to remember is just how skilled Sherman is as an opponent. You see Joe Johnston digging into these positions and then Sherman executes a turning movement and forces Johnson out of those positions to then retreat back to the next position. So if he wasn't up against Sherman, who was so offensively minded, maybe we would have seen Joe Johnston launch an offensive out of those dug-in positions.

Again, these are questions. I wonder, if maybe if Sidney Johnston would have lived past Shiloh, would we have also had critiques with him trying to defend some of these weaker areas, especially as troop numbers go down, prisoners go up, and supplies also go down.

Chris M.:   And Greg, I think that that's a great opening to talk about Albert Sidney Johnston's death because we've got a huge record that we can look at with Joe Johnston, and we can do a lot of armchair generalling, but Albert Sidney Johnston dies at what I would consider his "Jimi Hendrix moment"—he's at the peak of his success, and then dies. So we don't have a long record to judge. What kind of impact do you think that creates?

Greg M.:   Well, you're absolutely right. Usually people looking at Albert Sidney Johnston, seeing the very high reputation that he came into the Civil War holding, will comment that he died too early, before you can really tell whether he had a chance to live up to that. Davis would later write that Sidney Johnston's death was really the turning point of the Confederacy out in the West because there was nobody who could come in and take his place.

I do think there is a lot to see of what Sidney Johnston did during the battle of Shiloh, though, to help form a good idea of what kind of general he really was. First of all, Shiloh was the bloodiest battle in American history up to that point. The casualties at Shiloh, counting both sides north and south together, was as many as America had lost in all the wars combined before that point. So, it is a very, very severe test.

And Johnston does an excellent job of dealing with green troops. One of the first things we can note: He found some Arkansas troops that had just entered their first engagement ever, and they were repulsed. What does he do? Does he go and chew them out and say "You need to do better"? No. Because they're from Arkansas, he says, "Men of Arkansas. I understand that you have a great deal of prowess with the bowie knife. Today you wield a nobler weapon, the bayonet. Employ it well." So he fires them up and sends them back in.

When his troops take some of the first Union camps, and these green troops start to loot. Many of them had probably thought they won the battle. They drove the enemy back and now were in their camp. He sees some of the troops looting, and at first, he gets angry and says, "We have not come here for plunder!" And I'm not sure what kind of expression he saw on the face of the young officer he had just chewed out, but then he reaches down and grabs a cup off of the table, a tin cup, and says, "Let this be my share of the spoils," as if to say, "Okay, we take the enemy camp. Maybe if there's a piece of equipment that you need, or some food, grab it. But now let's rally back and continue the attack."

You mentioned Breckinridge before. Breckinridge does have some Mexican War experience as a major, but he showed up there after the fighting was over. He was inspired by reading the poem "The Bivouac of the Dead" when some of Kentucky's dead were brought back from the Mexican War and decided to go down. So, he's got some experience in the military, but basically, not much. He's commanding three different brigades in the battle, and he's given orders to launch his troops in an attack, but the men don't respond. And he goes to Johnston and says, "I can't get my men to move forward," and Johnson says, "Together, we'll do it." So this is kind of a teaching moment. Johnston is now going to show this inexperienced general how to rally the troops. He takes that tin cup he had and rides along the line, tapping the bayonets of Breckinridge's soldiers, and then sends them in the battle. It's about that time that Johnston receives his mortal wound, after he sent those men in.

So I see a lot of examples of Johnston displaying some good leadership techniques, if you will—a lot of talent. And knowing that he's got a green army, at that point—he's accomplished a great deal with a green army on that day.

So even though it is tough to say just where he is going to rank compared to people that have amassed more experience and more successes in the war, I am pretty impressed with what he did at Shiloh.

Kris W.: He could lift up his soldiers. He was one of those generals. Bragg was just the polar opposite of that out west. Lee, at the Wilderness and Spotsylvania, is able to lift up his soldiers—granted, by that point, they had a *lot* of faith in him. But Johnston's a guy who's willing to be seen and willing to lead from the front, which inevitably gets a lot of these generals throughout the war on both sides killed.

Angela R.: I don't want to be difficult, guys, because he *did* lead from the front, right? When you go to his death site, it's like "line of troops here," "shot," "bled out"— it's so incredibly close. But I wonder how much of this is memory construction. Many of these stories were written after Johnston died at Shiloh, so maybe there's a little bit of truth, but how much is *really* true? Because, of course, you want to tell a great story about your commander who was killed in battle. About a tin cup, and rallying, and these wonderful speeches. But I wonder, how much of that is really true? Because it turns him into some kind of mythic God who then later died at the height of his success. I wonder how much of that is soldiers crafting a particular narrative about Albert Sidney Johnston.

Some of these things are rooted in truth. We know they're generally good guys. We know that Johnston led from the front. We know he had a good relationship even with people who were difficult. But some of these stories that make them into these god-like individuals—maybe we have to question that a little bit because the second Johnston, Joe Johnston, doesn't ever have that happen and, instead, he's known for retreating and for surrendering.

Chris M.: And Greg, in your book [*Attack at Daylight at Whip Them: The Battle of Shiloh, April 6–7, 1862*], you write about the stump of the tree where Albert Sidney Johnston was supposedly shot and bled out. There used to be a sign that said, "Here's the tree where this all happened" and the Park Service was, like, "Bo, that never really happened." But it became part of the myth.

Angela R.: I've been to that tree! You have the giant monument, right, with all the cannonballs. And then you walk down the hill, and there's this tree, and it kind of opens up and there's an area for you to stand so you can take pictures and have a moment of silence. It has this aura to it.

Greg M.: The aspect of Sidney Johnston that I think had the greatest myth attached to it is what he would have done at Shiloh if he had lived. The Confederate monument there has a great deal of symbolism that is critical of Beauregard because Johnston fell at about 2:30 in the afternoon as his troops were collapsing the second of three different lines that the Union army will hold. And so the Union Army did fall back to a position known as Grant's Last Line, and Beauregard would call off the attacks around five o'clock or so. 5:30, maybe six o'clock in the evening. The monument includes a dejected officer who was looking down, and the reason he's dejected is because he has been told to stop the battle and feels that if they would just let him make one more attack, they will take that third position, just as they'd taken the first and second. And Johnston's own son, who was not there at the time, will write and say, "Oh, Beauregard ruined my father's plan at Shiloh by calling off that last attack."

So for a long time, there has been this feeling that if Johnston had only lived, the Confederates would have achieved a victory at Shiloh. I think there's a lot of analysis of that, and which historians today feel that, first of all, we don't know what Johnston would have done. And number two, the chances of him taking that last line were pretty slight considering the Confederates had put in all their reserves and then were running low on ammunition. They'd been fighting all day. They had a *huge* terrain feature that they would have had to cross, which had water at the bottom. Gunboats had now arrived on the battlefield and were on the river firing up that ravine Confederates would have had to cross. And then, if they make it across that ravine, there's a bunch of artillery lined up on the ridge, including some siege artillery the army had that was too big to haul around on the battlefield that were just planted there above that ridge virtually all day long. So that's the biggest myth about Johnston at the Battle of Shiloh.

Chris M.: And certainly that's a huge component of the Lost Cause. The "lost opportunity" at Shiloh is very central to all of that stuff.

One final point I want to make before we wrap things up. Greg, you've offered some great examples of what I think is positive leadership Albert Sidney demonstrates at Shiloh, apocryphal or real. He could inspire his men. And I keep thinking about Joe Johnston arriving in Jackson, Mississippi, in May and telling Pemberton, "You should come and concentrate here with me. Come down the railroad from Clinton and meet me," and he sends all these very conflicting orders, but all the while, he's retreating to the northeast. So he's telling Pemberton one thing while setting Pemberton up for failure.

Most people don't realize the Battle of Champion Hill is really an accident because Pemberton was blundering around out in the middle of nowhere, trying to fulfill these confusing orders Johnston sends him, and then he runs into Grant by accident. And Joe Johnston is so insincere, so disingenuous, in how he's dealing with Pemberton. He writes orders to suggest that Pemberton is disobeying his orders and, again, just sort of setting Pemberton up for failure, rather than lifting him up. Angela, you want to chime in on that?

Angela R.: Yeah. At Jackson, I think the reason we have all these conflicting orders is because Johnston is conflicted himself. He's confused. Where is Grant's army? They know they crossed south of Vicksburg, but they cut their supply lines. They're moving fast. We have Grierson's Raid moving through the center of the state. He only has so many troops that he can send trying to blunt his nebulous attack. So he is sending these conflicting orders because they're constantly getting more information, but a lot of that information is not reliable. They're coming in from scouts. They're coming in from Southern civilians. And so he's trying to deploy his forces against the Union, but the Union can be coming from anywhere at this point. So I think that's another reason that we have these conflicting orders.

But he also never takes responsibility for the conflicting orders. He always passes the buck, like it was *their* fault. They didn't listen. There's was *this* delay. And again, because he doesn't have enough people. It's always an external factor for his failure rather than his own failures.

Chris M.: So as we wrap up, I'll ask each of you to look at Joe Johnston and Albert Sidney Johnston. Was each one the right man for the right time in the right place?

Kris W.: Albert Sidney, yes, Joe Johnson, no. And since I was mean to him the entire time, I will at least say, he does have some wicked good facial hair.

Greg M.: Albert Sidney Johnston, yes. Emphatic yes. Joseph Johnston, no. The hard question, the next question is, who would have been the right person? Looking around, I can understand why he was placed there. It did end up he was the wrong person, but who else would you select? This is a difficult question, and I don't know.

Chris M.: And what we really haven't mentioned is that Joe Johnston did carry this tremendous reputation. He doesn't necessarily live up to it, but I can see why Davis, even though he didn't get along with Joe Johnston, he probably saw Johnston as someone he could count on.

Greg M.: And he comes back for the Atlanta campaign. He comes back for the North Carolina campaign. For somebody who seemingly did so horrible in the Vicksburg campaign, they go to him two more times.

Chris M.: So, Angela: right place, right time, yes or no?

Angela R.: I will say yes for Albert Sidney, again because of his relationships with his other commanders, his understanding of the area, and his relationship with Jefferson Davis. As they're feeling out this war, as they're feeling out who they're going up against, it's probably good that he had a great relationship with the president of the Confederacy. Definitely a great choice.

Joe Johnston? I don't think anyone would have done a good job in that situation from November 1862 through April 1865. I'm trying not to add into the Lost Cause, but it is incredibly difficult what he's coming into. But he does successfully delay by pulling back and forcing the Union to move away from supply lines. So, he doesn't do that bad of a job. I just don't know who else would have been better. Maybe someone who had better working relationships and a less cantankerous personality. I just don't know who that would be. He's prickly. Maybe Longstreet if Longstreet had a better communication style, but I feel like everyone in that theater is difficult.

Chris M.: The newspaper in Jackson says, "Send us Longstreet. Send us D. H. Hill. Send us Beauregard." And they get Joe Johnston. So, they were looking for options, for sure.

Angela R.: "Anyone else." That's probably what they're thinking.

Greg M.: Well, Richard Taylor.

Chris M.: And Taylor actually does pretty well, right? He could have been a good choice. Greg with the win!

Well, Angela. Greg, Kris. Thanks so much for chatting tonight. This has been a fun conversation. I appreciate you guys spend some time with us.

Thanks so much for joining us here on the Emerging Civil War podcast. I'm Chris Mackowski. We'll see you online and on the battlefield.

A Turning Point:
Assault on Battery Wagner by the 54th Massachusetts

by Phillip S. Greenwalt

*Originally published as a blog post at Emerging Civil War
on December 12, 2017*

Around a small hamlet in south-central Pennsylvania, Robert E. Lee's vaunted Army of Northern Virginia was stymied. They were driven back after three days of bloodletting at the battle of Gettysburg—July 1-3, 1863—a turning point in the Civil War.

On July 4, 1863, the Confederate bastion of Vicksburg, Mississippi, the "Gibraltar of the Mississippi River," capitulated to Union forces under Gen. Ulysses S. Grant—another turning point.

The evacuation of Tullahoma on the first of July and the surrender of the last Confederate stronghold on the Mississippi River at Port Hudson, Louisiana, on July 9, 1863, were two other significant actions that month. Both are turning points.

Yet, a more significant engagement, a Union defeat, also turned the tide of the Civil War. This assault took place on July 18, 1863, on Battery Wagner, part of the defenses of Charleston, South Carolina. In the waning moments of daylight, the 54th Massachusetts charged toward the sandy approaches and abates that formed Battery Wagner. Their assault failed with the loss of their commander, Col. Robert Gould Shaw. In this example, the heroism of the charge, the courage that these soldiers portrayed, and what their actions meant advanced the Union war effort.[1]

The 54th Massachusetts Regiment, an African American unit, was the brainchild of Massachusetts Gov. John Andrews. African American soldiers of the unit fought to thwart the misconceptions that blacks could only serve in labor and non-fighting positions. They wanted to assist in overthrowing the Southern slave oligarchy and institute universal freedom.[2]

Battery Wagner would be the pivot in which African American soldiers showed their fighting prowess and ability, like their fellow white soldiers, to uphold the standards of the American military. After the failed assault on July 18, 1863, the repercussions reverberated around the country, including the Confederacy.

"The negroes fought gallantly, and were headed by as brave a Colonel as ever lived," wrote Lt. Iredell Jones of the 1st South Carolina about the 54th Massachusetts attack.[3]

Even the *Charleston Courier's* editor grudgingly admitted that the African American soldiers showed "bravery" although he wished it was "worthy of a better cause."[4] In the North, descriptions such as "heroic conduct" came from the *Boston Transcript*; the *Cincinnati Daily Gazette* told its readership the 54th Massachusetts "fought with the desperation of tigers."[5]

"The experiment has begun," wrote a newspaper reporter for the *Washington Reporter,* a Pennsylvania-based publication. With the news of Battery Wagner, the 54th Massachusetts was "magnificent for their steadiness, impetuosity, and dauntless courage." As a fitting epitaph, the

1 "Fort Wagner," https://www.battlefields.org/learn/civil-war/battles/fort-wagner, accessed November 21, 2022.

2 "54th Massachusetts Regiment," https://www.nps.gov/articles/54th-massachusetts-regiment.htm, accessed December 10, 2017.

3 "Fighting for Freedom," https://www.alexandriava.gov/historic-alexandria/basic-page/fighting-for-freedom-black-union-soldiers-of-the-civil-war, accessed November 21, 2022.

4 Egerton, Douglas R., "Thunder at the Gates: The Black Civil War Regiments That Redeemed America" (Basic Books, New York City, 2016), 142.

5 Ibid.

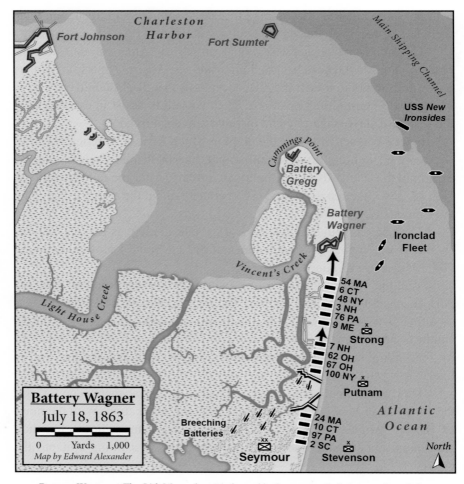

BATTERY WAGNER—The 54th Massachusetts charged in the vanguard of what was intended as a huge Federal fist. Its repulse served instead to bottleneck the column on the beach.

reporter wrote that if all Union troops, irrespective of skin color, showed "as single hearted as these soldiers, our difficulties would disappear."[6]

There were skeptics from the beginning of the "experiment" to arm and equip colored regiments, and the fighting on July 18, 1863, did not wholly dispel them. "Not myself a believer in the arming of negroes, free or

6 Ibid., 142–3.

contraband, as soldiers, I must do this regiment the credit of fighting bravely and well." Newspapers of the more Democratic Party persuasion, while still hesitant to embrace the Republican administration's African American soldier policy, admitted that the 54th Massachusetts and their bravery and courage under fire made the soldiers "entitled to assert their rights to manhood" and showed their "undaunted courage." They were "evidently made of good stuff."[7]

To conclude the importance of the assault in July, an *Chicago Tribune* editor summed up the cause of Union African American soldiers by writing:

> [The] government and the people have woke up to the importance
> of negro soldiers in the conduct of the war . . . [the] thing is now
> settled—the negroes will fight.[8]

The impact of the assault made the highest circles of the Federal government take note. The judge advocate general, Joseph Holt, in a letter to Secretary of War Edwin Stanton in August 1863, attested to:

> The tenacious and brilliant valor displayed by troops of this race
> has sufficiently demonstrated to the President and to the country
> the character of the service for which they are capable.[9]

Horace Greeley echoed the sentiment of how important that first test of combat was for the role and advancement of African American soldiers in the war effort. Writing in 1865, he looked back on that summer two years prior: "It is not too much to say that if this Massachusetts Fifty-fourth had faltered when its trial came, two hundred thousand colored troops for whom it was a pioneer would not have been put into the field."

The eyes of the nation, followed the black soldiers that courageously advanced along the South Carolina barrier islands. If these men had faltered,

7 Ibid.

8 Ibid., 143.

9 Ibid., 145–6.

balked on the advance, let fear of death and destruction deter them, the African American cause would have been severely hampered. Not only did they go in with gusto, but one of their number, Sgt. William Carney, earned the Medal of Honor for bringing the national flag out of the conflict, never letting it touch the ground.

Before the war's end, more than 179,000 African American soldiers would don Union uniforms, help defeat the Confederacy, and permanently end the "peculiar institution" of slavery and bondage. This number would constitute approximately 10% of the entire United States Army. Furthermore, another 19,000 African Americans served in the United States Navy. More than 40,000 succumbed to wounds or disease in defense of the Union. In addition to aiding the Union war effort, the removal of African American manpower affected the Confederate war effort, depriving them of manual labor, as enslaved men escaped north and joined the Union Army.[10]

When one discusses July 1863 and the turning points of the Civil War, the legacy of the 54th Massachusetts assault on Battery Wagner and what that created must be part of the discussion. This batch of occurrences in the summer of 1863 turned the tide of the conflict, putting the North on the footing to win the Civil War.

10 Black Soldiers in the U.S. Military During the Civil War" https://www.archives.gov/education/lessons/blacks-civil-war#:~:text=By%20the%20end%20of%20the,30%2C000%20of%20infection%20or%20disease, accessed November 21, 2022.

1. Decisions at Chickamauga

by Chris Mackowski, David A. Powell, and Dan Welch

This is an excerpted transcript of an Emerging Civil War Podcast episode that dropped on February 5, 2019. It has been edited for brevity and clarity.

Chris: Twenty-four critical decisions define the Battle of Chickamauga.

Dan: That's the premise of a new book by historian Dave Powell: *Decisions at Chickamauga: Twenty-Four Decisions that Defined the Battle,* published by University of Tennessee Press.

Chris: And joining us on the line today is our ECW colleague from the West. . . . Dave, tell us about your new book. . . .

Dave: *Decisions* is derived from all my other work on Chickamauga. It was a project I was asked to do by Col. Matt Spruill, U. S. Army, Ret., who has done a number of battlefield guides. He came up with this idea of "decisions at fill-in-the-blank." Pick your battle. The idea was to provide sort of a staff ride concept, where you would go to a spot on the battlefield—a critical turning point moment—and examine the situation. You explore the options available to the commander and then discuss the decision he arrived at, why he arrived at it, and the possible potential ramifications of that decision. In other words: did he choose to retreat? Should he have attacked? Should he have stood fast?

I chose something like twenty-four different decision points over the course of the Chickamauga Campaign, most of them centered on the three days of the battle, September 18, 19, and 20. . . .

Chris: Your three-volume study, *The Chickamauga Campaign*. which is an award-winning set, *I* think is the definitive study of Chickamauga.

Dan: Here, here.

Chris: And I think it will stand that way for a long, long time. So, as you wrote *Decisions*, was there new material for you to find? New insights for you to discover?

Dave: I won't say I discovered a lot of new stuff because I was such an obsessive researcher in the years leading up to the first publication. I will say that, doing the *Decisions* book, I initially was a little hesitant because I wasn't sure I had more new stuff to say. . . . Despite the fact that the trilogy runs to something like 1,300 pages, I found I could still say more and offer new things to say in doing so. So, I ended up enjoying the *Decisions* book quite a bit.

Chris: As I read this book didn't feel like it was a rehash of what I had read in the Chickamauga Campaign. Here, it was some really focused discussion and some sharp insights.

Dave: Well, thank you. That's pretty much what I hoped to achieve. The last thing I wanted to do was simply plug in old ideas from previous works into the book and have it come out with University of Tennessee and people say "Well, I've already read all this." So, I'm hoping it meets with that reaction, and I've already heard from a couple of people who have found it very useful in their own military staff ride, so I'm pleased about that.

Dan: You've got about two dozen decisions that you really spend time discussing, and some of the options that these decisions could have played out, and then their end result. Is there anyone on this battlefield that stands out as a great decision maker, or anyone that stands out that, time and time again during the multi-day battle, just can't seem to make a right decision?

Dave: I think the general who made the worst decision or set of decisions on the battlefield is probably Union Maj. Gen. James S. Negley, who was on the critical ground of Horseshoe Ridge on September 20, 1863. He lacked communication with his immediate superior, Maj. Gen. George Thomas, the corps commander, and in the end decided to leave the field. It cost him his military career, and it also greatly weakened the defense of Horseshoe Ridge at a critical time. I don't necessarily judge Negley too harshly, but I also think the decision was clearly, especially in retrospect, a disastrous one.

One of the commanders who I think made probably an unsung decision—well, really it's two men, General Thomas Wood, and General John Brannan, who together end up basically picking the defense of Horseshoe Ridge. They pick Horseshoe Ridge as their next position to stand, especially Brannan. Thomas gets the credit as "the Rock of Chickamauga" and standing on Horseshoe Ridge. And, certainly, he does reinforce that initial decision, but it sometimes gets overlooked that he didn't make the initial choice. When the Union right flank collapsed and a third of the Union army was in retreat, it was John Brannan riding back from Poe Field to identify that position, and also Thomas Wood, who turns around and leads Harker's Brigade back down the road to fight it out.

Dan: Do you ascribe that to a contemporary oversight of who made that decision, or more of a post-war mythology of the battle and Thomas's reputation?

Dave: One of the things I was fascinated about by Chickamauga is—and this goes back to how little literature there was on it—is that there's a great deal of misunderstanding and uncertainty about what happened and what caused the break-through, for instance, and I think the overall complexity of the battle has made it very difficult to write about for many people.

I know of one Civil War author, well-respected, who's written battle books, who I helped in the early 2000s—he started to write on the battle, and at one point after about 20,000 words, he told me, "Well, I'm gonna give it up. You can do what you want." I won't name names, although I don't think it's any scandal or anything like that. And I don't think it was a bad decision, but he did reach a point where it was just very difficult to untangle.

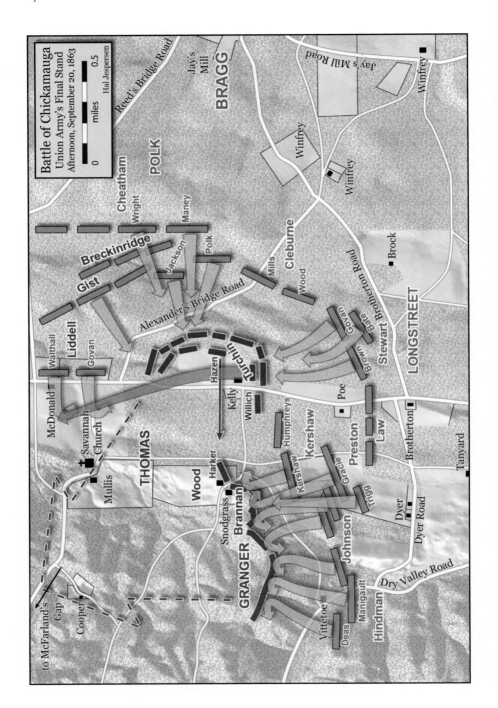

Battle of Chickamauga
Union Army's Final Stand
Afternoon, September 20, 1863

Hal Jespersen

miles   0.5
0

Reed's Bridge Road
Jay's Mill
Jay's Mill Road
BRAGG
Winfrey
POLK
Winfrey
Winfrey
Cheatham
Wright
Maney
Brock
Cleburne
Breckinridge
Jackson
Polk
Gist
Mills
Wood
Alexander's Bridge Road
Stewart
Brotherton Road
LONGSTREET
Liddell
Walthall
Govan
Govan
Bate
Brown
McDonald
Hazen
Turchin
Kelly
Willich
Poe
Savannah Church
Humphreys
Kershaw
Law
Brotherton
Tanyard
Mullis
Harker
Preston
Gracie
THOMAS
Wood
Snodgrass
Brannan
Trigg
Johnson
Dyer
Dyer Road
GRANGER
Manigault
Hindman
Dry Valley Road
to McFarland's Gap
Cooper
Vittetoe
Deas

OPPOSITE: BATTLE OF CHICKAMAUGA: UNION ARMY'S FINAL STAND—The selection of Horseshoe Ridge as a place for Union forces to make a final stand became fateful for a number of reasons, not least of all because it prevented a rout. The decision would have huge repercussions for Maj. Gen. George Thomas's historical reputation, defining him as "The Rock." *Courtesy of William Lee White*

I think a lot of the critical moments at the battle of Chickamauga are like that. Things are confused. On the Union side, we have the army commander, William Rosecrans, and two corps commanders riding off the field. The Confederate commander, Braxton Bragg, is largely out of touch with his front line for most of the three days of the battle. So, you get a lot of confusion.

Chris: I want to follow up on your comment there about the Union commander leaving the field, because I suspect that's probably one of the most second-guessed decisions of the entire war. How do you assess the decision that Rosecrans made?

Dave: Well, in the end, it's clearly a mistake. It costs him much of his military career. It's even fair to speculate that it cost him a shot at the presidency in the postwar years.

He was driven off the battlefield by James Longstreet's Confederate attack on September 20. He was caught up in the fighting with Sheridan's division, and then he fell back to the west and, as he turned around, they rode up towards Rossville—he was only accompanied by his chief-of-staff, James Garfield, and a couple of aides—and they reached the side road and the intersection of the main road between Rossville and Chattanooga. And had Rosecrans decided to turn right, go to Rossville and then go back to the battlefield, he would have found George Thomas and it would maybe be General Rosecrans who's the Rock of Chickamauga, not George Thomas.

Instead, Rosecrans decided that he had to go back to Chattanooga, which was, at the time, the Department of the Cumberland's new headquarters—it had just been established there on September 9—and that's where the apparatus of department command and where his main telegraphic connection were. Rosecrans decided to return to Chattanooga and control events as best he could from there.

Now, Rosecrans wrote—and after the war, he wrote many things about that decision, mostly to try and justify it. At the time, I don't think he was thinking all that clearly, frankly. I think he was exhausted and emotionally overwhelmed by the sudden collapse of a third of his army. His chief-of-staff pleaded with him not to go back to Chattanooga. Garfield was a politician, not a professional soldier even though he proved himself to be a fairly capable volunteer in uniform.

Dan: And a fine Ohioan, Dave. Don't forget that. [Dan is from Ohio.]

Dave: And a fine Ohioan. I cannot disagree. But Garfield, more than anyone, understood the political ramifications of leaving the battlefield. And Garfield also understood that Edwin Stanton, the Union Secretary of War in Washington, was not a fan of General Rosecrans, and, frankly, leaving the battlefield, going back to Chattanooga, would provide Stanton with sufficient ammunition to at least hurt Rosecrans. And as it turned out, ultimately, it cost Rosecrans command of the Army of the Cumberland.

Chris: How hard was it for you, through the lens of 150 years of hindsight, to try to sort through all of that mess? I mean, you've talked about how hard it was to see through the fog of war in studying the battle, knowing that there was a lot of postwar battle for memory over this particular decision.

Dave: Well, yes. I mean, there's a raft of competing and conflicting primary sources that talk about Rosecrans's state of mind, what he was thinking or not thinking, and, of course, this is all bound up in some postwar politics, as well, because James A. Garfield does run for president and has a very contentious campaign, as it were, against what a lot of people who thought it would be General Grant returning to the presidency in 1880. Grant doesn't run, Garfield does—and wins. So there's a huge swirl of good, bad, and just plain wrong information around this decision.

I always start by going to the most immediate sources I can, so that begins with a letter General Rosecrans wrote to his brother, a Catholic priest in Ohio, just a day after the battle. Rosecrans talks about that ride back to Chattanooga and his state of mind. In that letter, he says he's silently praying for guidance. Much different than, say, his postwar accounts written in the 1880s and published in things like the *Century Magazine* and the *National Tribune*, where he makes much stronger effort to justify his decision.

And there are letters from Garfield, and there are diary entries that record Garfield's conversations. And then I just try and take as much of the information as I can, and I figure out what seems most logical to me, most realistic. I find that the further you get away from an event in history, the more people have to say about it, and the more dialogue that's invented. Pretty soon you've got officers delivering soliloquies on the battlefield back and forth. Much of that is just simply unrealistic, it's impossible. That's not how things happen, even in what's a much more oratorical age than we have now.

Chris: So, Dave as you were compiling your list of critical decisions, was there something on your list that you think people will find a particularly surprising decision?

Dave: That's a good question, and I'm not sure I'm capable of answering it because, at this point, I'm very close to all those decisions. I'm a good 15 years of study in.

Perhaps I've made a pretty strong argument that Braxton Bragg did *not* make a mistake in not trying to pursue the Army of the Cumberland back into Chattanooga.

Dan: That will surprise a lot of readers.

Dave: Conventional wisdom has that as a blunder of the first order, right? In Confederate mythology, they have Nathan Bedford Forrest threatening to slap or duel Bragg over it. They have every Confederate general going, "What a terrible idea." And yet, once again, when you return to the immediate documentation—not the post-war justification, or even not the justifications a month later when all the Confederate generals and Braxton Bragg are feuding, and President Jefferson Davis has to come sort it out in October 1863—but when you look at what's written on September 21, September 22, by Longstreet and Polk and D. H. Hill, you come to realize that none of them knew that the Union army had retreated. None of them were really advocating an immediate pursuit because they didn't know where exactly the Union army was. They thought they would advance a half mile and find the Federals in a new position—and actually, they weren't that far wrong. The Federal army retreated to Rossville and took up a very strong position on Missionary Ridge.

So, there's just the problem of finding the Union army, and then you couple that with some almost unique logistical problems that Bragg faces. All of the reinforcements that come to Braxton Bragg double the size of his army within three weeks in September 1863—all of those troops without any of their wagons or transportation, or their horses, in many cases. And a nineteenth-century army without its wagons is immobile. It can't go very far, can't leave its railhead.

So all those factors add up to give Bragg very limited options on September 21, September 22, 1863. And those, of course, they all tend to be glossed over and overlooked when we even go forward a month and start looking at what people like D. H. Hill and Longstreet are writing.

Dan: It sounds like a very compelling argument to battle against the long-entrenched mythology and the historiography of this battle.

Dave: We'll see. It's been my experience that myths die a hard death. I suspect I'll be picking up books in 20 years or reading online in 20 years how Bragg failed to pursue and it cost the South the war.

Chris: Dave, before we wrap up, any final takeaways you want people to get when they read your book?

Dave: Try and put yourself in the mindset of the officers. The main thrust of the book is not to point out what decisions are right, what decisions are wrong, or who made good choices, who made bad choices. Instead, I want to point out how complex those choices were and the difficulties of making them under stress, under pressure, under fire, to give the reader a sense of what it is to be making those choices, as opposed to passing the judgment of history from our comfortable armchairs.

1. The Man in the Corner:
Anson Stager

by David A. Powell

Originally published as a blog post at Emerging Civil War on April 16, 2016

Colonel Anson Stager is not exactly a household name, even for many students of the Civil War.

If your reading has taken you into the arcana of military codes, or if you are a fan of late 19th Century industrialization, you probably *have* heard of him: he was an instrumental figure in both arenas. He invented the primary cipher adopted by the Federal armies during the war. He was also the first Superintendent of Western Union, and at various times, president of the Western Electric Corporation, Chicago Telephone, and the Western Edison Company. He died in 1885.[1]

For me, however, his name first popped up in the context of an important interview between James A. Garfield and Union Secretary of War Edwin M. Stanton on October 20, 1863.

Stanton was seeking details—some might say dirt—concerning the actions and behavior of Garfield's boss, Maj. Gen. William S. Rosecrans, during and immediately after the battle of Chickamauga. Rosecrans was driven from the field before the battle's close, and rode back to Chattanooga, 12 miles distant, leaving George H. Thomas to continue the fight.

---

1 "General Anson Stager Dying," *Rochester (NY) Democrat and Chronicle,* March 24, 1885.

Garfield, along with Gen. James B. Steadman, met with Stanton at Louisville. Garfield had left the Army of the Cumberland to take up a seat in Congress. In the wake of the Chickamauga crisis, Stanton rushed west from Washington to secretly confer with Ulysses S. Grant. Stanton offered Grant command of the entire Western Theater, which Grant accepted. Though the Grant–Stanton meeting had already occurred, and the order relieving Rosecrans already publicly announced. Rosecrans and his supporters would come to believe that Garfield's testimony had decided his commander's fate. Garfield, it was whispered, betrayed his old commander, suggesting that Rosecrans lost control of his emotions and was unfit to retain command. This testimony supposedly cemented Stanton's opinion that Rosecrans had to go.[2]

That last was certainly true. Immediately after meeting Garfield, Stanton wired as much to President Lincoln. Garfield's "representations," asserted Stanton, "more than confirm the worst that has reached us as to the conduct of the commanding general. . . ."[3]

Garfield would go to his grave insisting otherwise. Far from betraying Rosecrans, he did his best to defend his commander against Stanton's hostile accusations. In 1880, Garfield protested to Rosecrans that when Stanton "denounced you . . . I rebuked him and earnestly defended you against his assaults."[4]

How could that be? Who was right? Garfield would tell his friend and fellow Ohioan, Brig. Gen. Jacob D. Cox, that Stanton—a veteran courtroom lawyer and prosecutor—"not only had dispatches full of information from General [Montgomery C.] Meigs, who now also met with him at Louisville, [but also] . . . [Assistant Secretary of War Charles A.] Dana's . . . series of cipher dispatches giving a vivid interior view of affairs and of men." As a result, Stanton demonstrated "such knowledge of the battle . . . that it would

2 James R. Gilmore, "The Relief of Rosecrans," in *Burial of General Rosecrans, Arlington National Cemetery, May 17, 1902* (Cincinnati, OH: 1903), 85; *OR* 30, pt. 4, 478-479; Ulysses S. Grant, *Personal Memoirs,* 2, 26; William S. Rosecrans, "The mistakes of Grant," *The North American Review,* vol. 141, issue 349, (December 1885), 595-596.

3 William M. Lamers, *The Edge of Glory: A Biography of General William S. Rosecrans, U.S.A.* (Baton Rouge, LA: 1999), 411.

4 Garfield to Rosecrans, January 19, 1880, Rosecrans Papers, University of California, Los Angeles. Hereafter UCLA.

be impossible for Garfield to avoid mention of [those] incidents which bore unfavorably upon Rosecrans."

In short, Stanton was not fact-finding. He cross-examined Garfield, and like any good trial attorney, asked no question to which he did not already know the answer. The question remains, however, was Garfield a hostile witness, or a friendly one?[5]

Three other men were present at this meeting: Steadman, Military Governor of Tennessee Andrew Johnson, and Colonel Stager. Neither Steadman nor Johnson left accounts of this meeting.

But what of Stager? In 1881, one of Rosecrans's supporters, Col. Francis A. Darr (formerly a staff officer for George Thomas), claimed to have met Stager the previous year at West Point's annual military exercises, where, as Darr related to Rosecrans, Stager claimed that "Garfield . . . denounced Rosecrans as incompetent, unworthy of his position, as having lost the confidence of his army, and should be removed." Darr's quotation would seem to settle the matter pretty conclusively.[6]

Sort of.

Legally speaking, Darr's statement is hearsay, second-hand information. But we sit in the court of history, not law. Darr's statement has been used extensively by historians—most notably, Rosecrans's biographer, William Lamers—as clear-cut proof of Garfield's duplicity.

Even that much might not have come to light if not for the fact that in 1880, James A. Garfield became the quintessential dark-horse candidate for president. He won the election, only to be struck down by an assassin the next year and dying shortly thereafter. Election pressures in 1880 made the controversy between Garfield (the Republican nominee) and Rosecrans (running as a Democrat for congress) into headline news. As the rhetoric heated up, Rosecrans repeated Darr's assertions in his public comments. Garfield's subsequent death only gave the controversy greater legs. Well into 1882, newspapers reprinted stories about Garfield, Rosecrans, Stanton, and Stager.

5   Jacob D. Cox, *Military Reminiscences of the Civil War*. 2 vols, (New York: 1900), II: 7-8.

6   Francis Darr to Rosecrans, July 16, 1881, Rosecrans Papers, UCLA.

By then, Garfield was dead and beyond any hope of refutation. Stager was anything but. Stager was a respected businessman and public figure in his own right, living in Chicago. Naturally, the press turned to him for comment. In the June 15, 1882, issue of the *Chicago Daily Tribune*, when asked about Rosecrans's statements, Col. Stager replied, "that it is not in fact true that he [Stager] told Gen. Rosecrans or anyone else that what occurred at the Louisville meeting with Stanton was the reverse of what was stated by Gen. Garfield." Stager further asserted that he had never even met Rosecrans at West Point.[7]

When it was clarified that Rosecrans was not claiming to have met Stager personally, but instead quoting Francis Darr, Stager appeared in the June 17th edition of the *Tribune*, giving an even more emphatic denial. "'I never made any such statement,' said Gen. Stager . . . 'to Gen. Darr or anybody else. It wasn't a fact—Gen. Garfield did not denounce his superior officer—and I couldn't therefore have said he did. I met Gen. Darr at West Point; but if he says I made such a statement he misapprehended me.'" Stager's comments spread, via the wire services, to a few other papers—as far away as Sacramento. But though they seemed to get widespread play for a while, as the controversy faded, so did Stager's rebuttals.[8]

For decades, Darr's version of events has been widely cited as corroborating Garfield's duplicity. Stager's denials are strong evidence that Garfield was right all along: Far from denouncing Rosecrans, Garfield defended him.

Was Darr confused, mistaken, or duplicitous? How about Stager? Did Stager say one thing in private and another in print for public consumption? At this remove, who can be sure? However, at the very least, Stager's public statements cast much greater doubt on the question of Garfield's supposed treason.

William Lamers' outstanding biography of William S. Rosecrans was first published in 1961. Lamers extensively mined the voluminous

---

7 "Stager Denies," *Chicago Daily Tribune,* June 15, 1882.

8 "Garfield-Rosecrans," *Chicago Daily Tribune,* June 17, 1882; see also "Rosecrans receives another facer from General Stager," *Sacramento (CA) Daily Record-Union,* June 16, 1882; and "Stager's Statements," *Rock Island (IL) Argus,* June 15, 1882.

You might not have heard of Anson Stager, but he hobnobbed with an elite crowd. Here he is, back row, second from left, with the likes of Lt. Gen. Phil Sheridan (front, second from left), President Chester Arthur (seated, center) and Secretary of War Robert Todd Lincoln (front, second from right) on a fishing trip in Yellowstone in 1883. *Library of Congress*

Rosecrans Papers, where he found the Darr letter. He also plumbed a wealth of other sources, the *Chicago Tribune* among them. He lacked the tools of a more modern age: the combination of search engines and digitized, online newspaper databanks that place millions of articles at our fingertips.

With these tools and the proper search parameters, researchers can now reduce the endless hours once required to comb newspaper and additional archives to mere minutes. That ability leads to some fascinating discoveries.

I suspect that there are a great many more such interesting items waiting to come to light.

I. Tactical Innovations in the Civil War?

by David T. Dixon

*Originally published as a blog post at Emerging Civil War
on October 6, 2020*

Typing this title fills me with dread and nervous anticipation. As a historian who does biographies, I focus on the life story of my central character— how he or she developed social and political beliefs, changed over time, interacted with important people and events, faced and overcame challenges, and left some mark behind for us to study and evaluate. Having had no formal education or training in the military arts, writing battle narratives is daunting enough. Going deeper into strategy and tactics for a core audience of Civil War enthusiasts is like offering advice on shooting techniques to LeBron James. Thankfully, I have qualified, generous peers willing to review my drafts, and help save me from making an ignorant error or ten when describing combat maneuvers.

Disclaimers aside, accepting the challenge of writing about one of the most talented and interesting general officers in the Western Theatre required a deep dive into areas far from my realm of expertise. This is one of the great pleasures of research and writing. When Dave Powell and Eric Wittenberg urged me to tackle the biography of Army of the Cumberland General August Willich, I knew it would be a challenge. Besides being one of the most colorful and eccentric officers in the war, Willich had a well-earned reputation for tactical excellence. Whether his men were employing the hollow square formation to fend off a force of cavalry four times their size at Rowlett's Station, changing front nine times in five successive charges at Shiloh, or covering the retreat of two divisions at Chickamauga, Willich consistently demonstrated coolness under fire, the ability to think, adjust and act quickly, and the foresight to anticipate enemy moves, countering them with a blend of disciplined troop management and creative field leadership.

However, the origins of Willich's most heralded innovation, "advance firing," remain shrouded in mystery. Dave Powell describes the tactical opportunity:

> Advance Firing was Willich's own solution to the problem of advancing over contested ground. Typically, stationary infantry could fire 3 rounds a minute. Advancing troops had to cross the killing ground quickly and close with the enemy. When smoothbore ranges really limited infantry fights to 50 or 100 yards, defenders might rip off one good or two ragged volleys before that moment of closure. Rifles opened the range, and theorists, in turn, increased the rate of closure for advancing troops by doubling the pace. Willich found this answer unsatisfactory. Instead, he decided that it would be better to incorporate fire and maneuver while advancing.[1]

Advance firing required the battalion to right face, double into a column of fours, and then face back left. Instead of undoubling and reverting to a standard two-rank line, they stayed in fours, creating a line four ranks deep with an empty file on the left between each file of four. After the first rank fired, the fourth rank advanced several paces through the open file to the front and fired while the original first rank reloaded. The rear ranks moved to the front in successive order, having had plenty of time to reload. This created an advancing wall of fire that was, by the accounts of attackers and defenders, both surprising and overwhelming. As a captured Confederate sergeant described the first documented use of advance firing

---

1 David A. Powell, "Attention, Battalion! Advance, Firing!" *The Chickamauga Campaign* (blog), December 27, 2009, https://chickamaugablog.wordpress.com/2009/12/27/attention-battalion-advance-firing/.

by the 49th Ohio at Liberty Gap in Tennessee, "Lord Almighty, who can stand against that? Four lines of battle and every one of them firing?"[2]

Willich did not invent advanced firing out of whole cloth. Instead, he probably adapted it from tactics he had studied at the Prussian military academy. Powell mentioned a street fighting drill whereby German Jaegers advanced in four ranks in the American Revolution as one possible inspiration. My challenge was clear—find hard evidence of similar techniques in older military manuals that Willich was exposed to in Europe. Even though I could not pretend to carry Earl Hess's cartridge box or wear Brent Nosworthy's kepi, I plunged awkwardly into the deep end of infantry tactics. Here's what I discovered.

Initial clues came from Willich himself. He believed that most of the firing in battle should be done by heavy skirmish lines, reserving fire from the line as skirmishers were driven back or in the instance of a full-scale assault or retreat. Newspaper reports from 1863 describe the implementation of advance firing at Liberty Gap as a skirmishing drill executed at the battalion level by the entire regiment.[3] A few months later, at Chickamauga, Willich expanded the use of advance firing to the brigade level, with multiple regiments executing the technique simultaneously. They also performed the reverse technique when conducting a methodical withdrawal from the field, which Willich called "retreat firing."[4]

A Google search of these terms yielded intriguing results. An English skirmishing manual published in 1831, just three years after Willich earned his commission as a second lieutenant in the Prussian army, describes an battalion advancing in line with the leading ranks covering the front as skirmishers. Firing commenced as they advanced by alternate files.[5] This

---

2 David T. Dixon, *Radical Warrior: August Willich's Journey from German Revolutionary to Union General* (Knoxville; Univ. of Tennessee Press, 2020), 6. 170, 176, 182, 188—89, 196. David A. Powell and Eric J. Wittenberg, *Tullahoma: The Forgotten Campaign that Changed the Course of the Civil War, June 23 – July 4, 1863* (El Dorado Hills, Ca.: Savas Beattie, 2020), 156—57.

3 *Tiffin Weekly Tribune* 28 Aug. 1863.

4 Dixon, *Radical Warrior*, 197.

5 C. Leslie, *Instructions for the Application of Light Drill to Skirmishing in the Field: With Observations on Advanced and Rear Guards, and Flank Patroles* (Dublin: Pettigrew and Oulton, 1831), vii, 8, 17–18.

was not the same as Willich's technique. Some historians claim that similar methods of advancing and firing by alternate ranks were used throughout Europe for centuries. A glance at an English drill manual from 1635 revealed nearly the same four-rank advance firing technique that Willich used. They called it "firing by introduction." Here's a snippet from that manual:

> For the other way of firing by introduction, the first ranke (or file-leaders) are to give fire as before, and to stand, the last ranke (or bringers up) in the interim of their firing; marching up, and ranking even with the second ranke: the rest following their Bringers up; as they do when Bringers up double their front. The first ranke having fired, the Bringers up step immediately before them; present, and give fire; the rest stil, successively, doing the like, untill every rank have given fire once over.[6]

Conversations with historian Greg Biggs revealed that Frederick the Great's father used a four-rank infantry formation. His son reduced that to three ranks due to innovations with the Prussian musket that increased his rate of fire to five rounds per minute while advancing. Historians dubbed it a "walking battery."[7] Willich was a keen student of Frederick and Napoléon, claiming that lessons learned from studying the great military campaigns of the past were far more useful than "three ponderous volumes of Scott's tactics."[8] Ample evidence uncovered recently by 9th Ohio historian Andrew Houghtaling confirms that while Willich and other German American officers may have given lip service to strict comportment with American military manuals, their commanders often

6 William Barriffee, *Military discipline: or, the yong artillery man Wherein is discoursed and showne the postures both of musket and pike: the exactest way, &c. Together with the motions which are to be used, in the excercising of a foot-company* (London Thomas Harper, 1635), 203.

7 Email from Greg Biggs March 21, 2019. Biggs cites Christopher Duffy, *The Army of Frederick the Great*, 2nd Edition (Emperor's Press, 1996, Chicago); Jay Luvaas ed. and translator, *Frederick the Great on the Art of War* (Free Press, New York, 1966); Philip Haythornthwaite, *Frederick the Great's Army: Infantry* (Osprey Publishing, Oxford, 1991); Peter Hofschroer, *Prussian Line Infantry 1792-1815* (Osprey Publishing, Oxford, 1984).

8 Dixon, *Radical Warrior*, 224–8.

looked the other way while they maintained numerous practices derived directly from the Prussian drill manual.[9]

I will defer to the experts to debate the degree of tactical innovation during the Civil War. However, what made Willich a brilliant tactician was not his originality, but his ability to adapt to changing conditions, employing a much broader tactical repertoire than his West Point-trained counterparts. Willich made little effort to conceal his contempt for a professional officer corps, whom he criticized as composed of "the lurid intellect of a regular corporal or the scraps picked up from a half-digested compendium of a military school." Willich believed that a citizen army, with officers selected for their superior intelligence and morality and soldiers trained via compulsory military education and service, would serve the republic better than a system led by a class of privileged elites. His proposal for a national citizen militia was never seriously considered.[10]

General William S. Rosecrans was receptive to new ideas and left with the reputation of being one of the Union's most creative and resourceful strategists. Willich's revival of advance firing and other techniques plucked from the playbooks of the most talented European military leaders gained favor for a short time in the Army of the Cumberland. After the debut of advance firing at Liberty Gap, one solider reported, "I understand most of the brigades in the army are adopting the movement."[11] Indeed, two of Col. Charles B. Harker's regiments, the 64th Ohio and the celebrated 125th Ohio led by Col. Emerson Opdyke, employed advance firing on September 20 at Chickamauga.[12] However, when George S. Thomas replaced Rosecrans, such irregular maneuvers ended. The Rock of Chickamauga was a "by the book" army commander and had plenty of conventional tools in his arsenal that proved effective. Willich's advance firing technique, as devastating as it was, remains, as Powell so aptly put it, merely "a footnote in the history of the war."[13]

---

9 Andrew M. Houghtaling, *"Mit einem lauten hurrah-ruf": The use of "Prussian Drill" during the American Civil War*, unpublished manuscript, 2020.

10 Dixon, *Radical Warrior*, 224–8.

11 *Tiffin Weekly Tribune* 28 Aug. 1863.

12 Dixon, *Radical Warrior*, 196.

13 Powell, "Attention, Battalion!"

Pensacola's Advanced Redoubt

by Sheritta Bitikofer

Originally published as a blog post at Emerging Civil War on February 17, 2022

One of the fortifications I visited in 2019 while exploring the Pensacola forts (Pickens and Barrancas) was the Advanced Redoubt. It's located a short distance north of Fort Barrancas, to protect the inland approaches to the nearby Navy Yard. Construction on this Florida fort began in 1845, cost $150,000, and was part of the Third System of Coastal Forts following the War of 1812.[1] Its construction is typical for a fortification of the era, including a dry ditch or "kill zone" between the scarp and counterscarp, an underground passageway for access into the counterscarp, apertures for musket fire or cannon placements, and an open parade ground for drilling. While construction wasn't completed until 1870, it still experienced activity during the Civil War. Through these events, we see where Pensacola ranked in importance to the Union war effort along the Gulf Coast.

From 1861 to the spring of 1862, Pensacola was divided. Fort Pickens had remained in Federal hands while Confederates occupied Fort Barrancas, the Navy Yard, and Fort McRee. Numerous skirmishes occurred between the troops, including the Battle of Santa Rosa Island in September 1861,

---

1 George F. Pearce, *Pensacola During the Civil War: A Thorn in the Side of the Confederacy*, (Gainesville, University Press of Florida, 2000), 2.

Constructed between 1845 and 1870, Advanced Redoubt was the final
Third System Fort completed. *Sheritta Bitikofer*

and an artillery bombardment in November. The Confederate invasion
of Tennessee and the progression of Federal forces down the Mississippi
warranted evacuating 8,000 troops from Pensacola, leaving Col. Thomas
Jones in charge. On May 7th, Col. Jones received news of David Farragut's
fleet anchoring off Mobile Bay and prepared for evacuation. On May 9th,
as the final troops left Pensacola, he gave orders to "destroy all camp tents,
Forts McRee and Barrancas, as far as possible, the hospital, the [dwelling]
houses in the Navy Yard . . . in fact, everything that could be useful to the
enemy."[2] Per Jones' orders, Pensacola would remain untouched, though one
home was damaged when its neighboring oil factory was burned. Pensacola's
surrender was made official on May 10th between Acting Maj. John
Brosnaham—a local doctor—and Lt. Richard H. Jackson, aide-de-camp for
Brig. Gen. Lewis G. Arnold in charge of defending Fort Pickens. By May
12th, Federal forces had taken possession of Pensacola and its fortifications.
The South was deprived of a valuable port that could have been used for
blockade runners and facilities at the Navy Yard. The West Gulf Blockading
Squadron utilized the Navy Yard for repairs and resupplying, making it a
vital depot for the navy efforts in the gulf until the war's end.

2 *The War of the Rebellion: a Compilation of the Official Records of the Union and Confederate
Armies* (hereafter *OR*), Series 1, Vol. 6, 660-661; *Official Records of the Union and Confederate
Navies in the War of the Rebellion* (hereafter *ORN*), Series I, Vol. 18, 482-483.

Though some claimed that Pensacola's economy could "get along very well without foreign imports" the town felt the effects of depreciating Confederate money prior to Federal occupation.[3] Privation was common, as "there was want and suffering but we drank our coffee of parched potatoes or meal, took dirt from the smokehouse floor and boiled it to get salt; dyed Osnaburg for their dresses and smiled, knowing it could be worse."[4] Secessionists left town with the Confederates, and those remaining were forced to take the oath of allegiance or risk imprisonment at Fort Pickens. The much-needed manpower to rebuild the Navy Yard enticed citizens to Pensacola from the surrounding countryside for work and protection from Confederates that lurked in outposts.[5] Additionally, Pensacola became a beacon of freedom for the enslaved. By 1863, a school was established for the newly freed blacks.

Military activity within Pensacola before the spring of 1863 was limited to the regular occupation of the city. A picket line was established five or six miles encircling the city, and expeditions to ascertain Confederate strengths pushed into the outlying communities of Oakfield and Milton. These intermittent skirmishes ensured the protection of Pensacola from any danger for the time being.

As efforts intensified to conquer the Mississippi River, Federal forces pulled out of Pensacola. They abandoned the city, keeping the forts and Navy Yard garrisoned. The evacuation was completed on March 22, 1863, and many citizens followed the troops to Warrington and Woolsey near the Navy Yard, benefiting from their protection. Secretary of the Navy Gideon Welles sympathized with the refugees, stating that "loyal citizens should be protected and not permitted to suffer."[6] By early 1864, Unionist refugees were encouraged to enlist in the Federal Army, and many joined the 7th Vermont or the 14th New York Infantry at Barrancas. The condition of the city degraded after the evacuation. According to one observer after paying a

3 *Pensacola Daily Observer*, January 30, 1862.

4 Mary Crary Weller and Marrie Crary Coley, "Civil War Reminiscences," P. K. Younge Library of Florida History, Manuscript Collection, University of Florida, Gainesville.

5 George F. Pearce, The *U.S. Navy in Pensacola: From Sailing Ships to Naval Aviation, 1825-1930,* (Gainesville, University Press of Florida, 1980), 82.

6 *ORN*, Series I, Vol. 20, 134.

visit, "Everything looks gloomy where once so much life and spirit prevailed, and a feeling of sadness seizes one to witness so much desolation."[7]

The first—and only—assault upon the Navy Yard and Fort Barrancas occurred on October 8, 1863. Brigadier General James H. Clanton led 200 Confederates from the 57th and 61st Alabama Infantry, and the 6th and 7th Alabama Cavalry to the south side of Bayou Grande just north of Barrancas. A short-lived skirmish occurred around the Advanced Redoubt with the 7th Vermont Infantry, and 14th Regiment Corps d'Afrique under the command of Col. William C. Holbrook ended in a Confederate retreat. Another skirmish occurred the following day, though neither side suffered recorded casualties. Intelligence from Old Tom, a black cook who had been captured during the skirmish, and later released, suggested Clanton had led the expedition. He was scouting the position of black pickets and "was only after the negro soldiers; that he would not fire on the white pickets, but that every black picket that could be seen would be shot."[8] A regiment of black infantry 500 strong arrived from New Orleans as reinforcements, and another was promised within a few days. Other freedom seekers arriving at the forts were incorporated into the 14th Regiment Corps d'Afrique. The skirmish proved to Clanton and his 1,000 troops around Pollard, Alabama, that they would not be able to contend with Holbrook at Barrancas without sufficient firepower.

A false alarm sent the troops around Barrancas, the Redoubt, and the Navy Yard into a hurried effort to fortify their position. Commander of the District of West Florida Brig. Gen. Alexander Asboth heard rumors of an impending assault in November 1863, spurring the reoccupation of Pensacola. Special Order No. 10 detailed the extensive preparations, including round-the-clock manning of the fortifications, and strengthening the trenches that stretched from Bayou Grande to the seashore.[9] By December, no assault came, and Asboth admitted that the Confederate activity around Pollard was defensive. Troops were again withdrawn from Pensacola.

These efforts prepared Asboth for a more serious threat in April 1864, with reports of 10,000 Confederates concentrated at Pollard. Asboth wrote that his command was "entirely inadequate to secure a long resistance to

---

7 *Santa Rosa News Boy*, June 15, 1863.

8 Ibid., 617-618.

9 *OR*, Series I, Vol. 26, part 1, 822-823.

a tenfold superior force." He requested reinforcements, cooperating with Commandant William Smith on plans to evacuate the Navy Yard. He was denied reinforcements but was ordered to hold Barrancas "to the last extremity."[10] By May, Confederate forces were diverted north to assist Gen. Joseph Johnston in protecting Atlanta from Gen. William T. Sherman. Only two cavalry units, the 15th Confederate and 7th Alabama, remained at Pollard, and the 82nd United States Colored Infantry arrived at Barrancas, relieving some of Asboth's anxieties.

However, frustration over his denied requests for more troops and supplies only grew. Without additional manpower, he could not launch an offensive against the Confederates who lingered around Bayou Grande. Through 1863 and 1864, Asboth gradually received more regiments and cavalry for raiding, either west toward Mobile or east toward Milton, and sustained few casualties. After the battle at Marianna, Asboth was temporarily replaced by Bvt. Brig. Gen. Joseph Bailey, who led successful raids to Milton and Bagdad. Bailey's replacement, Brig. Gen. Thomas J. McKean, also raided westward against forces under Brig. Gen. St. John R. Liddell out of Blakeley, Alabama. Most raids harassed outposts or disrupted supplies trying to make their way to or from Confederate lines.

A rapid troop buildup took place in Pensacola in January 1865. Shortly after, Asboth resumed his command from McKean over the District of West Florida. As preparations were made for troops at Barrancas to embark with Maj. Gen. Frederick Steele in the Mobile Campaign, all passage between Barrancas and Pensacola was restricted to military purposes only. Supplies for the expedition were routed to the storehouses around the Navy Yard. Steele's command comprised a total force of 12,114, concentrated at Pensacola before setting out on March 20th.[11] These troops fought in the Battle at Fort Blakeley on the evening of April 9, 1865, the same day Robert E. Lee surrendered the Army of Northern Virginia to Ulysses S. Grant at Appomattox.

On April 22, Asboth received a letter from Gen. Clanton that he would take the next available boat arriving at Barrancas by the 26th. Cautious of any plot to attack the fort, Asboth ordered the new Navy Yard commandant, James Armstrong, to send an armed escort to bring Clanton to him. Asboth

10 *OR,* Series I, Vol. 35, part 2, 56-57; Ibid., 84.

11 Pearce, *Pensacola During the Civil War,* 226.

Advanced Redoubt, now (top) and then (bottom).
Sheritta Bitikofer/Author's collection

was authorized by Gen. E. R. S. Canby to accept the surrender of Confederate troops in his district on the 29th, and that the parolees could return to their homes and would "not be disturbed by the authorities of the United States so long as they continue to observe the conditions of their paroles."[12] In May, Asboth declared both Pensacola and Milton military posts, offering safe havens for citizens from Escambia and Santa Rosa counties to take the oath, accept five days' rations, and restart their lives.

Troops from Barrancas were sent to Mobile and Blakeley for occupation duty, leaving around 60 men to garrison. By 1866, no troops remained at Barrancas or the Advanced Redoubt. Due to changing technologies in the latter half of the nineteenth century that made these forts nearly obsolete, the Advanced Redoubt suffered neglect and vandalism.

When the fortification became part of the Gulf Island National Seashore in 1971, measures were taken to stabilize and restore the structure, and add signage explaining the redoubt's history. The Trench Trail from the Fort Barrancas parking lot to the Advanced Redoubt takes visitors through the woods along Taylor Road, pointing out remnants of the entrenched line that Federal soldiers had used in 1863 and 1864. The interior was not accessible during my visit. Currently, Barrancas, the Redoubt, and other historical locations on the Naval Air Station in Pensacola are closed to the public due to security incidents. There is hope that a private civilian entrance will be constructed and allow the forts to reopen for visitors.

---

12 Edwin C. Bearss, *Fort Barrancas: Gulf Islands National Seashore,* (Denver, Denver Service Center, National Park Service, 1983), 461.

Captured at Missionary Ridge
The "Traitor" Vice President's Son

by Sarah Kay Bierle

The battle of Missionary Ridge fought on November 25, 1863, resulted in the reported capture of 4,146 Confederate soldiers. Among that number was Lt. Joseph Cabell Breckinridge, a teen whose runaway venture had created a political price for his father in 1861 and whose sudden disappearance from the battlefield in 1863 made his parents fear the worst. Young Breckinridge's story serves as a reminder of youth's impetuosity in the early days of the American Civil War and the intense mental and emotional strain the conflict placed on families. The moment of his capture at Missionary Ridge provides a lens to re-examine his choices and how they impacted both his family and the Confederate cause.

Joseph Cabell Breckinridge had been born on December 29, 1844. His father, John C. Breckinridge—a rising lawyer with a talent for politics—proudly welcomed his first-born child, even as he worried about his wife Mary's precarious health after "the extraordinary sufferings of her confinement."[1] But with each passing day, both baby and mother survived, and the bond of family was firmly established.

As the nation's "familial bonds" stretched toward a breaking point in the 1850s, John C. Breckinridge served in the U.S. House of Representatives

---

1 William C. Davis, *Breckinridge: Statesman, Soldier, Symbol* (Lexington: The University Press of Kentucky, 2010) 31.

and later as the youngest vice president in American history. The Buchanan administration left much to be desired, and the country looked to the presidential election of 1860 as a hint for the future. Many southerners rallied around Breckinridge, one of three candidates on the Democratic Party ticket, but Abraham Lincoln from the newly formed Republican party won the presidency. Leaving the vice president office, Breckinridge became a senator from border-state Kentucky. By the summer of 1861 with eleven states in rebellion and the first battles of the American Civil War already fought, Breckinridge struggled to navigate the situation in

John C. Breckinridge as fresh-faced vice president of the United States. *Library of Congress*

Congress and represent his state. The actions of his eldest son did not help matters or his reputation in Washington City.

By 1861, Cabell—as the family called the firstborn—had reached the age of 16 and threw his alliance toward the Confederacy. Ignoring his father's counsel and wishes, Cabell repeatedly ran away, trying to get out of neutral Kentucky and enlist in a Confederate regiment. Twice, Cabell was caught and brought home. His third private rebellion ended in his success (from his perspective). He reached Tennessee, lied about his age, and on July 13, 1861, enlisted himself in the 2nd Kentucky Infantry.[2]

Federal authorities sought to detain Breckinridge Sr. by mid-September 1861 since they did not approve of his political stance and questioned his loyalty — partly taking his son's actions into the equation. Facing arrest for

2 Ibid., 278.

an indefinite period or officially joining the Confederacy, the father followed the son's trail to Tennessee. John C. Breckinridge took command of the Kentucky "Orphan" Brigade on November 16, 1861. The brigade included the 2nd Kentucky, bringing Cabell under his father's authority once again.

The Breckinridge family name became a target to Federal authorities. At the end of 1861, Breckinridge Sr. was formally declared a traitor by the United States Senate, and a federal district court had indicted him for treason. If General Breckinridge or anyone in his immediate family fell into the grip of Union soldiers, the outcome looked uncertain.

Meanwhile, Cabell joined his father's staff, often performing messenger duties. Soldiers remarked that the general did not show favoritism or spare his son from dangerous circumstances. "I must not shield my son from the dangers of his comrades," General Breckinridge explained.[3] During the battle of Shiloh in April 1862, Cabell's horse had been shot under him.[4] The next year at the battle of Chickamauga in September 1863, another officer begged the general to not send Cabell into heavy fire to deliver a message. Emotional but resolute, the general instructed his son to carry the orders.[5]

By the end of 1863, Cabell had significant battle experience and had become accustomed to going to the battle lines to witness, report, and guide the fighting at his father's direction. On November 25, brigades from Union General Joseph Hooker's command surged toward the steep slopes of Missionary Ridge. Toward the top of the high ground, General Breckinridge's thin lines stretched to meet the attack. Cabell rode toward the crumbling position while his father and other officers tried to find reinforcements and rally the soldiers further back.

Colonel James A. Williamson of the 4th Iowa Infantry commanded the Second Brigade of the First Division in the XV Corps. His regiments had gone "forward to the valley, and then moved out by the flank, through the gap, down the pass to the open ground, when I was ordered to make a short halt. While at the halt, 2 men of the Ninth Iowa captured

---

3 James C. Klotter, *The Breckinridges of Kentucky, 1760-1981* (Lexington: The University Press of Kentucky, 1986) 122.

4 William C. Davis, *Breckinridge: Statesman, Soldier, Symbol* (Lexington: The University Press of Kentucky) 307.

5 Ibid., 374.

Lieutenant Breckinridge, a son of Maj. Gen. John C. Breckinridge, of the Confederate Army."[6]

In the confusion of the battle, General Breckinridge only knew that his son had not returned. That night he collapsed on the floor of General Bragg's headquarters, giving Bragg reason to claim that Breckinridge had been drunk. More likely, exhaustion and sorrow over his missing son contributed to the reaction.[7]

The uncertainty of the young man's fate extended to the homefront. His mother, who had just recovered from a near fatal malaria illness, wrote, "I just made a promise that if I could hear he was not wounded I would never shed another tear, but sometimes in the silent hours of the night unbidden tears will steal down my cheek."[8] Within a week after the battle of Missionary Ridge, the general knew his son was a prisoner, but otherwise unharmed; he started writing to the U.S. War Department, seeking to arrange a prisoner exchange.[9] Cabell's prisoner of war journey sent him to Louisville, Kentucky, then to Johnson's Island on Lake Erie where he arrived on December 5.

By early spring 1864, Cabell had been exchanged and rejoined his father, now in the Trans-Alleghany Department which encompassed parts of Virginia, West Virginia, and Kentucky claimed by the Confederacy.[10] That summer Cabell was accidentally wounded by friendly fire while destroying track along the Baltimore & Ohio Railroad, but the injury proved unserious.[11] The war took its toll on Cabell, and his habits of carousing with cavalrymen and drinking excessively worried his father.[12]

Richmond, the capital of the Confederacy, fell in April 1865, and Breckinridge Sr. and Jr. hurried further south, evading capture. With an

---

6 *Official Records of the War of the Rebellion*, Series 1, Volume 31, Part 2, Reports. Page 615.

7 William C. Davis, *Breckinridge: Statesman, Soldier, Symbol* (Lexington: The University Press of Kentucky) 397.

8 Ibid., 401.

9 Ibid., 400.

10 Ibid., 409.

11 Ibid., 451.

12 Ibid., 498.

indictment to his name and the official label of "traitor," John C. Breckinridge needed to get out of the country and his escape took him to Florida and then Cuba. Cabell, following his father's orders, left the escape party and surrender himself in Tallahassee, Florida.[13] In the immediate post war years, Cabell struggled to keep a job, suffered from health complications, drank heavily, and rarely maintained regularly contact with his parents.[14] A few years later he tried to improve his life and eventually married the daughter of a U.S. Senator in 1869.[15]

Like many young men, Cabell Breckinridge eagerly sought action in the Civil War and quickly found that war had its horrific realities and dangers. However, most young recruits' runaway antics did not endanger their fathers' political careers, adding pressure and questions of his loyalty. The pending judicial case against John C. Breckinridge must have added an additional level of worry when he realized his son had been captured. The specific note about Lieut. Breckinridge in a Union battle report suggests they knew the potential importance of their prisoner.

In some respects, Cabell's flight from home to the Confederacy paved the path for his father's journey from U.S. Senator to refugee to Confederate general to Confederate Secretary of War and to defeated refugee. Quotations from family letters suggest the close bond and the emotional stress between father and son, especially when seeing each other under battle fire. For this family, their personal war experience hit a tense moment when General Breckinridge could not find his son on Missionary Ridge and the son found himself surrendering at gunpoint to Union soldiers.

13 Ibid., 529.

14 Ibid., 552.

15 Ibid., 597.

7. A Missed Opportunity: The Confederates' Lost Chance at Chattanooga

by Patrick Kelly-Fischer

Originally published as a blog post at Emerging Civil War on January 7, 2022

In September 1863, the Confederates executed one of the largest strategic troop maneuvers of the entire war, setting themselves up to potentially destroy a major Union field army. They shifted Lt. Gen. James Longstreet and approximately 15,000 troops of his First Corps of the Army of Northern Virginia by railroad to northern Georgia.

Once there, Longstreet joined Gen. Braxton Bragg's Army of Tennessee. The gamble achieved parity in numbers, if not an outright advantage. Rosecrans's Army of the Cumberland advanced into the mountains of northern Georgia.

The resulting battle of Chickamauga, the second bloodiest battle of the war, ended in a major Union defeat. The Army of the Cumberland might have been effectively destroyed on that field, as Confederates broke through their lines and could have cut off their retreat. As Maj. Gen. George Thomas held on until dark, earning the nickname "The Rock of Chickamauga," Bragg didn't grasp the opportunity. With the chaos of a 19th-century battlefield, the Army of the Cumberland survived to fight another day. Beaten but not destroyed, they staggered back to Chattanooga, where they were quickly besieged.

One area that makes the Civil War so compelling is the number of distinct moments one could easily imagine having altered the war's course. However, was Chattanooga truly an opportunity for the South to have changed the outcome?

For starters, Chattanooga was perhaps the only time in the war when a major Union field army was besieged and seemingly at serious risk of being destroyed. This is not to diminish the garrison's capture at Harper's Ferry in 1862. Longstreet believed that the Army of the Cumberland was primed to continue retreating, whereas the South could finish the job they started at Chickamauga. After the war, he wrote, "General Rosecrans prepared, no doubt, to continue his retreat, anticipating our march towards his rear, but finding that we preferred to lay our lines in front of him, concluded that it would be more comfortable to rest at Chattanooga, reinforce, repair damages, and come to meet us when ready for a new trial."[1]

Major General Ulysses S. Grant, recently promoted to command of Union armies across the West and dispatched to salvage the situation in Chattanooga, agreed. He wrote in his memoirs:

> In the course of the evening Mr. Stanton received a dispatch from Mr. C. A. Dana, then in Chattanooga, informing him that unless prevented Rosecrans would retreat, and advising peremptory orders against his doing so. . . .
>
> A retreat at that time would have been a terrible disaster. It would not only have been the loss of a most important strategic position to us, but it would have been attended with the loss of all the artillery still left with the Army of the Cumberland and the annihilation of that army itself, either by capture or demoralization.[2]

Union Maj. Gen. William T. Sherman, commanding the Union Army of the Tennessee, painted a similarly grim picture of the situation when he arrived in November. "Bragg had completely driven Rosecrans's army into

1 James Longstreet, *From Manassas to Appomattox: Memoirs of the Civil War in America.* Da Capo Press, 1992, 462-463.

2 Ulysses Grant, *Personal Memoirs of U.S. Grant.* Gutenberg Project.

Confederates squandered their chance at Chattanooga by taking a passive approach to its capitulation, quickly outmatched by the much more active approach Ulysses S. Grant took when he arrived on the scene. *Library of Congress*

Chattanooga; the latter was in actual danger of starvation, and the railroad to his rear seemed inadequate to his supply."[3]

Backing the Army of the Cumberland into a corner was one thing. The question now was how the Confederates could capture or destroy it. Storming the fortified city would be costly, and not a sure thing. Starving the Union Army out was safer, and the route that Bragg largely opted for. However, it took too long in the face of stiffening Union resolve and significant reinforcements being brought in from across the North.

I've found no evidence that Longstreet, for his part, ever argued for a direct assault on fortified lines. In this instance, he advocated for crossing the Tennessee River to get between Rosecrans and his remaining supplies. This would force him to retreat or fight out in the open, which paralleled what he wanted to try at Gettysburg.[4]

3 William T. Sherman, *Memoirs of Gen. William T. Sherman*. Pantianos Classics, 2021, 144.

4 James, Longstreet *From Manassas to Appomattox: Memoirs of the Civil War in America*. Da Capo Press, 1992, 461-466.

This was the exact scenario that Grant feared, writing: "If a retreat had occurred at this time it is not probable that any of the army would have reached the railroad as an organized body, if followed by the enemy."[5]

Like any memoir, one should take Grant, Sherman, and Longstreet's writings with a grain of salt, recognizing they served an implicit postwar agenda. The worse Rosecrans's situation was, the greater Grant and Sherman's heroics in rescuing him. Longstreet maneuvered to replace Bragg during the siege, which could only be justified if Bragg fumbled an opportunity that Longstreet might exploit.

In his history of the Army of Tennessee, historian Larry J. Daniel dismisses Longstreet's proposal to cross the river and threaten Nashville. He argues that there was no pontoon bridge available to make the crossing. Additionally, the Confederates did not have the supplies, transportation, or logistical resources for such a maneuver.[6]

Instead, in the siege's early days, political infighting hamstrung the Confederate Army. Bragg sought to leverage his victory at Chickamauga into a purge of his political opponents in the army. Others, including Longstreet, sought to oust Bragg. The situation devolved , forcing Jefferson Davis to travel from Richmond to mediate the latest feud among the Army of Tennessee's high command. Ultimately, he left Bragg in charge.

Even as the Union's position improved, the Confederacy could barely support its siege army. Food was scarce, and morale cratered. "Daily starving soldiers crave of us permission to pick out of the dirt around the horses the soiled and trodden grains of corn that remained after feed time," wrote Adolphe Chalaron of the Washington Artillery.[7]

As the Confederate high command burned valuable time feuding and their soldiers starved, the Union situation continually improved. Rosecrans was relieved of command of the Army of the Cumberland, replaced by Thomas, who resolved to "hold the town till we starve."[8] Grant took

5 Ulysses S. Grant, *Personal Memoirs of U.S. Grant*. Gutenberg Project.

6 Larry J. Daniel, *Conquered: Why the Army of Tennessee Failed.* (Chapel Hill: University of North Carolina Press, 2019), 191-192.

7 Nathaniel Chears Hughes, Jr. *The Pride of the Confederate Artillery: The Washington Artillery in the Army of Tennessee,* (Baton Rouge: Louisiana State University Press, 1997), 152.

8 Ulysses Grant, *Personal Memoirs of U.S. Grant.* Gutenberg Project.

overall Union command in the West. He rushed in reinforcements from Virginia and Mississippi. They reopened supply lines and defeated Bragg in November, driving him back into Georgia and opening the door to the Atlanta Campaign.

Like any counterfactual, we'll never know how history might have played out differently. Even if the Army of Tennessee found victory quickly at Chattanooga, either by capturing the city, or inducing Rosecrans to retreat and then attacking him on the road, it's hard to imagine Bragg suddenly rampaging to the Ohio River with his half-starved, badly bloodied army.

It is possible that he might have forced Burnside back from Knoxville, moving the war's front lines back to Nashville. The command team of Grant, Sherman, and Thomas would have been able to concentrate reinforcements, safely supplied by the Union's Navy along the Cumberland and Tennessee Rivers. They certainly would have resumed the offensive within months, but this course of events, and setbacks, might have changed the public's perception of the war by the 1864 elections.

Interestingly, the Army of the Cumberland may not have been the most valuable prize the Confederates lost. Grant recounted how he met a Southern soldier wearing a blue (probably captured) uniform:

> I rode up to him, commenced conversing with him, and asked whose corps he belonged to. He was very polite, and, touching his hat to me, said he belonged to General Longstreet's corps. I asked him a few questions—but not with a view of gaining any particular information—all of which he answered, and I rode off.[9]

9 Ibid.

Chattanooga:
More Than Just Another Victory for Grant

by William Lee White

Originally published as a blog post at Emerging Civil War on December 10, 2017

In the late summer and early fall of 1863, all eyes seemed to focus on the small railroad town of Chattanooga, Tennessee. The disastrous defeat at Chickamauga in September and its huge casualties turned what had nearly been for Union commander Maj. Gen. William S. Rosecrans a victory almost as significant as the fall of Vicksburg into an embarrassing defeat. However, in the defeat, Rosecrans still held onto Chattanooga, the objective of his campaign. His army, the Army of the Cumberland, soon found itself under siege.

Rosecrans held on, thanks to a 60-mile supply line to his forward supply base of Bridgeport, Alabama, only 25 miles away. Due to the Confederate army's cannon placement on Lookout Mountain and sharpshooters along the banks of the Tennessee River, direct access was impossible. Rosecrans continued to work on the town's defense, planning to open up another, shorter route of supply, although word of this did not make its way to the War Department. The assistant Secretary of War, Charles Dana, feeding a growing panic about Rosecrans, sent false reports of an eminent withdrawal. Already reinforcements were on the way to aid Rosecrans: Joe Hooker marched with the XI and XII Corps of the Army of the Potomac from Virginia, and William T. Sherman was coming with a portion of the Army of the Tennessee from Mississippi. Suddenly, another move was made that would tremendously impact the rest of the war, and fatally wound Rosecrans' career.

Major General Ulysses S. Grant had steadily grown into the hero of the Union cause. From the first so-needed victories at Forts Henry and Donelson, the snatching of victory from the jaws of defeat at Shiloh, and the hard road to capture Vicksburg, Grant seemed to provide the desperately needed Union victories. Grant proved to be a tough-as-nails commander, and his maxim of "when I started to go anywhere, or to do anything, not to turn back or stop until the thing intended was accomplished" served him well.[1]

However, Grant displayed some very human flaws. He was sometimes jealous of the attention the press gave other officers and displayed some misplaced paranoia. This resulted in a bitter rift with Rosecrans, destroying a decades-long friendship in the wake of the battles of Iuka and Corinth.

Grant's accomplishments, though, shined brightly now that the Mississippi once more, through his efforts, ran "unvexed to the sea," severing the Confederacy. With this latest accomplishment, Grant received notification of his promotion. He would command the newly created Military Division of the West, covering a massive expanse of ground: the three military departments between the Appalachians and the Mississippi, including his old command, the Army of the Tennessee, now commanded by his good friend and loyal subordinate, William T. Sherman, and that of the seemingly collapsing Rosecrans, the Army of the Cumberland.[2]

Grant was tasked with ensuring that Chattanooga remained in Union hands. The War Department gave him two sets of orders related to the fate of his old friend, Rosecrans. He held Rosecrans's fate in his hand. One set of orders retained him, and the other removed him from command, replacing him with Maj. Gen. George H. Thomas.

There never was any doubt: Rosecrans was done.

---

1 Ulysses S. Grant, *The Personal Memoirs of Ulysses S. Grant* (New York: Charles Webster and Sons, 1885), 50.

2 For more on the relationship between Grant, Vicksburg, and Chattanooga, read Dan Davis's essay "Vicksburg: The Victory That Unleashed Ulysses S. Grant" in *Turning Points of the American Civil War*, part of ECW's "Engaging the Civil War" Series (Southern Illinois University Press, 2018).

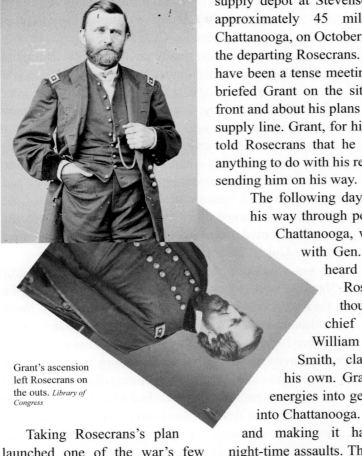

Grant's ascension left Rosecrans on the outs. *Library of Congress*

Grant arrived at the Union supply depot at Stevenson, Alabama, approximately 45 miles west of Chattanooga, on October 22nd, met by the departing Rosecrans. In what must have been a tense meeting, Rosecrans briefed Grant on the situation at the front and about his plans for opening a supply line. Grant, for his part, falsely told Rosecrans that he did not have anything to do with his removal before sending him on his way.

The following day, Grant made his way through pouring rain to Chattanooga, where he met with Gen. Thomas and heard more about Rosecrans's plan, though, the army's chief engineer, William F. "Baldy" Smith, claimed it was his own. Grant turned his energies into getting supplies into Chattanooga.

Taking Rosecrans's plan and making it happen, Grant launched one of the war's few night-time assaults. The amphibious attack, known as the battle of Brown's Ferry, broke the Confederate siege of Chattanooga. What became known as "the Cracker Line" was now open, and a steady stream of supplies moved into Chattanooga.

Along with the supplies, a path was open for the reinforcements that began arriving. Hooker's men had arrived only eleven days after they were dispatched, playing a big part in opening the "Cracker Line," and defending it in a series of skirmishes that are collectively called the battle of Wauhatchie. Grant waited for Sherman to arrive.

In the interlude, the Confederate commander, Braxton Bragg, dispatched part of his army to deal with the third army under Grant's command. Major General Ambrose Burnside's Army of the Ohio captured Knoxville, Tennessee, after the city's garrison had rushed to reinforce Bragg before the battle of Chickamauga. Now wanting to eliminate Burnside as a threat and retake Knoxville, Bragg sent Lt. Gen. James Longstreet with his corps for this mission. When Sherman finally arrived at Chattanooga in mid-November, Bragg initially discounted him as a local threat. He thought Sherman's men were on the way to Knoxville. This prompted him to order more of his army to that front. Ironically, that move compelled Grant, now growing worried about Burnside, to act against Bragg.

Receiving a report that the Confederates were leaving his front, Grant ordered a reconnaissance in force on November 23rd against Confederate picket lines near Orchard Knob, a prominent hill between Chattanooga and Missionary Ridge. Confederate defenses ran along a long portion of the base. That reconnaissance soon turned into the first of what would become three days of fighting. The Confederates were still in their lines, and a short skirmish ensued, with the Union forces capturing Orchard Knob.

Grant saw that it was time to act. He ordered the main assault to occur the following day. Sherman would attack the Confederate right, rolling up the line, and sweeping the Confederates away from Chattanooga and into North Georgia. Hooker would then attack Lookout Mountain in a diversionary action.

However, November 24th was a day of frustrating success and failure. Hooker's attack was a success, forcing the Confederates to abandon the seemingly impregnable Lookout Mountain. In contrast, Sherman, due to poor reconnaissance and even poorer maps, attacked what proved to be an undefended set of hills slightly in front of Missionary Ridge. Grant needed to draw up new plans for November 25th, even as Bragg pulled his men back to defend Missionary Ridge. The following day, Sherman would attack what he now knew was the Confederate right on the portion of the ridge known as Tunnel Hill. Hooker would move off Lookout Mountain, cross Chattanooga Valley, and attack the Confederate left, crushing the Confederates between the two forces as the Army of the Cumberland loomed as a diversion in their front.

Once again, luck seemed to abandon the Union forces. Flooded creeks and a burned bridge delayed Hooker as he moved eastward, while Sherman was handed several humiliating repulses in his attacks.

Finally, late in the day, having received erroneous reports that Bragg had reinforced his right, Grant committed Thomas and the Army of the

Cumberland. The Cumberlanders moved forward with orders to attack the Confederate defenses at the foot of the ridge. It was an easy move, but they came under heavy fire from the Confederate main line on top of the ridge, and the men surged forward without orders. Clambering up the side of the ridge, they repeatedly shouted, "Chickamauga!" Using the name of their defeat as their battle cry, they soon had the summit, and quickly broke the Confederate line, sending the Rebels into full retreat. Grant had his victory.

In the battle's aftermath, Grant was again hailed as the great victor, this time having opened the gateway into the heart of the Deep South. In four months, Grant had delivered two of the most significant victories of the war, and he was destined for even greater things. Grant was again promoted, this time to take command of all of the Union Armies. He, in turn, promoted Sherman, despite Sherman's failures, to command of the Military Division of the West. The team was now being assembled to win the war.

Grant traveled to Virginia the following spring to try his luck against Robert E. Lee. Sherman moved through the gateway into Georgia, beginning a campaign that would lead to both his fame and infamy, but all of it leading to the Confederacy's death.

Chattanooga was not just another victory for Grant. The event enabled him to assemble his winning team—a team that won the war.

Longstreet Goes West

by David A. Powell

*Originally published as blog posts at Emerging Civil War
August 23, 2016–January 4, 2017*

Machiavellian or Misunderstood?

Confederate General James Longstreet remains one of the war's most controversial figures. Detractors see him as a scheming subordinate whose ambition overreached his talents; supporters hail him as a realist who understood the changes in warfare better than most of his contemporaries, and tried to change with the times.

Short of Gettysburg, no aspect of Longstreet's Civil War career stirs more controversy than his trip west to reinforce the Army of Tennessee in September 1863. Was this a duplicitous effort to get out from Robert E. Lee's thumb, undermine Braxton Bragg's command, and let Longstreet take his rightful place in the sun? Or was it motivated by the disastrous course of the western war, a feeling that no matter how well the South did in Virginia, the war was being lost in the Old Dominion State?

On one level, that question is easily answered. By the fall of 1863, it was apparent to every Southerner that something must change to reverse the course of western defeat. Vicksburg was gone, leaving the Mississippi River in Union hands, rendering 30,000 Rebels prisoners of war at a stroke.

Lieutenant General James Longstreet would be yet one more "rock star ego" for Braxton Bragg to deal with. As Robert E. Lee's "Old War Horse" from the vaunted Army of Northern Virginia, Longstreet had also once been a protégé of Joseph E. Johnston. *Library of Congress*

Tennessee had been lost. At August's end, when the Union Army of the Cumberland crossed the Tennessee River, opening a new drive to capture Chattanooga, a new crisis was brewing.

The response was to send James Longstreet's Corps, two divisions strong to help Bragg. However, when Longstreet reached the scene, Bragg had already been forced out of Chattanooga, and was prepared to give battle in North Georgia.

That battle, of course, was Chickamauga. Only half of Longstreet's troops participated, with the general not arriving until late on September 19th, after two days of fighting had concluded. After a brief midnight conference, Bragg granted Longstreet command of half the army. Longstreet's attack the next day proved devastating, and the defeated Federals fell back into Chattanooga.

That moment of discussion in the late hours of September 19-20 proved to be the high point of Bragg's and Longstreet's wartime relationship. Henceforth, almost every moment of interaction between the two men would be characterized by misunderstanding, recrimination, and acrimony. It would be one of the more fateful command relationships of the war, with negative repercussions for the cause of Confederate independence.

This relationship fascinates me, and not just because I believe it to be one of those "turning point" moments.

Longstreet's history of controversy, tainted by fellow Confederates' efforts to scapegoat him for several blunders, real and imagined, complicates modern efforts to untangle fact from speculation. It didn't help that Longstreet experienced a popularity boom beginning in the mid-1970s when Michael Shaara cast him as a sympathetic character in his seminal, Pulitzer-prize-winning Civil War novel *Killer Angels*. A sudden spate of Longstreet fans produced the inevitable backlash as the opposition pushed back on Shaara's portrayal.

The pro-Longstreet crowd got a statue of him erected at Gettysburg, the only Confederate general so honored there besides Lee. Even that statue became controversial.

I find that Longstreet's detractors come in several flavors. Fans of Stonewall Jackson tend to dislike Longstreet, while those who favor the Western Theater seem to resent Longstreet as an interloper, all the more so for his role at Chickamauga.

But what of the real James Longstreet? Where should he fit into the war's cast of characters?

Through the following paragraphs, I intend to explore Longstreet's western experience, and where it fits in Civil War historiography.

Westward Ho!

The decision to reinforce Bragg came after many debates, and after every other expedient had been exhausted. While President Davis believed the Confederacy needed to use interior lines to achieve localized concentrations of force, that theory did not extend to Virginia. Generally, troops flowed into Virginia from other theaters, not the other way around. By the spring of 1863, a growing group of soldiers and politicians felt that Davis was neglecting the Western Theater. These men included Louis T. Wigfall, Joseph E. Johnston, P. G. T. Beauregard, and James Longstreet.

In May 1863, after Lee's victory at Chancellorsville, these men began pressing to shift troops westward, responding to Ulysses S. Grant's worrisome operations around Vicksburg. Since half of Longstreet's Corps had not fought at Chancellorsville, due to operating near Suffolk, Virginia, the idea was to send one or two divisions under Longstreet to Mississippi or Tennessee.[1]

---

1 Archer Jones, *Civil War Command and Strategy,* (New York: 1992), 173-180.

In Richmond, Longstreet broached the idea of a strategic concentration in Tennessee to Confederate Secretary of War James Seddon on May 6, 1863. He argued that he take Hood's and Pickett's Divisions, and join Bragg, while Joseph E. Johnston brought troops from Mississippi. This combined force could assail William S. Rosecrans's Union Army near Nashville. Johnston, as the senior man, would have overall command. Once Rosecrans was defeated, the Rebels could move north or west. Either way, Grant's operations would cease.[2]

Davis and Lee resisted this plan, arguing for a concentration of force under Lee. General Lee wanted to force an offensive into Pennsylvania. Lee prevailed. The result was Gettysburg.

In June, almost as a footnote to this decision, Lee marched north. There was some discussion of bringing P. G. T. Beauregard to Virginia, with enough reinforcements to add a fourth corps to Lee's Army. Longstreet favored this plan. It came to nothing, though it makes for a fascinating alternative to the Gettysburg campaign.[3]

Longstreet's support for the Tennessee concentration or of bringing Beauregard to Virginia is interesting. In each case, Longstreet was not necessarily agitating for an independent command. He was junior to both Johnston and Beauregard. This fact undermines the idea that Longstreet had become overly ambitious, creating scenarios that would expand his independence and authority.

Before Gettysburg, the South worked to some extent from a position of strength, at least in the east. With Hooker defeated, Lee held the initiative. After Gettysburg, everything changed. Lee lost his Pennsylvania gamble, Vicksburg and one Confederate army were gone, and Bragg, outnumbered, could not retain a hold on Middle Tennessee.

The decision to send Longstreet west came at the last minute after Knoxville fell to one Federal Army and Chattanooga to another. The resulting concentration, including Longstreet's Corps and a large number of troops from East Tennessee and Mississippi, came more from desperation than design.

---

2 James Longstreet, *From Manassas to Appomattox, Memoirs of the Civil War In America* (Philadelphia: 1896), 327.

3 *OR* 27, 3, 925.

Perhaps the most interesting aspect of this discussion is found in Longstreet's various communications with Joseph E. Johnston, which was maintained after Johnston left the Virginia Army in May 1862. By the time Johnston recovered from his battle wound in October, Lee was in command of the Army of Northern Virginia. Johnston then headed west to help "co-ordinate" affairs there. Longstreet also made the interesting offer to yield his position as corps commander to Johnston, who would then serve under Lee. "I have no doubt," said Longstreet, "that you would command this army by spring."[4]

At other times, Longstreet offered to go west and serve under Johnston. In September, as he was departing, Longstreet penned a 15-page missive to Davis, urging for a larger concentration, with Johnston in command. As late as March 1864, Longstreet again proposed the same strategic western concentration under Johnston, who headed up the Army of Tennessee at Dalton. He wanted to use his men and Beauregard's force. The idea was to raise Johnston's numbers to 80,000 and seize the initiative.

It is clear that Longstreet was reluctant to serve under Bragg. At one point, Longstreet suggested to Seddon and Davis that he take three brigades from the Richmond defenses (about 6,000 men), going west in Bragg's stead. It would allow Bragg to come east, and take command of the First Corps under Lee. Longstreet seemed to favor such "swaps," however unrealistic they might be. Before heading west in September 1863, Longstreet informed Lee that he wished Lee were coming west with him to take overall command. That, too, seemed unlikely. Lee, for one, did not want any part of that plan.

Writing to Confederate Senator Louis T. Wigfall, in September 1863, Longstreet elucidated his opinion of Bragg: "I don't think that I should be under Bragg, and would fight against it if I saw any hope of getting anyone in the responsible position except myself."[5]

This statement has been widely interpreted as Longstreet's clearest statement of his naked ambition. Personally, I am not sold. Given how hard

---

4 Longstreet to Johnston, October 6, 1862, Longstreet Papers, Duke University, Raleigh, NC.

5 William Garrett Piston, *Lee's Tarnished Lieutenant, James Longstreet and his Place in Southern History* (Athens, GA: 1987), 68.

and often Longstreet lobbied for the man he wanted to see in that job, Joe Johnston, it seems unlikely that this lobbying was just a smokescreen.

In the following sentence of that letter to Wigfall, Longstreet admitted that he knew exactly how such a fight would be interpreted: "If I should make any decided opposition the world might say that I was desirous of a position which would give me fame. So I conclude that I may be pardoned if I yield my principle under the particular circumstances."

The evidence of Longstreet's supposed overweening, destructive ambition seems sparse. The evidence that Longstreet did not trust Bragg's generalship is stronger, and by the fall of 1863, many other generals, southern politicians, and civilians did not trust Bragg's generalship. Many even served in the Army of Tennessee.

The evidence that James Longstreet wished to be serving under Joseph E. Johnston is perhaps the strongest of all.[6]

On to Nashville?

Longstreet's move to Georgia took nine days. Some of the trailing elements in his corps, such as Anderson's Brigade and several Georgian soldiers, arrived much later after returning from much-needed leave after two years. The leading elements arrived on September 17th. Three of his nine brigades saw combat on the 19th, under John Bell Hood's command. Longstreet arrived at Catoosa Platform that afternoon, but he did not reach Bragg's headquarters until 11:00 p.m.[7]

Braxton Bragg promptly gave Longstreet a wing command, consisting of six divisions—his own two, plus four from the Army of Tennessee. Longstreet's mission was to support Leonidas Polk's wing when that officer attacked at dawn on September 20.

Polk, of course, ran late. Longstreet spent the morning organizing his command, attacking around 11:00 a.m. He achieved a staggering success,

---

6 See Piston, *Lee's Tarnished Lieutenant*, 66-68; and Jeffry D. Wert, *General James Longstreet, The Confederacy's Most Controversial Soldier, A Biography* (New York: 1993), 300-303, for examination of Longstreet's motives.

7 Longstreet, *From Manassas to Appomattox*, 438.

aided partly by a fortuitous Federal blunder committed on his front at the Brotherton farm.

Near 3:00 p.m., Longstreet and Bragg conferred. Longstreet reported his success and asked for reinforcements. To Longstreet's later recollection, he found Bragg angry and pessimistic, based on the failings of Polk's wing. Polk had repeatedly assaulted Union Gen. George Thomas's defenses around Kelly Field, each time being repulsed. Longstreet also recorded that Bragg seemed defeated and believed the army was as well. He didn't want to hear of Longstreet's victory. Longstreet first described this meeting to Daniel Harvey Hill in the 1870s and, in his 1904 memoir. Subsequent events certainly influenced Longstreet's memory of that meeting.[8]

Whatever happened, this encounter marked a turning point in Bragg and Longstreet's relationship. During the first approximately 17 hours in which Longstreet and Bragg served together, the Army of Tennessee won the most complete battlefield success ever achieved by that force. From there, things went steadily downhill.

Discord

In the aftermath of Chickamauga, an uncertainty gripped Bragg and his generals. Early on, it appeared Rosecrans might abandon Chattanooga, falling back to his railhead at Stevenson, Alabama. As the days passed, and it was clear the Federals would remain, entrenching furiously, the uncertainty gave way to frustration.

In one aspect, the reaction within each army, both the victors and vanquished, was similar: a purge ensued.

The defeated Yankees shed one divisional commander, two corps commanders, and, ultimately, Rosecrans. On the southern side, Bragg retained command, but rid himself of a divisional commander, Thomas C. Hindman, and two corps commanders, Leonidas Polk and D. H. Hill. He also reshuffled his organization, hoping to minimize the effectiveness of his

---

8 David A. Powell, *The Chickamauga Campaign. Glory or the Grave: The Breakthrough, the Union Collapse, and the Defense of Horseshoe Ridge, September 20, 1863* (El Dorado Hills, CA: 2015), 455.

remaining critics. Bragg created such havoc within his army that President Jefferson Davis would travel west to try and resolve the crisis.

There has been a tendency among some historians to view the post-Chickamauga discord within the Army of Tennessee as a power struggle between James Longstreet and Braxton Bragg—fueled, in part, by Longstreet's ambition. I view this as a mistaken interpretation.

It was really a power struggle between Bragg and his principal subordinate, Episcopal Bishop & Lt. Gen. Leonidas Polk. This struggle began in the spring of 1862. It blew up into the army's first command crisis the following year in the spring of 1863, the result of fallout from both the Perryville and the Murfreesboro campaigns. Much to Bragg's frustration, Polk, though popular among the men, proved consistently incapable as a commander. The Bishop paid little attention to military discipline, relying instead on the fact that he was a West Point classmate and personal friend of Jefferson Davis to paper over any missteps.

Bragg had nearly been relieved of command in March 1863, saved only by Joseph E. Johnston's reluctance to assume that position, thus appearing to scheme against Bragg for his own gain. However, Davis's decision to retain Bragg while sustaining Polk, resolved none of the Army's core issues.[9]

This time, Bragg intended the showdown to be final. As he told his wife, Elise: "Again I have to complain of Genl Polk for not obeying my orders, and I am resolved to bring the matter to an issue this time. One of us must stand or fall."

On September 22, Bragg dictated a tersely worded formal note to the Bishop: "GENERAL: The General commanding desires that you will make as early as practicable a report explanatory of your failure to attack the enemy at daylight on Sunday last in obedience to orders."

Polk, fully understanding what was coming, immediately began marshaling resources. On the 23rd, he visited D. H. Hill and James Longstreet, soliciting support. Polk intended to write to Jefferson Davis and wanted to name Hill as a supporter. Polk also wanted Longstreet to write to Davis, an independent corroboration of his criticism. Hill, certain he was about to be "scapegoated," agreed to let Polk list him as in agreement. Longstreet

---

9 Thomas Lawrence Connelly, *Autumn of Glory, The Army of Tennessee, 1862-1865,* (Baton Rouge, LA: 1971), 85.

chose not to write Davis directly. However, on September 26th, he penned a lengthy letter to Confederate Secretary of War James G. Seddon, knowing Davis would see any such letter within minutes of it arriving.

Unaware of Polk's plot, Bragg struck first. On September 25, in a private letter to President Davis, Bragg detailed the problem officers. In McLemore's Cove, wrote Bragg, Hill and Hindman "fail[ed] to execute" their orders. On September 20th, the fault lay with Polk. "Genl Polk . . . is luxurious in his habits, rises late, moves slowly, and always conceives his own plans the best. He has proved an injury to us on every field where I have been associated with him."

And Hill? "Genl Hill is despondent, dull, slow, and tho gallant personally, is always in a state of apprehension, and upon the most flimsy pretext makes each report of the enemy about him as to keep up constant apprehension, and require constant reinforcements. His open and constant croaking would demoralize any command in the world. He does not hesitate at all times and in all places to declare our cause lost."[10]

Bragg reserved praise for four officers; Patrick Cleburne, the badly wounded John B. Hood, James Longstreet, and Simon B. Buckner.

Polk's letter to Davis warned of Bragg's "incapacitation," suggested his incapable leadership, and asked Davis to "send Lee or some other" to replace Bragg.

Longstreet's letter to Seddon was scathing. After setting forth a litany of detailed complaints, Longstreet closed with a sweeping indictment of Braxton Bragg. The head of the Army of Tennessee, he observed, "has done but one thing he ought to have done since I joined this army. That was to order the attack upon the 20th. All other things that he has done, he ought not to have done."

Polk and Longstreet also wrote separate letters to Robert E. Lee, appealing for him to come west and replace Bragg. Lee declined.

On September 28, having launched his covert salvo against Bragg, Polk provided the demanded explanation. Unhesitatingly, the Bishop threw his ally, D. H. Hill, under the proverbial omnibus. In a detailed response, Polk

10 David A. Powell, *The Chickamauga Campaign, Barren Victory: The Retreat Into Chattanooga, the Confederate Pursuit, and the Aftermath of the Battle, September 21 to October 20, 1863* (El Dorado Hills, CA: 2016), 109-111.

listed multiple points where Hill was to blame for the delayed attack. Bragg remained unswayed. On September 29, Bragg suspended Polk and Hindman. General Hindman was already absent, recovering from a neck wound, while Polk departed for Atlanta. A court-martial now seemed in the offing.

Longstreet and Hill remained with the army. However, when Hill saw Polk's explanation of the September 20th failure, he was upset to discover that he was the main target of Polk's blame-finding. Polk's departure resolved nothing. Bragg determined to squash all opposition, which, only hardened the dissension among Bragg's remaining senior officers.

Chief of Staff William Mackall foresaw what was to come. On September 29, in a private letter to Joseph E. Johnston, Mackall predicted that "if Bragg carries out his projects, there will be great dissatisfaction. I have told him so, but he is hard to persuade when in prosperity, and I do not think my warning will be heeded until too late."

Bragg and Davis exchanged lengthy telegrams over the first few days in October. Davis said that Bragg had exceeded his authority by suspending Polk. As commander, Bragg could arrest and prefer charges, but not unilaterally relieve officers, which was the president's prerogative. Bragg suggested swapping Polk for Hardee, then in Alabama, which would come up again later. Davis was worried about the suspension of two officers, while leaving Hill alone, which seemed like selective judgment.

From this turmoil stemmed the infamous "Petition." This document was prepared as an indictment of Bragg's performance. It informed President Davis of several items. First, that the Army of Tennessee was in a state of "complete paralysis," allowing Rosecrans to retreat safely into Chattanooga. Second, the Confederates needed reinforcements. Finally, a request that Bragg be relieved of command for the "sufficient reason" that "the condition of his health unfits him for the command of an army in the field."

Who wrote it? In 1890, William Polk, Leonidas's son, provided a copy for the official records, which, he wrote, was "supposed to have been written by [Simon B.] Buckner." Another suggested author was Daniel Harvey Hill, who denied authorship but later confirmed that he "signed it willingly." In his memoir, written eight years after Hill's death, Longstreet stated that Hill confessed he had indeed authored it. Whatever the origin, Hill kept it at his headquarters, where several officers eventually signed it. These included Longstreet and Hill, as the army's ranking corps commanders;

divisional commanders Bushrod R. Johnson, William Preston, and Patrick R. Cleburne; and six brigade commanders. John C. Breckinridge declined to sign, arguing that his well-known pre-existing troubles with Bragg would only prejudice the document.

The petition's existence was an open secret. Trouble was in the wind, and the whole army now talked about discord in the senior ranks. On October 5th, Brig. Gen. James R. Chesnut, Davis's personal aide and envoy in the west, telegraphed the alarm from Atlanta: "Your immediate presence in this army is urgently demanded."[11]

The showdown was at hand.

Davis Hurries West

President Jefferson Davis departed Richmond on October 6, 1863, to Atlanta. James Chesnut's urgent appeal had borne fruit. Davis boarded, passing through Petersburg by 8:30 a.m. He made short speeches in Weldon and Wilson, North Carolina, along the way. Two aides, William Preston Johnston and G. W. C. Lee accompanied him. Davis also brought Lt. Gen. John C. Pemberton, the man who had surrendered Vicksburg. Davis had not lost faith in Pemberton, hoping to find him a command in Bragg's army.

Davis reached Atlanta on October 8. There, he met with Polk. He also had a chance to read a follow-up letter written by Polk on October 6th, which he either received while en route or upon arriving in Atlanta. Polk reiterated all the main points of his quarrel with Bragg: the failed orders, Hill's failings, and Bragg's own inadequacies. Davis attempted to reassure Polk that any pending charges would come to naught, attempting to convince Polk to return with him. Polk refused. On the subject of Bragg, Polk remained harsh. As he stated in his October 6th letter: "No Sir, General Bragg did not know what had happened. He let us down as usual and allowed the fruits of this great but sanguinary victory to pass from him by the most criminal incapacity, for there are positions in which weakness is wickedness."

---

11 Powell, *Barren Victory,* 112-115.

On October 9th, Davis rode the Western & Atlantic rails northward to the Army of Tennessee. According to the newspapers, Generals Longstreet and Breckinridge rode with him, having arrived to meet him the day before. Certainly, the anti-Bragg men hustled to get their licks in.

After all this personal discussion, it is hard to imagine how Jefferson Davis could be so out of touch concerning the animosity that divided Bragg and most of his senior commanders. But, out of touch he was. A rude awakening awaited.

That evening, Davis met privately with Bragg. Not all the details of this discussion were preserved, but two facts stand out. First, Bragg offered to resign, which Davis refused. Davis probably pled Polk's case again, and unwilling to back down, Bragg offered to step aside. It was a gamble, but a calculated risk on Bragg's part. It was unlikely that Davis, having sustained Bragg previously, would dump him after Chickamauga. Davis then offered John C. Pemberton instead of Polk.

If additional evidence were needed of Davis's obliviousness to the army's mood, this hit the target. Though Bragg averred that Pemberton was "as true and gallant as any man in our service," he tactfully informed Davis that no division would accept the man who surrendered Vicksburg as their commander. It fell to William Mackall to inform a forlorn Pemberton that he was not wanted.

That session concluded, Davis next chaired a group meeting between the army commander and his four corps commanders, Longstreet, Hill, Buckner, and Benjamin F. Cheatham, standing in for Polk. What ensued must have been mortifying. Davis asked each man, in Bragg's presence, what they thought of the army's commander and future operations. In his memoir, Longstreet recalled feeling so embarrassed that he tried to duck the question, but Davis insisted.

With Longstreet leading, each man expressed dissatisfaction. Hill, who had been sitting in a corner trying to look "inconspicuous," came last. According to Longstreet, everyone agreed that Bragg "could be of greater service elsewhere than at the head of the Army of Tennessee." Davis listened carefully but gave no indication of his thoughts.

For a few days, uncertainty prevailed. Buckner told Longstreet that he thought Bragg was on the way out. Conversely, Mackall believed that Bragg seemed buoyed; "evidently [he] thinks he has the Prest. on his side."

The next day, Davis toured the Confederate lines, giving speeches and holding private discussions. One of those sessions was with Longstreet. In his 1896 memoir, Longstreet advanced the controversial claim that Davis offered him Bragg's job, but that he declined. This claim, unsupported by other sources, came almost certainly from either a case of faulty memory or of outright ego-padding. At the time of their meeting, Davis had already decided to sustain Bragg, not replace him. Then, in a more accurate passage, Longstreet again asked for Joe Johnston to come take command.

If the Army of Tennessee could be combined with the troops in Alabama and Mississippi, Longstreet reasoned, all under Johnston's direction; "I said that under him I could cheerfully work in any position."

Davis seemed angered. Longstreet had misread his audience. Davis and Johnston were semi-publicly feuding over who was responsible for Vicksburg. With Pemberton in tow, Davis was clearly siding against Johnston. Did Longstreet, a regular correspondent of Johnston's, not know this? In any case, Davis seemed so offended that Longstreet offered to resign, or transfer to the Trans-Mississippi. With so many offering resignations, Davis rejected both suggestions.

On October 12th, Davis ended the suspense. Bragg would stay. In what was clearly a face-saving move for everyone, Polk would transfer to Mississippi, while William J. Hardee would return to the army in his place. The charges against Polk and Hindman would be dropped. Once again, Davis displayed a sense of naiveté when he confided that he hoped Hardee would heal the breach between Bragg and his senior generals. It was a sentiment no one outside of Richmond shared.

D. H. Hill was also shown the door. On October 15th, Hill received orders sending him to Richmond. Bragg charged that Hill "weakens the morale and military tone of his command." Outraged, Hill asked for a court-martial, or a full explanation of why he was being relieved. He never got either.

Additional changes followed. Buckner was reduced to divisional command. Cheatham's old division shuffled, breaking up what Bragg viewed as an anti-Bragg power block. Longstreet would remain, but he and Bragg would have as little to do with each other going forward as possible.[12]

12 For Davis's visit, see Powell, *Barren Victory*, 113-115, and Connelly, *Autumn of Glory*, 235-246.

Midnight Madness

Trapped in Chattanooga, October 1863 was a lean month for the Union Army of the Cumberland. Joe Wheeler's Rebel cavalry kicked off the month by destroying a Union supply train of nearly 800 wagons on Walden Ridge. Though chased away, more trouble lay ahead. Rain fell. Rivers and creeks rose to flood stage. Roads were churned to mud. The 60-mile round-a-bout trip from Chattanooga to Bridgeport became all but impassable. By mid-month, it was obvious that either the Federals open up the Tennessee River to bring in supplies or they would have to leave. Starvation was another option.

"The Cracker Line" came as the answer to the Union's resource woes, transporting the supplies to Kelly's Ferry, bridging the Tennessee twice, first at Brown's Ferry and then opposite Chattanooga proper, to relieve the supply pinch. At 3:00 a.m. on October 27, a Union brigade in 50 pontoon boats floated downstream to Brown's Ferry, seized the landing in a *coup de main*, and driving off the two Confederate regiments defending that site. They erected a bridge, and soon a second brigade crossed.

On October 28, a second Union column appeared. It was Joseph Hooker's combined XI/XII Corps command, marching from Bridgeport to link with the Brown's Ferry force. By that afternoon, 10,000 Federals occupied Lookout Valley, the bulk camped around Brown's Ferry. Hooker left one small division, around 1,700 men, of the XII Corps at the rail junction of Wauhatchie to guard the entrance to Running Water Canyon.

When Braxton Bragg heard about the Union crossing at Brown's Ferry, he decided to personally examine the state of affairs. Early on the 28th, he ventured from his headquarters on Missionary Ridge, meeting James Longstreet on Lookout Mountain. Bragg, angry that the Federals had secured a lodgment, wanted Longstreet to counter-attack and drive the Brown's Ferry Federals back into the Tennessee River. The two generals still conferred when a courier brought word of Hooker's appearance in the valley below.

From a vantage on the western brow of Lookout, Bragg and Longstreet gaped at Hooker's column as it joined the Brown's Ferry force. Bragg, already furious that the Federals had achieved a lodgment at the Ferry, now fumed as more blue troops established control over the rest of the valley. Unless they could be driven away, the siege of Chattanooga was over.

How had the Confederates lost Lookout Valley so easily? Why were there so few Confederates in the valley to begin with? Longstreet placed one brigade there, under Brig. Gen. Evander Law. Half of the command was inopportunely withdrawn just before the Yankees struck.

There has been a great deal of historical debate over the exact reason for this lack of a significant Confederate presence west of the mountain. Most historical commentators blame Longstreet's carelessness, arguing that he was too busy pouting over his supposed failure to supplant Bragg. In most analyses, Longstreet is portrayed as neglectful and out of touch with what was happening on his own front.

I find this argument unconvincing. There are two very good reasons why the Confederate presence west of Lookout was confined to a token force. These reasons tend to be dismissed or are overlooked by modern analysis.

First, there is the matter of logistics. Bragg's Army of Tennessee lacked an adequacy of wagons *before* all the reinforcements started to arrive. None of the new troops brought transports with them. Those wagons were promised to arrive later, but few ever did, and certainly not by October's end. Fortunately, Bragg's railhead now extended to Chickamauga Station. With most of his army on Missionary Ridge, hauling supplies to them and to the men occupying Chattanooga Valley was manageable. However, the overall capacity of the railroad was strained to meet the daily needs of 70,000 men.

It proved even more difficult to supply the men atop Lookout Mountain. Fortunately, holding Lookout's north and west faces required fewer troops, which eased that strain, but a strain it remained. Throughout the siege of Chattanooga, the Rebels never held the Mountain with more than 5-6,000 men.

What about those troops sent to hold Lookout Valley? Supplying those forces proved to be exceedingly difficult. Why? Moccasin Bend. Within days of the Union retreat into Chattanooga, William Rosecrans dispatched two artillery batteries to hold the hills on Moccasin Bend. An infantry brigade supported those guns, but the 18th Ohio and 10th Indiana Batteries were the keys to constraining Rebel movements in and out of the valley.

These ten artillery pieces; six 3-inch Ordnance rifles from the 18th Ohio and four 10-pound Parrott rifles from the Indiana 10th, later augmented by two 20-pound Parrotts, collectively dominated the only road between Chattanooga and Lookout Valleys. This road, the Wauhatchie Pike ran across the northern shoulder of Lookout Mountain. The road lay within easy cannon-shot of Moccasin Bend. Accurate Union gunnery soon made daylight transits impossible, and nighttime crossings became perilous.

Denied virtually all use of the Pike, the Confederates faced severe logistics challenges. The next road into Lookout Mountain's rock-walled western escarpment lay 20 or more miles to the south, in Johnson's Crook, on the road leading to Trenton. Any Confederate wagon train hauling supplies into Lookout Valley from Chickamauga Station via this route would face an arduous 100-mile round-trip, climbing and then descending the mountain each way. This was impossible given Bragg's limited and much-dilapidated rolling stock.

The primary reason why no more than one brigade of Confederates ever held Lookout Valley was simple. Any larger force placed there would eventually starve.

The second reason was that Bragg and Longstreet also differed on the nature of the next Union threat. Longstreet believed, even after Union troops swarmed up the riverbank at Brown's Ferry, that the most likely Federal effort to seize Lookout Mountain would come from the south. There Union troops could ascend the palisade well south of the Mountain's tip, through Johnson's Crook again, and drive north along the plateau. Though he understood this danger, Bragg dismissed it. However, Longstreet's assessment contained valid, unarguable points. A successful Union attack against the north or west faces of Lookout would be exceedingly difficult. Even the Craven House plateau could be held by a brigade or so.

But if the Federals ascended the mountain at Johnson's Crook, and then turned north as Longstreet feared, defending against that threat would require Longstreet's entire corps. Who then would be left to hold Chattanooga Valley?

This was not mere speculation on Longstreet's part. When the Federals maneuvered Bragg out of Chattanooga back in September, Thomas's XIV Corps did exactly that. Later, when Bragg ordered Confederate cavalry commander Joseph Wheeler to capture the summit of Lookout Mountain, he approached from the south.

Additionally, if Lookout Mountain were to fall, any force placed in Lookout Valley would be completely cut off. Longstreet could lose the Mountain, the Valley, and perhaps most of his corps in one single bad day. Not only did more troops in the Valley mean fewer troops to hold the already-overtaxed lines atop the Mountain, but it potentially represented a large bag of prisoners for the Union.

In short, the southern approach was the most logical and likely direction for Grant to attack. It certainly promised the best chance of success. Therefore, Longstreet focused his primary attention on that threat.

However, Longstreet was proven wrong. The Federal commanders opted for the more daring course. But that did not mean Longstreet was careless. It is very hard to see how he could have placed more strength in the valley without gravely weakening his defenses, especially considering the existing Confederate supply limitations.

With the Federals now firmly ensconced in that same valley, Bragg demanded a response. He expected Longstreet to counter-attack with his entire corps and even authorized Longstreet to use William H. T. Walker's Division of Hindman's Corps, giving the commander up to four divisions, or 20,000 men to use. Further, Bragg expected the main blow to land against the large Union force now securing Brown's Ferry, driving the Union bridgehead back into the river. With that, Bragg returned to his headquarters.

Once again, the fundamental flaw in Bragg's thinking was logistics. How was Longstreet to move four divisions over the Wauhatchie Pike, in full view of the Union artillery, under fire, and deploy? The Confederates might be able to move a single division during the course of a single night, but not an entire corps. Even if he could move that many troops quickly, how could Longstreet sustain a force that size in Lookout Valley once it arrived?

Instead, Longstreet settled for the possible. He ordered Micah Jenkins to take the four brigades of Hood's division—5,000 men—over the pike once darkness fell on October 28th. Rather than attacking the estimated 10,000 Federals defending Brown's Ferry, Longstreet instructed Jenkins to assault the smaller, unfortified Union command at Wauhatchie Junction. Their goal was to capture the large wagon train accompanying Geary's command.

It took Jenkins several hours to move his command into position. Two brigades, under Law, headed to the right, ordered to hold a hill overlooking Brown's Ferry Road. Their mission was to block any Union reinforcements that might be sent to help Geary. Jenkins assigned Law this command because he was the second ranking brigadier, and because he already knew the terrain. A third brigade, Benning's Georgians, was detailed to guard another hill just south of Law's position. Benning could then defend the bridge over Lookout Creek, Jenkins's only path of retreat.

This left only Jenkins's brigade of South Carolinians, currently under Col. John Bratton's command, to make the main assault. The odds were even: Bratton carried about 1,700 men into action, roughly equal to Geary's strength at Wauhatchie.

The battle was a confused affair, which was hardly surprising, given the conditions. It took Jenkins longer than expected to move and deploy his command, which led Longstreet to cancel the whole operation. However, it was too late as the orders reached Jenkins after the fighting began. Bratton's men achieved some initial success, but Geary's Federals mounted a stalwart defense. Geary lost his son, a lieutenant in an artillery battery, which left Bratton's initial effort short of routing the Union command. Bratton rallied for a second charge when word came to retreat.

Law, commanding his and Robertson's brigades on what would become known as Smith's Hill had his own night fight with the Union XI Corps. The men moved south towards Wauhatchie in response to hearing the fighting there. Law resisted an initial assault, however, a second Union effort broke part of his line atop the hill. Law then ordered a retreat, having received word that Federals were manuevering around his southern flank to interpose themselves between his line and the bridge over Lookout Creek. A third Union charge all but routed the rear-guard elements of Law's brigade as they filed off the hill.

Jenkins would blame Law for retreating too early. Law, in turn, insisted he retreated only after Bratton's men withdrew. In his account, Longstreet charged Law's men with "abandoning" their position to the enemy, which caused Jenkins to break off his own action. Jenkins' order instructing Bratton to fall back seems to have come before Law's retreat, though Bratton's South Carolinians did not precede Law's people back across Lookout Creek.

For many, the entire affair was disappointing. Longstreet believed it was a forlorn hope, while Bragg felt that Longstreet flagrantly disobeyed his orders. Jenkins, in his first taste of command, found failure instead of victory, and Law thought the attack was foolish from the start.

Recriminations a-plenty would follow.[13]

13 For the best discussion of Wauhatchie, see Douglas R. Cubbison, "Midnight Engagement: John Geary's White Star Division at Wauhatchie," *Civil War Regiments,* vol. 3, no. 2 (1993) 70-104.

A Parting of Ways

On October 30, Bragg dispatched an angry telegram to Jefferson Davis, then in Savannah, headed back to Richmond. Bragg outlined his frustrations with Longstreet, and the lack of effective action in Lookout Valley. On the 27th, wrote Bragg, Longstreet was ordered to attack with three divisions. No attack followed. "That night, . . . Longstreet asked for another division as a support. . . . It was given. He informed me he [Longstreet] should attack with one brigade. I ordered him not to do so with less than a division. He moved a division to the vicinity, but attacked with one brigade. . . . We have thus lost our important position on the left."

The following day, after another round of acrimonious dispatches between Bragg and Longstreet, the outraged commander sent a follow-up to Davis: "Further correspondence of a more disrespectful and insubordinate character is received from the general. Copies will be sent."

Davis must have been dismayed. The Confederate President had strong views on what *should* have occurred once the Federals crossed the Tennessee. On October 29, before he even knew of Longstreet's repulse at Wauhatchie, Davis detailed those ideas: "As you have a shorter and better road . . . [between Chattanooga and] Bridgeport, that you will be able to anticipate him, and strike with the advantage of fighting him in detail."

As we have seen, this was an unrealistic expectation, given the Confederate logistical limitations. Either Bragg failed to fully explain those limits, or perhaps Bragg himself did not fully realize the extent of those limits. If the latter is true, it was a damning indictment of Bragg's own negligence.

So far, Longstreet had largely escaped any consequences of his opposition to Bragg. Other generals were relieved or re-assigned, but Davis generally preferred to smooth troubles rather than confront them. In that same October 29th dispatch, Davis explained: "The removal of officers of high rank, or important changes in organizations, usually work evil, if done in the presence of the enemy. . . . I prefer to postpone the consideration of any further removal of general officers from their commands, and relying on the self-sacrificing spirit which you [Bragg] have so often exhibited, must leave you to combat the difficulties arising from the disappointment or discontent of officers by such gentle means as may turn them aside." [14]

In other words: 'General Bragg, you figure it out. I've got a war to run.'

However, by November 1st, and with Bragg's latest complaints, Davis suddenly seemed more fully in Bragg's corner. The botched fight at Wauhatchie, said Davis, "is a bitter disappointment. . . . Such disobedience of orders and disastrous failure as you describe cannot be consistently overlooked. I suppose you have received the explanation due the Government, and I shall be pleased if one satisfactory has been given."

Longstreet seemed on the brink of losing his command. However, it did not happen. Somewhere between October 29th and November 3rd, Longstreet and Bragg seemed to work through some of their difficulties. Bragg showed Longstreet Davis's October 29th letter, and Longstreet withdrew his "disrespectful" and "insubordinate character" communications. Additionally, Hardee and Howell Cobb's arrival, which were designed to heal the ongoing rifts between the officers assisted in working past the disruptions.

Cobb was a former Speaker of the U. S. House of Representatives, a former Secretary of the Treasury under President Buchanan, a former president of the Confederate Provisional Congress, and a Confederate major general. He had Davis's ear, carrying sufficient gravitas in the political and military realms as to gain everyone's attention. In the fall of 1863, Cobb commanded the Georgia State Troops, whose mission included protecting Bragg's lifeline, the Western & Atlantic Railroad.

Cobb and Hardee arrived on the 1st or 2nd of November. Cobb spent "several days" with the Army of Tennessee. In a confidential letter to Davis written on November 6th, Cobb described the current state. "It is very unfortunate," Cobb admitted, "that there does not exist more cordiality & confidence between Genl Bragg and Genl Longstreet—If that difficulty could be overcome, I believe all would be well." More encouragingly, however, "I have reason to believe that the feeling is better than it has been."

---

14 See Connelly, *Autumn of Glory,* 263; Lynda Lasswell Crist, Kenneth H. Williams, and Peggy L. Dillard, eds. *The Papers of Jefferson Davis* 14 vols. (Baton Rouge, LA, and Houston, TX: 1971-2015), 10: 35-45.

Hardee proved his worth. Hardee, said Cobb, was "laboring earnestly (and I think successfully) to bring about cordiality & confidence where there had been the greatest need for it."[15]

Besides, there might be a better solution to heal the rift between Bragg and Longstreet, first proposed by Davis in his October 29th letter. Bragg "might advantageously assign General Longstreet with his two divisions to the task of expelling Burnside, and thus place him in position . . . to hasten or delay his return to . . . General Lee."

Back in mid-October, Bragg dispatched a division toward Knoxville. It was under the command of Maj. Gen. Carter L. Stevenson, who assumed control over those elements of Joe Wheeler's cavalry corps operating in East Tennessee. Stevenson's mission was to prevent Burnside from joining with Rosecrans, and forcing the Federals back toward Knoxville if possible. Stevenson's weak division, which numbered less than 4,000, and adding another 2,000 with the cavalry, could do little more.

These Confederates won a small but heartening victory at Philadelphia, Tennessee, on October 20th, killing or capturing 479 Federals with about 100 Confederate casualties. Sensing an opportunity, on October 22nd, Bragg decided to reinforce Stevenson with a second division under John K. Jackson, numbering another 6,000 troops. Now came Davis's idea of sending Longstreet into East Tennessee.

Exclusive of cavalry, on October 31st, Bragg's army numbered just under 53,000 present for duty. Around 10,000 were in East Tennessee. Longstreet and his two divisions numbered just over 11,000 troops. If Bragg swapped Longstreet for Stevenson, the net loss in combat power would be negligible. Even better, following Hardee from Mississippi were at least two more infantry brigades, roughly another 3,000 to 3,500 men, so even without Longstreet, Bragg's forces would increase slightly.

The Confederates understood that large numbers of Federals were either headed for or already in Chattanooga. In addition to Hooker's column, now in Lookout Valley another 25,000 Yankees made their way from Grant's old command, the Union Army of the Tennessee, now led by Sherman. Without including Burnside's men, Grant would soon have perhaps 85,000 men, and Bragg would be outnumbered two to one.

15 Crist, *Papers of Jefferson Davis,* 10: 54-57.

Over the years, Davis and Bragg have come under a great deal of criticism in sending Longstreet away. Even Ulysses S. Grant leveled scornful remarks at Davis's supposed "military genius" in his memoirs. However, the concept was not devoid of strategic promise. Outnumbered armies have been beating larger foes since ancient times; attacking disparate or isolated elements of the enemy force with locally superior numbers, one after another. Militarily, the term is "defeat in detail."

But doing so successfully requires not just a better strategic sense. Such victories also require consummate operational skill, superior timing, and superior execution. Was the Army of Tennessee capable of that expertise?

Knoxville, and Huzzah!

On November 3rd, Bragg, Longstreet, Hardee, and the Army of Tennessee's other senior officers gathered at Bragg's headquarters to discuss their next move. In what by now should come as no surprise, accounts vary as to the exact details of this conference.

Longstreet opened with a plan that aligned with his current worries. He proposed crossing the Tennessee River near Bridgeport, and through threatening or destroying the Army of the Cumberland's forward supply base, compel a retreat from Chattanooga. In theory, this was the soundest strategy, but the idea foundered on the by-now obvious logistical difficulties. It probably received no more than a cursory discussion, as Longstreet didn't mention it in his official report. Only a letter from William Hardee to Longstreet, written in April 1864, provides us with the details.

Tabling the Bridgeport plan, everyone moved to the meat of the matter: East Tennessee. Here, Longstreet made a more daring proposal. Instead of merely swapping Stevenson for Longstreet and maintaining the existing perimeter around Chattanooga, the Army of Tennessee should fall back. Not far, Longstreet cautioned, but behind the "Chickamauga River." Such a retreat would have two benefits: tightening Bragg's defensive lines and shortening his supply path beyond his existing railheads. By giving up any idea of defending Lookout Mountain, such a move would free up troops and wheeled transport, enough to make a realistic strike at Knoxville.

Lookout, as we have seen, was more liability than asset. It was not even a good artillery platform, as it was too high, at 2,100 feet, for effective artillery fire. Longstreet's favored artillerist, Porter Alexander, noted as much. While Rebel guns atop Lookout could lob random shells at Brown's Ferry, Moccasin Bend, or even Chattanooga, they could not deliver an effective, sustained fire capable of disrupting enemy activity. The range and elevation were simply too great.

In a letter to Gen. Buckner, two days after this meeting, Longstreet explained his thinking. With "our army in a strong (concentrated) position," Longstreet noted, the Confederates could "make a detachment of 20,000 to move rapidly against Burnside and destroy him, and by continued rapid movements continue the threaten the enemy's rear . . . to draw him out from his present position."

According to Longstreet, Hardee, at least, thought it an idea worth considering. Any Confederate strike against Burnside needed to be done quickly, with sufficient enough force to overwhelm any Federal defenders. The Federals concentrated a great strength at Chattanooga, and if given enough time, would grow too strong to resist. The idea of using interior lines was to deal a damaging or mortal blow to one enemy, then turn, re-unite, and face the next.

Longstreet certainly understood this. There were already 10,000 Confederates halfway to Knoxville in the form of Carter Stevenson's two divisions. If Longstreet united his two divisions to Stevenson's force, this would raise his strength to 21,000, further augmented by Wheeler's cavalry. While his troops were hastening up the railroad, which was operating as far as Cleveland, to the Hiwassee River, Stevenson could gather supplies to support the move.

The Confederates estimated Burnside's strength at 15,000 infantry and artillery, plus perhaps 8,000 cavalry, for a total of 23,000. In fact, these estimates were a bit conservative, but not by much. On October 31st, Burnside reported 26,060 troops present for duty, equipped, out of 30,300 aggregate present. Of course, not all of these men were deployed to face Stevenson, or Longstreet, when he arrived. Roughly one-third of the force stayed northeast of Knoxville, watching the Confederates in southwest Virginia, commanded by Maj. Gen. Samuel Jones. Burnside would always be facing the prospect of a two-front war. He could never deploy his whole

force against a single threat, unless he simply abandoned virtually all of east
Tennessee by retreating within the defenses of Knoxville.

   This was all to the Confederates' advantage. Burnside might have to
face Longstreet's assumed 20,000 infantry and artillery with a force of no
more than half that size.

   How well did Longstreet articulate this argument? We don't know. In
that same November 5th letter to Buckner, Longstreet thought that few of
those present paid attention. "The only notice my plan received was a remark
that General Hardee was pleased to make: 'I don't think that this is a bad
idea of Longstreet's.'" However, in a letter Hardee sent to Longstreet the
following April, he did not recall this proposal, so how forcefully Longstreet
articulated his point remains open to question. As the conference concluded,
Bragg issued verbal orders, instructing Longstreet to begin his movement,
with written orders to follow the next day. [16]

   When those written orders arrived, they were silent on the question of
Stevenson's force, and contained an inherent contradiction. Bragg asserted
that "every preparation is ordered to advance you as fast as possible, and the
success of the plan depends on rapid movement and sudden blows." Food
and forage, asserted Bragg, there would be aplenty; so much so that there
would be "a large surplus of breadstuffs." Your object should be to drive
Burnside out of East Tennessee first, or better, to capture or destroy him."

   All well enough so far. However, those same instructions closed
with a troubling injunction: "You will please keep open . . . telegraphic
communications with us here and see to the repair and regular use of [the]
railroad to Loudon [where the East Tennessee Railroad normally bridged
the Tennessee River, about two thirds of the way to Knoxville.] The latter
is of the first importance, as it may become necessary in an emergency
to recall you temporarily. I hope to year from you fully and frequently,
general, and sincerely wish you the same success which has ever marked
your brilliant career."

   Bragg's emphasis on the railroad was significant, as it was not in good
shape. The tracks from Chickamauga Station to the downed bridge over the

---

16 For the decision to send Longstreet to East Tennessee, see Connelly, *Autumn of Glory,*
262-264; Peter Cozzens, *The Shipwreck of their Hopes, The Battles for Chattanooga* (Urbana,
IL: 1994) 101-104.

Hiwassee ran for 42 miles. Beyond that, Sweetwater lay another 20 miles, and Loudon a full 44 miles, before another destroyed bridge would halt traffic again.

Longstreet was understandably confused. A series of written notes followed. Longstreet asked after Stevenson's men; would they be part of his command or not? "It was never my intention," returned Bragg, "for Stevenson's division to remain on your expedition . . ." Only a single brigade would remain to hold Cleveland and guard the Hiwassee bridge once repaired. Curiously, Bragg asserted that "your force will without Stevenson [still] still exceed considerably the highest estimate placed on the enemy. . . ." Suddenly, Bragg was using a different math than that presented at the command conference, where Longstreet's 11,000 might expect a slight edge over the Federal 10,000, and that if Burnside remained cautious about his rear, facing Virginia.

As for maintaining close communications with Bragg, Longstreet wrote, "if I am to move along the line of the railroad repairing and building bridges, &c., it is not at all probable that I shall even overtake the enemy. . . . If I am to attempt to overtake the enemy, with a view to destroy him, I must of necessity break the railroad communications with Chattanooga."

Longstreet also made another plea for Stevenson's men. He argued that while Bragg would indeed be taking a greater risk by augmenting the East Tennessee force, in the short term, the Federals did not in fact outnumber the Rebels. This was true as far as it went, but reinforcements were approaching. In fact, the greater risk would be NOT to reinforce Longstreet—"If I am feeble [in strength] my movements must be slow and cautious. This would give the enemy warning and time to strike. . . ."

Finally, Longstreet pointed out other deficiencies in his command: poorly conditioned, broken-down horses; incomplete and worn-out harnesses; and above all, insufficient wagons. He needed good maps, guides who knew the terrain, more and better wagons, and commissary and quartermaster officers to maintain the flow of supplies to his expeditionary force.[17]

In the end, none of these things were forthcoming. Bragg ignored the contradiction inherent in "destroying" Burnside and repairing the rails in case Longstreet had to be recalled quickly. He assured Longstreet that all other needs would be met, but they never were. Longstreet's detractors have largely ridiculed the Georgian for itemizing his needs. Judith Lee Hallock,

17 *OR* 31, pt. 3, 634-637.

Bragg's biographer, suggested that Longstreet had lost his nerve when confronted with an independent command, and was merely setting up pre-positioned excuses for his anticipated failure.

Privately, Longstreet was certainly disillusioned. In that same November 5th letter to Buckner, he confided "that this was to be the fate of our army— to wait till all good opportunities had passed, and then, in desperation, to seize upon the least favorable one." As things stood, "we thus expose both [forces] to failure and really take no chance to ourselves of great results."

Nevertheless, Longstreet's requests were hardly unreasonable. In reality, he would have been accused of gross negligence if he *failed* to address the shortcomings.

Far from executing "rapid movements and sudden blows," it took Longstreet's command a week to move the 42 railroad miles just to their departure point on the Hiwassee. On November 11th, now at Sweetwater, in East Tennessee, 20 miles past Cleveland, Longstreet sent Bragg an angry message: "I regret to report the entire failure of the preparations ordered by you to advance and facilitate our operations. Our railroad affairs have been so badly managed that my troops could have marched up in half the time . . . . our artillery horses were sent through by road, leaving the guns, &c., to be transported by rail." It got worse. "The supply train has not joined us, and General Stevenson tells me that he was ordered not to have rations on hand here. Instead of being prepared to make a campaign, I find myself not more than half prepared to subsist."

That same day, in a separate message to Col. George Brent, Bragg's chief of staff, Longstreet complained that "the quartermaster and commissary [officers] . . . for this department, whom the commanding general promised to order here, have not yet reported."[18]

In fact, not only had Stevenson been ordered not to stockpile rations for Longstreet's move, but he had been ordered to evacuate supplies from Cleveland. They were destined for Bragg's army, or, even more incredibly, for Virginia. East Tennessee foodstuffs were still being reserved for Lee's army.

Bragg responded by blaming Longstreet. He claimed that Longstreet had been given authority over the railroad and should have straightened out any mess; a claim which Longstreet knew nothing about. On the face of it,

18 *OR* 31, pt. 3, 680-81.

nothing makes sense. Longstreet was a corps commander, and his command was detached to reinforce the Army of Tennessee. His headquarters staff were not capable of or prepared to assume control over the logistics of Bragg's supply line, and the continued absence of the promised additional officers only highlighted the absurdity of Bragg's reasoning.

So, what happened? Mostly, more internal army politics. While Longstreet orchestrated this move, Buckner and Bragg busily sent their own angry telegrams to Richmond. They were squabbling over whether Buckner's department still existed or had been fully subsumed into Bragg's sphere of authority. Buckner and his staff knew the terrain and logistics of East Tennessee, far better than an outsider like Longstreet. Had Buckner's headquarters been placed in charge of the rails and Longstreet's supply depot might things have been accomplished much faster?[19]

History cannot answer that question. We know is that Bragg never made any effort to do so or to support the East Tennessee movement properly.

In the end, it might be that all Bragg wanted to accomplish was what he confided to Confederate Brig. Gen. St. John Liddell: "to get rid of [Longstreet] and see what he could accomplish on his own resources."[20]

The November of Our Discontent

Bragg and Longstreet—indeed every Confederate from Richmond on down—understood that to be successful, any movement into East Tennessee must be conducted quickly and with sufficient strength. The idea was to deliver a rapid knock-out blow against Ambrose Burnside, and then deal with Grant.

The fundamental military advantage gained by interior lines, however, is negated if the requisite speed and force needed to gain that knock-out blow are not also part of the equation. In East Tennessee, Longstreet was neither fast enough nor strong enough.

---

19 For the Buckner-Bragg feud, see *OR* 31, pt. 3, 650-668.

20 Nathaniel Cheairs Hughes, Jr., ed., *Liddell's Record. St. John Richardson Liddell, Brigadier General, CSA, Staff Officer and Brigade Commander, Army of Tennessee* (Baton Rouge, LA: 1997), 157.

We have already touched on the logistical complications of Longstreet's movement to Sweetwater. The rail movement, theoretically the easiest portion of that redeployment, proved a nightmare. The condition of the locomotives, cars, and track were all dire. Engines could not haul the loaded cars up certain grades. This forced the men to halt and march alongside the tracks, while the empty trains wheezed alongside. Wood for fuel was in short supply, forcing stops to forage for timber—often at the expense of nearby farm fencing. The bulk of Longstreet's men did not assemble at Sweetwater until November 12th, with his artillery and supply trains still arriving.

By the 12th, Longstreet's force numbered 12,000 infantry and artillery. It included "portions" of four brigades of cavalry of around 5,000 men, under the command of Joseph Wheeler. He described his force as "much worn and depleted by . . . arduous service." Though the overall Federal force was considerably larger (25,600, by the November 30th) they were also more scattered. Burnside could only bring around 12,500 infantry and 3,000 of his 8,000 available cavalry against Longstreet.

Union intelligence also greatly exaggerated the Rebel threat. Charles A. Dana, dispatched to Knoxville in mid-November by Grant to report on conditions there, wired at 4:00 p.m. on the 13th that "it is certain that Longstreet is approaching from Chattanooga with from 20,000 to 40,000 troops." Though his numbers were not inaccurate Dana could not know that Stevenson was being recalled, or that Wheeler's cavalry were in a parlous state.[21]

Despite these difficulties, Longstreet resolved to move on November 13th. The big Georgian wanted to sidle up the south bank of the Tennessee River, outflanking Burnside's advance guard, and fall on Knoxville unexpectedly. Once again, his plans foundered on logistics.

Moving up the south bank required three major river crossings. First came the Little Tennessee River, then the Little River, and finally, cross to the north bank of the Tennessee River somewhere close to Knoxville. Each crossing would require pontoons. While he had sufficient pontoons, Longstreet lacked the animals to draw them. His pontoon bridge could only

21 *OR* 31, pt. 2, 258.

be moved by rail. There was no rail line, operable or otherwise, running along the south bank.

Longstreet could float the pontoons directly off the train cars downstream to cross to the north bank of the Tennessee near Loudon. This would put him on the same side of the river as Knoxville, and the rail line he was charged with repairing. However, it would also mean confronting Burnside's main strength head-on, instead of turning Burnside's flank. He had no other choice.

Not ready to entirely give up on his preferred strategy, Longstreet settled for sending Wheeler up the south bank. The Rebel cavalry could capture the town of Maryville and threaten Knoxville from the south. Even if he failed to take the city, Wheeler might draw away some of Burnside's force.

At dusk on November 13th, South Carolinians from the Palmetto Sharpshooters crossed the Tennessee at Hough's Ferry. By dawn on the 14th, a bridge was up. Moxley Sorrel, Longstreet's chief of staff, described that rickety structure as "a sight to remember. The current was strong, the anchorage insufficient, the boats and indeed entire outfit quite primitive, and when lashed finally to both banks it might be imagined . . . [to be] a huge letter 'S.'"[22]

Still, it worked. Longstreet's main body crossed on November 14th, though navigating that torturous bridge took most of the day. Alerted by the activity, Gen. Burnside rode the rails to Lenoir Station, assembling about 9,000 troops. He hoped to catch Longstreet while crossing, but that did not happen. Instead, Burnside cautiously advanced in the afternoon. However, the only conflict came when a small Union force skirmished with Bratton's brigade of Confederates. Eschewing any larger assault, Burnside decided to fall back to Lenoir's Station, and retire to Knoxville.

On November 15, Longstreet rushed to Lenoir's, attempting to flank Burnside before he could retreat. That maneuver failed. Longstreet had no useful maps, his guides seemed inept, and his remaining cavalry, John Hart's Georgia Brigade, provided no useful reconnaissance. The weather was also a factor, though it affected both sides. The mud was so bad that Union guns could only be moved by assigning platoons of infantrymen to

---

22 G. Moxley Sorrel, *Recollections of a Confederate Staff Officer* (New York: 1905), 206.

help push them along. Burnside possessed the direct road to Knoxville and the railroad. Any flanking effort by Longstreet, assuming he figured out the roads, required lengthier and even more arduous marches than those faced by Burnside's men.

Unsurprisingly, Longstreet failed to catch the Federals, though they did fight a sharp action at Campbell's Station on November 16th. There, Longstreet's column caught up with the Union rearguard and attacked. Aggressively, Longstreet attempted a double envelopment. McLaws's division delivered a spirited attack, but Jenkins' division failed to arrive on time. The Federals got away, while the Rebel miscue only fed more internal dissent between Jenkins and Evander Law.

Meanwhile, Joseph Wheeler's cavalry captured Maryville. Skirmishing with the Union cavalry along the way, they reached the south bank of the Tennessee opposite Knoxville by the afternoon of the 15th. That night and the next morning, Rebel cavalrymen probed the Federal defenses, well-sited on the town's southernmost heights, but failed to achieve any results. Late on the 15th, Wheeler received a dispatch from Longstreet, who wrote that "unless you [Wheeler] are doing better service by moving along on the enemy's flank than you can do here, I would rather you should join us and co-operate."

Despite later reporting that he had routed the opposing cavalry quite handily, Union defenders had clearly stymied Wheeler. He elected to move back downstream. On November 17th, he crossed to the north bank of the Tennessee at Louisville, about halfway between Knoxville and Campbell's Station. He rendezvoused with Longstreet at 3:00 p.m.

By that time, Burnside's entire force had successfully fallen back within the defenses of Knoxville. Behind Union Engineer Orlando Poe's excellent works, Burnside's army now outnumbered Longstreet's expeditionary force. They were also better provisioned, preparing for a potential siege for some weeks and possessed of far more decent living quarters than the Confederates, a significant factor during the cold, rainy November ahead.

Despite the logistical difficulties, Longstreet's small army made surprisingly good time. They covered the 45 miles between Sweetwater and

Knoxville in around 72 hours, which included skirmishes at Lenoir's and a stiff fight at Campbell's Station.[23]

It was all for naught. Longstreet lacked the force to encircle Burnside, meaning that the Federals were never cut off from re-provisioning, and his 9,000 effective infantry (the Rebels suffered nearly 600 casualties so far, and illness was also taking a toll) were too few for a direct assault. He postponed the effort on November 20th. Somewhat surprisingly, over the next week, Bragg proposed to send him another 3,500 men under Bushrod Johnson, and, more daringly, one of the Army of Tennessee's finest commands, Patrick Cleburne's division. The lead elements of Johnson's force departed for Knoxville on November 23.

Then disaster struck in the form of Ulysses S. Grant. Opening with an advance to Orchard Knob on the 23rd, following with an attack on Lookout Mountain on the 24, and concluding with a series of devastating assaults against Missionary Ridge on the 25th, Grant shattered Bragg's army, driving it back to Dalton in a disorganized, chaotic retreat. If Bragg had not stopped Cleburne's departure in the nick of time, that officer would not have been present to first stop William T. Sherman's attack on the 25th, and then save Bragg's whole army with a valiant rear-guard action at Ringgold on the 27th.[24]

One of the lesser-known but important actions of Grant's plan involved sending 1,500 Federal troopers under Col. Eli Long of the 4th Ohio Cavalry to destroy or damage the East Tennessee Railroad at Cleveland. Long reached Cleveland on November 26th, and after driving off a brigade of Confederates, proceeded to wreak considerable havoc. Long's men destroyed a copper rolling mill, large quantities of foodstuffs and ammunition, and tore up considerable distances of track. This last bit of destruction was the most important, as it became impossible for Longstreet to return to Chattanooga, either to help Bragg or to fall on the Union flank.[25]

On November 23, Longstreet also received Brig. Gen. Danville Leadbetter, chief engineer for the Army of Tennessee, who had originally

---

23   See Earl J. Hess, *The Knoxville Campaign, Burnside and Longstreet in East Tennessee* (Knoxville, TN: 2012) 37-76 for a detailed description of these movements and combats.

24   For details, see David A. Powell, *The Impulse of Victory: Ulysses S. Grant at Chattanooga* (Urbana, IL: 2020).

25   Powell, *Impulse of Victory,* 167-68.

laid out the Confederate defenses at Knoxville. Leadbetter conveyed Bragg's views, and he was supposed to help Longstreet find a way to attack Knoxville and overwhelm the defenders, thus avoiding a long siege. If that was not possible, he would instruct Longstreet to rejoin Bragg.

Leadbetter's effect on the campaign was curious. His advice to Longstreet was ambiguous, waffling between two objectives. On the northwest corner of the Union line stood Fort Sanders. On the northeast corner, Mabry's Hill. Leadbetter could not decide which was more vulnerable. The truth was that there were no good approaches, but Fort Sanders was the most likely of a bad bunch. On November 28, Longstreet ordered McLaws to attack.

The assault on Fort Sanders represents a nadir of both Confederate planning and execution. One key issue was the depth of the ditch in front of the fort's glacis. Leadbetter told Longstreet that the Confederate Fort Loudon, upon which Sanders was built, had no ditch. Confederate observers saw men and animals routinely cross the ditch easily, suggesting that it was no more than waist-deep on a man. McLaws's staffers dismissed the ditch as "a mere scratching." It wasn't.

Of course, the Confederates had little else to go on but wishful thinking. McLaws proposed building fascines out of shocks of wheat, but the Confederates couldn't find wheat. Scaling ladders were also proposed, but the troops had no tools to make them. Once again, planning foundered on a lack of even the simplest resources.

The attack was a bloody failure. The Rebels lost 813 men. The Yankees lost 13. The ditch was 12 feet deep and 8 feet wide. Longstreet's suggestion that the attackers dig hand and footholds in the fort wall in lieu of ladders was impractical.[26]

Adding to the pressure to make the assault was the understanding that Bragg had been defeated at Missionary Ridge. The first intimation that affairs at Chattanooga had taken an active turn came with Leadbetter. Barely an hour after the repulse at Fort Sanders, Longstreet received a relayed telegram from Jefferson Davis, ordering him to break the siege and immediately rejoin Bragg.

Longstreet took steps to comply the next day but soon had second thoughts. Even Bragg had doubts that Longstreet could join him at Dalton.

26 See Hess, *Knoxville Campaign,* 151-174.

Bragg's force numbered no more than 40,000. Longstreet had perhaps 18,000, counting the reinforcements and cavalry. Grant's army, now around 80,000, lay directly between Longstreet and Bragg, controlling the only good route through East Tennessee. The railroad was no help, badly damaged, and in Union hands. Longstreet's options would be to march against Grant head-on with a vastly inferior force, or to slip southwest through barren mountain country, without adequate wagons and forage along the way. Davis's order was an invitation to complete disaster.

Instead, after several more days of siege, Longstreet retreated farther northeast, towards Virginia, where he still had a viable rail connection. His decision to linger at Knoxville also drew some benefit; for as Bragg retreated, Grant dispatched 25,000 men northward to succor Burnside and lift the Knoxville siege. As it turned out, Burnside was never in any danger of starvation or surrender. But those 25,000 Federals would not be moving against Bragg's badly disorganized force at Dalton.[27]

Longstreet's small army lingered in East Tennessee until the end of February, and eventually rejoined Robert E. Lee in Virginia. Throughout the winter, Longstreet's presence continued to be a thorn in Grant's side, with the Union commander under pressure to clear East Tennessee of Rebel troops once and for all. Threatening moves and one more battle at Bean's Station, on December 14th, which produced 700 Union and 900 Confederate casualties, marked the rest of the campaign. Nothing much came from any of it. When, on March 8, 1864, Longstreet boarded a train taking him east to confer with Lee at Orange Court House, his sojourn in the west ended.[28]

So, too, was Braxton Bragg's tenure as commander of the Army of Tennessee. Bragg offered his resignation on November 29, as McLaws's men were unsuccessfully storming Fort Sanders. Davis accepted Bragg's offer immediately. Within two months, Joseph E. Johnston, the man Longstreet had agitated for so long to serve under, took command at Dalton.

27 Powell, *Impulse of Victory*, 175-179.

28 Hess, *Knoxville Campaign,* 207-220.

Conclusions

James Longstreet's time in the Western Theater has not garnered historical accolades. The prevailing western-centric view casts him as a haughty eastern interloper, coming to further his ambitions at Bragg's expense. Historians of a more eastern bent tend to regard this period as proof of his long-suspected lurking incompetence, which is useful in undermining his relationship with Lee.

Here, then, are my own final thoughts on several of the most significant questions concerning Longstreet's time west of the Appalachians.

Did Longstreet come west intending to replace Bragg?

I think the answer to this question is clearly, no. While he evinced no great admiration for Bragg, James Longstreet thought that the proper man to command the Army of Tennessee was Joseph E. Johnston. Virtually all of Longstreet's arguments were pitched to this end. He flirted with other solutions, including suggesting that Lee come west and offhandedly suggesting that he and Bragg trade places. However, the only man he consistently and repeatedly put forward was Johnston. Was this merely adroit maneuvering, a smokescreen on Longstreet's part to provide cover for his ambitions? For that to be true, Longstreet would have to be certain that Davis would never place Johnston in command of the Army of Tennessee— thus clearing his own path.

The great flaw in that line of reasoning is obvious. On December 27, 1863, despite admitted misgivings, Davis appointed Johnston to command of the Army of Tennessee.

I think Occam's Razor applies here: Longstreet liked, admired, and valued Johnston as a man and a soldier. Johnston shared similar views about how the war in the West should be conducted. Those facts are straightforward. Too much Herculean mucking around in Longstreet's psychological stables looking for unhealthy ambitions and resentments doesn't make for good history.

Was Longstreet the chief instigator agitating for Bragg's removal?

This is an easy one: No. The cabal against Bragg organized itself long before talks of sending Longstreet west arose. The genesis of the anti-Bragg movement can be found at Perryville, in October 1862, while the first command crisis arose in the spring of 1863. The movement's leader was Leonidas Polk, of that there can be no doubt.

But it is equally certain that Longstreet did become an important player in the drama once he arrived.

The evidence for Longstreet's leadership comes primarily from two sources. Mackall's comment that Longstreet had done more damage to Bragg than all the other generals combined is telling, as is Lafayette McLaws's charge that Longstreet was the ringleader of the post-Chickamauga plot.

For various reasons, I think McLaws overlooks the roles played by Polk, Hill, and Buckner, but Longstreet's prestige counted for a great deal. He had influence based on his reputation, and once he threw that influence behind the movement to oust Bragg, it gave greater weight to the scheme. As for being the ringleader, he inherited this mantle because Polk was absent, sent packing by Bragg in the wake of Chickamauga. But Polk didn't travel far, only to Atlanta, where he could intercept Davis in early October and plead his case before Bragg would lay out the prosecutorial evidence.

It is also worth noting that Longstreet's memoirs work against him. In *Manassas to Appomattox,* James Longstreet claimed that Jefferson Davis privately offered him command of the army in Bragg's stead, which he refused. There is no contemporary evidence of this, nor is it likely to have been made, given how hard Davis worked to sustain Bragg and heal the rifts in the army's leadership. Such an offer doesn't square with the facts known at the time. It does seem more like the faulty recollections of an old, much-assailed man salving his wounded pride.

Did Longstreet bungle his portion of the Chattanooga campaign? Specifically, Wauhatchie?

As I have tried to point out, there were no good solutions for the Confederates in Lookout Valley, mainly due to logistic inadequacies. The loiter time there of any Confederate formation larger than a brigade was extremely limited, and could be measured in days, not weeks. The Federals could pick the time and place of their attack, and mass far more combat power west of Lookout Mountain than the Confederates. Thus, Longstreet, or any commander who replaced him, such as Carter Stevenson,, was always going to be forced to defend too much ground with too few troops. Longstreet's most significant mistake was in misreading Union intentions. He assumed Hooker's column would ascend the mountain well to the south, attacking north along the crest. That was, after all, the gist of previous Federal efforts.

Tactically, Bragg faulted Longstreet for not using more force. Bragg expected Longstreet to take as many as four divisions into Lookout Valley and crush the newly formed Union bridgehead. Naturally enough, historians have followed suit. But Bragg should have known better. It was all but impossible to move more than a division across the northern point of Lookout in a single night and moving during daylight was risky. Taking several nights to shift additional strength would have meant not only the complete loss of surprise, but also that the first troops would be out of rations by the time the whole force was assembled. Bragg's concept was never feasible. As the army's commander, Bragg should have known that.

Did East Tennessee demonstrate Longstreet's incompetence?

East Tennessee is often held up as proof of Longstreet's incapacity at independent command. It is a judgment reached without understanding the logistics of the campaign. As shown, every Confederate believed that to be successful, the Rebels needed to move quickly, unexpectedly, and in great force. None of those things happened, primarily because Bragg's logistics were already failing. It took more than a week for Longstreet to transfer his men to Sweetwater. The lack of transport for his pontoon bridge dictated where Longstreet must cross the Tennessee, ruling out any chance of surprise. Longstreet also never had more than numerical parity; there was never any hope of applying overwhelming force. The actual result was the most likely outcome: a stalemate at Knoxville.

The attack on Fort Sanders was flawed, both in planning and execution. But like many such efforts during the war, it was driven by frustration, impatience, and the need to act rapidly. Thus, the Fort Sanders affair is reminiscent of many other wartime attacks: Grant's attacks at Vicksburg on May 22nd and at Cold Harbor, Sherman's effort at Kennesaw, or Lee's repeated assaults at Malvern Hill. All were marked by frustration and miscommunication. Longstreet's attack cost his army 813 men, a sizeable butcher's bill, but hardly without precedent, and far from the costliest of blunders. I suspect that had Longstreet slipped away from Knoxville without an attack, history might fault him for not making a token effort at storming the Federal lines.

Longstreet's ability to return his troops to Lee the next spring, despite the hardships and logistical shortcomings of wintering in East Tennessee, meant that he managed some success—even if in just subsisting his force. It is hardly proof of incompetence.

*   *   *

In the end, I think that the greatest damage done to Longstreet's reputation was that he lived through the war. Had he died at Gettysburg, we might well remember him differently. However, it was a different war by the Fall of 1863. Gone were the Confederate glory days of 1862 when Stonewall Jackson could rampage through a different valley, confounding every Federal he faced.

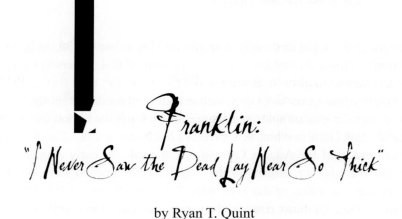

1. Franklin:
"I Never Saw the Dead Lay Near So Thick"

by Ryan T. Quint

*Originally published as a blog post at Emerging Civil War
on the 150th anniversary of the battle, November 30, 2014*

It was a near-run thing. John M. Schofield's Federals steadily marched down the Columbia Pike towards Franklin through the night of November 29th while sitting nearby, close to their campfires, were John B. Hood's Confederates. The former West Point roommates, Schofield and Hood, were pitted against each other as they battled through Tennessee.

The onset of darkness had ended the November 29th fight at Spring Hill, 12 miles south of Franklin. Pushed close to the brink, Schofield's XXIII Corps of the Army of the Ohio and the IV Corps of the Army of the Cumberland needed to escape the closing noose. Because of a complete snafu from the high Confederate leadership, the beleaguered Unionists had their way out.[1]

Leaving the Columbia Pike uncovered, the Army of Tennessee left the escape open to Franklin, and the Federals quickly took the advantage.

---

1 The "snafu" was that of capturing the Columbia Pike and thus sealing it off to traffic. This did not happen, creating controversy to this day. See Stephen Hood, *John Bell Hood: The Rise, Fall, and Resurrection of a Confederate General* (Savas Beatie, 2013), 112-131.

Throughout the night and early morning of November 29–30, Schofield's men trudged toward Franklin. The six regiments of Col. Emerson Opdycke were left behind to cover their march.

At thirty-four-years-old, Opdycke had no formal military training, but had seen his fair share of combat. As a lieutenant, he fought at Shiloh then helped raise the 125th Ohio, in which he served as a lieutenant colonel. Chickamauga, Chattanooga, and the Atlanta Campaign followed. By early August 1864, Opdycke had his own brigade in the Fourth Corps' Second Division. With this brigade, consisting of the 36th, 44th, 74th/88th Illinois, 125th Ohio and 24th Wisconsin, Opdycke covered the army's movement to Franklin.[2]

Around 8:00 a.m., on November 30th, Opdycke's regiments began to skirmish with Confederate cavalry commanded by Nathan B. Forrest. The Federals leapfrogged, presenting a two-regiment front, firing, and falling back through each other. In this form, Opdycke's men were able to cover the distance to Franklin without having to shake the entire brigade into a battle formation.[3]

This literal running gun battle lasted about four hours until Opdycke's tired soldiers arrived outside Franklin. By now, the other Union soldiers had started digging their entrenchments that would become useful in the coming action. David Stanley, commanding the IV Corps, said that Opdycke had "rendered excellent service, skirmishing all the way with the rebel force following us and forcing our stragglers . . . to make a final effort to reach Franklin."[4]

Opdycke's men were tired and hungry, and the constant skirmishing with Forrest's cavalry had diminished their cartridge box supplies. As Opdycke's men closed in on the main Federal works, he was met by his division commander, George D. Wagner. Wagner ordered the colonel and his six regiments to form along an elevation about half a mile from the main Federal works. Wagner's other two brigades were already filing into position. However, Opdycke saw the folly of such a position and was in no mood to follow Wagner's commands. The position was isolated, and the Federals could see swarms of Confederates already appearing on Winstead

---

2 Mark M. Boatner III, *Civil War Dictionary* (David McKay Publishing, 1959), 609.

3 Wiley Sword, *The Confederacy's Last Hurrah: Spring Hill, Franklin & Nashville* (University Press of Kansas, 1992), 158-159.

4 *OR*, Vol. 45, pt. 1, 115. All series are 1.

Hill. An attack was imminent, and there was no chance for Wagner's small force to stop the assault. So Opdycke kept his men marching and headed for the opening in the Federal lines.[5]

Wagner turned after him angrily. He and Opdycke rode side-by-side into the opening, yelling back and forth. Opdycke did not seem to care that Wagner outranked him. Opdycke said, according to an observer, "Troops out on the open plain in front of the breastworks were in a good position to aid the enemy and nobody else."[6]

Later, in his official report, Wagner wrote that "I directed Colonel Opdycke to form in the rear of Carter's house to the right in rear of the main line of works, to act as a reserve. . . ." This was not true. The same observer who had narrated the two officers' discussion said that Wagner gave up on telling Opdycke where to go with a dismissive, "Well, Opdycke, fight when and where you damn please. We all know you'll fight." That observer, Capt. John K. Shellenberger of the 64th Ohio, was one of the men placed in front of the Federal lines. Shellenberger added that Opdycke made the right choice in refusing to form up alongside Lane and Conrad, claiming that "his persistence in thus marching his brigade inside the breastworks about two hours later proved to be the salvation of our army."[7]

The six regiments in Opdycke's brigade stacked their arms about 200 yards from the red house belonging to Fountain Branch Carter. There they made some cooking fires to prepare their coffee and await further developments.[8]

They would not have long to wait. Two miles ahead of the Federal works, John B. Hood was forming his Confederate in preparation for a massive attack. Close to 20,000 rebels lined up in their battle formations, stretching for around two miles. Around 4:00 p.m., with bands playing them forward into the dying sunlight, the Confederates advanced.[9]

Half a mile in front of the main Federal lines, Wagner placed his two remaining brigades into position. The brigades of John Lane and Joseph

5 Eric A. Jacobson and Richard A. Rupp, *For Cause and Country: A Study of the Affair at Spring Hill and the Battle of Franklin* (O'More Publishing, 2008), 229.

6 *Confederate Veteran*, Volume 36, 1928, 380.

7 *OR*, Vol. 45, pt. 1, 232; Confederate Veteran, Volume 36, 381.

8 *OR*, Vol. 45, pt. 1, 240.

9 Jacobson and Rupp, 255-256.

OPPOSITE: CLEBURNE AND BROWN ATTACK—The double hammer-blow of Cleburne and Brown, with some of the most battle-hardened veterans of the Army of Tennessee, drove the advanced Federal position back and resulted in intense hand-to-hand combat. Opdycke's fortuitous counterattack turned the tide of the battle. *Courtesy of William Lee White*

Conrad stared wide-eyed as the rebels came on—first in columns of brigades, and then, as they neared the Federals, expertly maneuvered into the traditional battle lines. The two brigades were hopelessly outnumbered. They fired a couple nervous volleys that seemed to stymie the rebels at first, but then the Confederates rallied and dashed forward with bayonets extended.

Under the immense rebel attack, spearheaded by the veterans of Patrick Cleburne, Lane's and Conrad's brigades were shattered. The men raced for their main lines, about half a mile away. The Confederates followed closely, using their Federal foes as human shields. One historian writes, "[The rebels] were intermixed with Wagner's fleeing troops in a wedge-shaped mass of humanity, veering haphazardly toward the gap in the pike. Suddenly a cry rang out amid the gray ranks: "Let's go into the works with them!""[10]

For the Federals behind their breastworks, the "mass of humanity" presented a moral conundrum. If they fired their rifles and pulled their taught lanyards, the stream of lead would cause huge numbers of casualties amongst their fellow Unionists. However, if they waited, the Confederates would be upon them and in the works. They waited for as long as they could, and then, with only 100 yards separating the sides, the Union infantry fired. In the blast that followed, surely some of Wagner's men were killed by "friendly fire," although the volley did little to stop the rushing Confederates.[11]

By about 4:30 p.m., only half an hour after the attack started, the Confederates had punctured the center of the Union lines. The rebels now occupied about 200 yards of the main Federal works, and more Confederates were arriving. If the break was not sealed now, disaster would follow.

David Stanley, commanding the IV Corps, reported that he rode up to the "left regiment" of Opdycke's brigade and "called the them to charge; at the same time I saw Colonel Opdycke near the center of his line urging his

10 Sword, 193.

11 Jacobson and Rupp, 307.

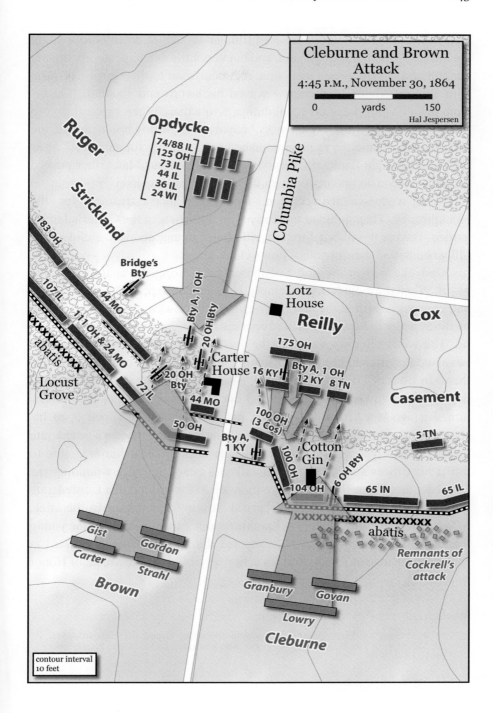

Cleburne and Brown
Attack
4:45 P.M., November 30, 1864

0   yards   150

Hal Jespersen

Ruger

Opdycke

74/88 IL
125 OH
73 IL
44 IL
36 IL
24 WI

Columbia Pike

Strickland

183 OH

107 IL

Bridge's
Bty

44 MO

111 OH & 24 MO

xxxxxxxxxx
abatis

Locust
Grove

72 IL

20 OH
Bty

Bty A. 1 OH

20 OH Bty

Carter
House

44 MO

50 OH

Bty A,
1 KY

Lotz
House

Reilly

Cox

175 OH

16 KY

Bty A, 1 OH

12 KY   8 TN

Casement

100 OH
(3 Cos)

100 OH

Cotton
Gin

6 OH Bty

5 TN

104 OH

65 IN

65 IL

XXXXXXXXXXXXXXXXXXXX
abatis

Remnants of
Cockrell's
attack

Gist

Carter

Gordon

Strahl

Brown

Granbury

Govan

Lowry

Cleburne

contour interval
10 feet

men forward."[12] A soldier in the 73rd Illinois wrote that, seeing the break in the lines, "Without one command, and but very little excitement—by mutual consent and almost as one man—the regiment went to their guns. . . ." The 73rd Illinois' Major Motherspaw waved his sword and shouted, "Go for them boys!" Opdycke, with equal drama, wrote that "When I gave the word 'First Brigade, forward to the works,' bayonets came down to a charge, the yell was raised, and the regiments rushed most grandly forward. . . ." Near the brigade's right flank, nineteen-year-old Maj. Arthur MacArthur pushed his 24th Wisconsin into action with the order "Up Wisconsin."[13]

In a wedge-shaped echelon, Opdycke's men streamed for the breakthrough. They collided violently with the rebels in the Carter's family garden. Bayonets stabbed forward, rifle butts swung about like clubs, and officers emptied their pistols at point-blank range.

Opdycke was in the midst of the carnage, firing the chambers of his pistol. When the cylinders were empty, he grabbed the pistol by its hot barrel and cracked its butt at the rebels. The violent blows damaged the pistol, so he threw away the gun and picked up a musket to continue fighting.[14]

The wild melee continued in the yard and garden of the Carters, who were huddled in their basement, listening to the whirlpool of violence above them. In front of the 24th Wisconsin, Arthur MacArthur saw a rebel battle flag. Rushing toward it, the teenaged major's horse was shot from under him. Rising, MacArthur was then shot, and the "bullet ripped open his shoulder." Continuing, MacArthur neared the rebel flag when a Confederate major shot the young officer square in the chest. MacArthur was able to thrust his officer's saber into his assailant's torso, mortally wounding the Confederate officer. But, as the two men fell to the ground, the Confederate got one parting shot off from his pistol, striking MacArthur in the knee. MacArthur's extreme bravery at Franklin was another example of the young man's fighting spirit—he had already led the 24th Wisconsin forward at Missionary Ridge as its adjutant, an action he would get the Medal of Honor

12 *OR*, Vol. 45, pt. 1, 116.

13 *A History of the Seventy-Third Regiment of Illinois Infantry Volunteers* (1890), 461, 444; *OR,* Vol. 35, pt. 1, 240; Douglas MacArthur *Reminiscences* (Douglas MacArthur Foundation, 1964), 10.

14 Sword, 203.

for. Remarkably, MacArthur recovered from his wounds and later fathered Douglas MacArthur of Second World War fame.[15]

Elsewhere, other men from Opdycke's brigade continued the fight. Soldiers from the 44th Illinois recaptured some Federal guns that were overwhelmed in the initial Confederate onslaught. Manning the guns, the Illinoisans began to fire canister into the faces of their foes. The 44th's commanding officer reported that, "Our colors suffered very much from the terrible fire of the enemy, the flagstaffs were partially cut away . . . and the flags badly cut and torn."[16]

Under Opdycke's counterattack, the Confederates began retreating outside the works. The horrible confrontation in front of the Carter House only lasted about 15-20 minutes. Opdycke wrote in his report, "I twice stepped to the front of the works on the Columbia pike [sic] to see the effect of such fighting. I never saw the dead lay near so thick. I saw them upon each other, dead and ghastly in the powder-dimmed star-light."[17] In a letter to his wife, Opdycke added, "On came fresh columns of the enemy and the musketry exceeded anything I ever heard; the powder smoke darkened the sunlight. . . . The carnage was awful."[18] Coming from a man with as much combat experience as Emerson Opdycke, his words point to the horrifying nature of the battle of Franklin.

The fight continued into the night, and it was not until around midnight of December 1st that Opdycke's men were pulled out of their works. For their gruesome work, they had suffered 216 casualties, but those losses were offset by the nine battle flags it had captured as well as an estimated 394 prisoners.[19] Opdycke wrote in a somewhat bragging tone to his wife, "Every one here says 'Col. Opdycke saved the day.' Stanley, [Thomas] Wood, and Wagner assert it. Genl [Jacob] Cox said the same to me, and to day the immortal [George] Thomas pressed my hand and repeated it."[20]

15 MacArthur, *Reminiscences*, 10; Jacobson and Rupp, 322-323.

16 *OR*, Vol. 45, pt. 1, 246-247.

17 *Ibid.* 241.

18 Emerson Opdycke, *To Battle for God and the Right: The Civil War Letterbooks of Emerson Opdycke.* Edited by Glenn V. Longacre and John E. Haas. (University of Illinois Press, 2003), Kindle file, 6425.

20 Opdycke, Kindle file, 6425-6426.

George Wagner had forgiven Opdycke for his insubordination in refusing to form alongside his other brigades, with good reason. Wagner had seriously threatened the integrity of the entire Union line with his foolish deployment of Lane's and Conrad's brigades. Those two brigades had the casualties to show for the poor deployment. Lane's brigade had almost double the casualties that Opdycke's men had suffered, even with the savage hand-to-hand combat in the Carter's front yard. Perhaps realizing that Opdycke had saved the threatened Federal line, Wagner wrote, "I desire to bear testimony to the gallantry and fitness of Col. Emerson Opdycke . . . for his position, and he should by all means be promoted at once. There is no man in the army more worthy to be a brigadier-general."[21]

The battle of Franklin is famous for the extreme casualties suffered by the attacking Confederate forces, and the deaths of six Confederate generals— foremost Patrick Cleburne. However, it is also worth remembering the sacrifices of the Federal soldiers, whether it be the brigades of Lane and Conrad, who stood to their posts even as the tidal wave of rebels advanced, or the nearly unimaginable endurance exemplified by Arthur MacArthur. Above all, how the foresightedness and quick-thinking of Emerson Opdycke saved a Union army, with its back to the overflowing Harpeth River, from utter destruction.

---

21 *OR*, Vol. 45, pt. 1, 232.

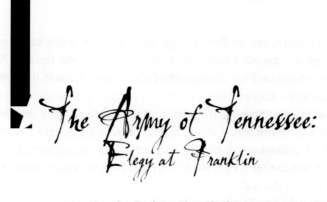

The Army of Tennessee: Elegy at Franklin

by Robert Lee Hodge

Originally published as part of a two-part post at Emerging Civil War on December 18 & 19, 2019

November 30 continues to be a meaningful date for me.

On that day in 1864, at Franklin, Tennessee, came the swan song of the main "western" Confederate fighting force, the Army of Tennessee. In five hours, the 30,000-man army suffered 7,500 casualties—attacking seventeen times, according to one Federal witness. Fourteen Confederate generals became casualties, as well as 55 regimental commanders. Afterward, the leadership and administration of the once-powerful Southern army ceased to exist. The attack at Franklin dwarfs Gettysburg's Pickett's Charge—all the more reason to bring attention to the memory of the event.

I commemorate the battle annually by retracing, on foot, the route Confederate soldiers took on that fateful day.

In 2019, I marched off from Winstead Hill at 4:00 p.m.—the same time the Army of Tennessee stepped off in 1864. Unlike other years, the police changed the official march time for "safety reasons" to 2 p.m.—I am not sure what that meant, but I did not get the memo. If you are not going to do the march in "real-time," I feel the effort loses its impact.

Maybe the march change was due to a huge storm front coming in. Within moments of stepping off from Winstead Hill, I was smacked with a

"Biblical" rain. It was a real Rebel Baptism, and a violent and angry wind kicked up with it. The rain came in torrents, a "big ole fat rain," to use Forrest Gump parlance. The moment was severe and surreal—nothing like the "Indian summer" day in 1864.

I had a hard time staying upright, and the rushing cars on Columbia Pike splashed me thoroughly. I could not have been wetter if I had attended a water park. A gentleman from Indiana who was my companion in this deluge said, "I will never forget this!" At least his exclamation came with a positive tone.

We marched by the Chick-fil-A, where skeletal remains, with Civil War "eagle" buttons, were found around ten years previously. Further on, we passed a big swath of now-rare undeveloped land on the west side of Columbia Pike. This land should be saved as part of the original stone wall remains. In 1999, this land of open fields was part of a 72-acre parcel for sale. At that time, I called the realtor, to ask about the price, but $4,500,000 was too steep for my pocketbook. Since then, the land has been subdivided and chipped away with several poorly planned structures, adding to the sea of sprawl.

Although the march was cathartic, it was sometimes awkward marching in my Rebel attire with my 16th Alabama flag. The two of us weren't in any group. I thought about the more recent hostility towards Confederate memory. I certainly meant no offense to anyone regarding what I was doing—just remembering dead folks I had never met that I somewhat look up to. Twenty years ago, this wouldn't have been something I thought about, but perhaps I should have.

I struggled through the rain, passing the controversial library, and shrugged. That building was a big hit to preservation, but as a result, it helped spark the movement toward saving other parcels on the battlefield.

Marching past the old Pizza Hut land, I smiled. Now it was a park with a pyramid of cannonballs, marking where the popular Confederate Irish General, Patrick Cleburne, had perished.

Splashing up to the Carter House, I stood in awe at the pock-marked farm office and smokehouse buildings filled with bullet holes, reminding me of Swiss cheese. These structures are some of the most important to preserve in the United States—their scarring is a weighty witness to the horrific actions "in the vortex of Hell" of November 30th.

Franklin's Confederate cemetery is, by far, the most sobering site on the battlefield, and is maintained by the United Daughters of the Confederacy. The burial ground is a transcendental testament to the sad day—an exclamation point in the sentence of the Army of Tennessee. The nearly 1,500 headstones are arranged by state. Over the last twenty years, I have always finished my Franklin hajj by going to this resting place. Everyone buried there died or was mortally wounded between 4:00 p.m. and 9:00 p.m. on Wednesday, November 30th, 1864, making it a very specific cemetery. That specificity adds to the gravitas of the place.

This year, in the soaking rains, I faced the columns of headstones at the cemetery. I felt as if they were my audience, or perhaps I was theirs. I thought of the myriad of stories that rest there. What would their judgment be of me? For more than 30 minutes, I stood in the storm in my ratty Rebel attire, reflecting on them. I was also reflecting upon myself, asking, *Why was I there? Why did I have an interest in these long-dead men?*

I also thought of my Franklin journey over the years. I thought about how good my life has been. I did not have to deal with anything close to the suffering of those giants in gray and blue.

Perhaps the experience was somewhat Buddhist; I was meditating in the dark in a blinding rainstorm. What is the future of their memory? Some may call them villains. Some have called them evil. The en vogue presentism has never added up in my mind. I could not help but think the judgment of today on people we never met was mathematically illogical; it felt akin to trying to put a round peg in a square hole.

However, I am defensive towards such things. "Confederama" has been a massive part of my life since I was four. It would be hard to let go of so much that has defined me. The current attacks on the dead drive me to think and read more.

I reckon I will be at Franklin next November 30 to pay homage to the gray ghosts that haunt my mind. It would feel weird not to be there.

A Very Ugly Episode: The Battle of the Cedars

by William Lee White

Originally published as a blog post at Emerging Civil War on December 7, 2014

There was no rest for the weary after the slaughter at Franklin. John Bell Hood ordered most of his army to continue pursuing Schofield's forces to Nashville. Along the way, on December 2, 1864, Gen. William Bate received the following orders: "General Hood directs . . . that the citizens report some 5,000 Yankees at Murfreesborough. General Forrest will send some of his cavalry to assist you. You must act according to your judgment under the circumstances, keeping in view the object of your expedition . . . to destroy the railroad."

It was a return to what Hood had done in North Georgia: strike the railroad and take out bridges and blockhouses to disrupt Union operations. They meant to attempt isolating the nearly 8,000-man Murfreesboro Federal garrison under Gen. Lovell Rousseau and prevent reinforcements from arriving from Chattanooga.

Bate moved his command cross country, arriving at the Murfreesboro Turnpike near Overall's creek about five-and-a-half miles north of Murfreesboro to strike the Nashville and Chattanooga Railroad. Confronting a blockhouse, Bate sent part of his Florida Brigade under Col. Robert Bullock and the 5th Company Washington Artillery to deal with it.

Lieutenant General Nathan Bedford Forrest (left) enjoys an almost mythical reputation—in part because it overlooks ugly episodes like the battle of the Cedars. Major General William Bate (right), unintimidated by the cavalryman's reputation, which was even then fierce, took strong issue with Forrest's performance at the battle. *Library of Congress*

The garrison put up a spirited defense, and the arriving troops from Murfreesboro foiled the attempt, driving off the Floridians after wounding Bullock. Bate withdrew and was soon joined by Forrest with two Confederate cavalry divisions and two additional infantry brigades. Forrest took command of the whole force.

Forrest decided to move against Murfreesboro. However, he realized the town was guarded by the impregnable Fortress Rosecrans. He decided to try and lure them out of the fortification, thereby delivering a crushing blow in the open. Bate's infantry would be the bait.

Bate moved toward Fortress Rosecrans on December 6, engaging the Union picket line, digging rifle pits, and entrenching his main line. Forrest then sent orders to withdraw further to the west at daylight.

Bate ordered his men back at dawn. They made their way back to a hill at Wilkinson and Salem Pikes intersection near Overalls Creek. There, Bate joined Palmer's Tennessee Brigade and Sears's Mississippi Brigades, and word arrived that Union troops were approaching from the south. Gen. Robert Milroy, commanding two infantry brigades, was sent to engage the

Confederates. Forrest ordered the infantry to build temporary works and face the threat.

Fighting soon began as Milroy's two brigades emerged from a cedar forest, advancing into a cornfield ahead of the Confederate position. After a short while, Milroy ordered his men to withdraw. Once under the forest's cover, he ordered them to move around the Confederate left, forming on their unsuspecting flank.

Late in the afternoon, Milroy ordered his force forward. Forrest, hearing the opening of the attack, ordered Bate to shift and confront the new threat, but it was too late. Milroy's troops smashed into the lines, sending them reeling. Finley's Floridians stampeded from the field, and the remaining Confederate line collapsed.

Riding among the fleeing men, Bate and Forrest tried vainly to rally them. Forrest was enraged. Drawing his revolver, he shot one color bearer and took up the flag. "Men, for God's sake, rally!" Forrest reportedly cried. "Don't run off the field & leave the artillery to do all the fighting!"

One witness noted that Forrest, "finding his pleadings did not accomplish anything—threw the flag to one of them—saying take the damned dirty rag & go to the rear!" Another account has Forrest throwing the flag on the ground in his rage. Either way, it was an ugly scene.

The ill will did not rest there. Bate was also enraged, but not at his men as much as Forrest, whom he blamed for leaving his flank unprotected. "Generals Forrest and Bate had a big row about some parts of the line giving way too soon," a member of the 1st Florida recorded, "and I thought they would shoot one another, but some other officers got between them and stopped the row."

Thus ended an ugly episode.

Forgetting Nashville

by Sean Michael Chick

*Originally published as a blog post at Emerging Civil War
on December 16, 2019*

Among the 25 bloodiest battles of the Civil War, Nashville, fought December 15-16, 1864, stands among the most "forgotten." Only two major works, by Stanley F. Horn and James Lee McDonough, have currently chronicled the engagement. The reasons for this are multi-faceted, explaining the complications of Civil War memory and historiography.

On the surface, it seems clear why Nashville is forgotten. John Bell Hood's Army of Tennessee lost the Tennessee Campaign at Spring Hill, while the carnage at Franklin ended his last slim chances of victory. Nashville comes off as a bloody postscript, a ludicrous attempt to save a long-lost cause. The battle did not seem equal. In two days, George Thomas, the best tactician in either army, lined up his Union troops and pounded Hood's men.

On December 15th, Thomas attacked Hood's right and left flanks, avoiding the Confederate center. On Hood's right, a mixed force of U.S. Colored Troops (U.S.C.T.) and white troops were repulsed. However, Thomas' main attack pushed against Hood's left. Federals overran five redoubts, and the Confederate line nearly crumbled, saved only by nightfall. At that point, all hope of a tactical defensive victory was gone, but Hood remained outside the city. Again, his flanks were attacked, but the right held under an attack by U.S.C.T. and white troops. The left collapsed as James

Wilson's cavalry turned Hood's flank, and the XVI overran Compton's Hill. The Confederates were routed from the field, with night again saving them from a larger defeat.

Few Confederates wanted to remember or celebrate that day. Franklin was a Confederate defeat, but the attempt could have been an example of valor. Of Nashville, Hood once wrote, "I beheld for the first and only time a Confederate army abandon the field in confusion."[1]

Nashville also came after Abraham Lincoln had been reelected, William Tecumseh Sherman neared the gates of Savannah, and Philip Sheridan burned the Shenandoah Valley. The war was decided, and Nashville seemed like a tragic afterthought.

Lastly, there is no battlefield park in Nashville, and preservation has been limited. In 1910, Nashville's citizens had a lukewarm response to a motion on creating a park. Some was due to the quality of the land, which is now mostly dotted by suburban housing. They didn't want to see markers of a hopeless battle, particularly when the battlefields of Shiloh and Chickamauga were already covered in monuments to a side they saw as conquerors. With no park to draw in veterans, their descendants, and tourists, the battle eroded into the mists of time, known only by a few markers, and the Battle of Nashville Monument Park, boasting two acres of land. Today, Nashville hardly cares that thousands fought and died over much of the current city. Given the current animus towards Civil War history not in line with the Just Cause, there is little hope this will reverse course. A few Nashville sites are maintained by the Battle of Nashville Preservation Society and the Sons of Confederate Veterans, and that later organization appears to be declining.

The above reasons have some merit, but they do not explain how thoroughly the battle has been forgotten. To understand, one should consider how both sides viewed the war and the competing mythologies and interpretations they crafted. Neither the Lost Cause nor the Just Cause had any major reasons to recall this battle, allowing it to fade into historical memory.

The Lost Cause obsessed over Southern valor and the generalship of Virginia's "holy trinity" of Robert E. Lee, James "Jeb" Stuart, and Thomas "Stonewall" Jackson. None of these men were connected to Nashville.

---

1 John Bell Hood, *Advance and Retreat* (New Orleans: Hood Orphan Memorial Fund, 1880), 302.

Lost Cause favorites for the Western Theater were also absent. Nathan Bedford Forrest rode elsewhere, and Patrick Cleburne was already dead. Benjamin Cheatham was the only comparably popular figure at the battle. While he was celebrated in Tennessee, his fame did not extend elsewhere. Hood, the Confederate commander at Nashville, made for an imperfect Lost Cause hero. His role was cast as a tragic figure, tainted by bitter memoirs, machinations against Joseph E. Johnston, and hopeless battles where he seemed like an unfeeling monster. Hood took a neutral stance during Reconstruction, ignoring politics to concentrate on his family and business. He also advocated for aid for crippled veterans.

The Confederates fled Nashville in disorder. Sam Watkins of the 1st Tennessee wrote that attempts to rally the men "was like trying to stop the current of Duck river with a fish net."[2] If one wanted to play up Southern fortitude, Nashville certainly was not ideal, outside of few moments such as the stand by William Shy on Compton's Hill. The Rebels did well in repelling attacks made by the U.S.C.T. on the right, but the racial aspect of this fighting and its bitterness forced Lost Cause peddlers to downplay it to gain more sympathy in the North, particularly among Union veterans.

The Just Cause, which is a current ascendant memory of the war, would seem to have much to be proud of. The battle featured U. S. C. T. regiments at their best on December 16th. A Rebel army fled, while Union troops showed great pluck. Minnesotans recalled the battle with a magnificent painting. Two future governors, Lucius F. Hubbard and William R. Marshall, led brigades up Compton's Hill. The battle played a crucial part in determining the Confederacy's fall. In the words of Col. Henry Stone of Thomas's staff, "the whole structure of the rebellion in the Southwest, with all its possibilities, was utterly overthrown."[3]

Yet, the battle featured two inconvenient aspects that complicate the Just Cause narrative. The U. S. C. T. performed poorly, at least on December 15th. While their attack was over rough and poorly scouted ground, they vanished quickly under fire, as did nearby white troops. Their actions did

2 Sam R. Watkins, *Company Aytch or a Side Show of the Big Show* (New York: Simon and Schuster, 1990), 241.

3 Henry Stone, "Repelling Hood's Invasion of Tennessee." *Battles and Leaders of the Civil War*, 4 (New York: Century, 1888), 464.

not impress anyone. The popular narrative of black soldiers fighting an impossible battle, but winning respect from white soldiers, didn't apply to December 15th. However, it does apply to December 16th, so it could be argued the two cancel each other out. Either way, it is not the main reason the battle fell forgotten in the North.

The Just Cause's holy trinity is William T. Sherman, Phillip Sheridan, and, most of all, Ulysses S. Grant. None of them were in Nashville. To make it worse, Thomas *was* there, and he gained victory, but Grant did not like him. However, one should not say Grant despised Thomas; Grant reserved that feeling for William Rosecrans and Gordon Granger.

Grant favored friends and punished enemies, and he did the latter with palatable malice. Nothing shows this more than Nashville. He wanted Thomas to attack immediately, despite bad weather and his unprepared cavalry. Toward his favorites, Grant showed consideration. For instance, he did not rush Sheridan into the Shenandoah Valley, and he gave Sherman latitude in 1864. With Thomas, a proven battle commander, Grant barraged him with impossible orders and plotted his fall. He was unwilling to remove a beloved officer, wanting Henry Halleck to do it. After the victory, Grant falsely claimed that Thomas was slow in his pursuit. He also opposed Thomas's promotion to major general, relenting only when it was clear that Abraham Lincoln and Edwin Stanton would force it. To study Nashville is to see the less savory aspects of Grant's personality and military thinking (he somehow thought Hood was getting stronger), just as studying Vicksburg or Appomattox show Grant at his best. Yet, one must reckon honestly with both to avoid the current vogue of Grant hagiography.

Suppose Grant, Sherman, or Sheridan had been in command at Nashville. If that were the case, there would no doubt be at least six books in the last sixty years, discussing the Union victory as a work of genius by a military commander, setting the template for "modern war." To avoid the tropes of Civil War history, and the traps of causes Lost and Just, we must consider areas we do not like about the people we cover, and study battles that do not feature the cast of Ken Burns' *The Civil War.* Most of all, we should seek to place the Civil War in the wider context of its era of warfare.

"The Uproar of the Damned Was About Us": The Battle of Spanish Fort

by William Lee White

*Originally published as a blog post at Emerging Civil War
on April 8, 2015*

The situation was grim across what remained of the Confederacy on April 8, 1865. Lee's vaunted Army of Northern Virginia was nearly cut off. Along the banks of Mobile Bay, a remnant of the Army of Tennessee faced a blue juggernaut in the form of Maj. Gen. Edward Canby's Department of West Mississippi—a force of more than 45,000 men.

Canby began his campaign in late March, moving the bulk of his forces northward along the eastern shore of Mobile Bay, while another column moved out from Pensacola, Florida. Canby's ultimate goal was to take Montgomery, but he decided that he could also force the evacuation and capture of Mobile, one of the Confederacy's last remaining cities. To confront him, the Confederate commander at Mobile, Maj. Gen. Dabney Maury, moved men from the city's garrison across Mobile Bay to reinforce the meager garrison at Spanish Fort and Fort Blakeley.

The troops sent to Spanish Fort, slightly more than 2,000 men, were largely men from the Army of Tennessee who had been sent to Mobile instead of North Carolina as spring dawned in 1865. They encompassed the men of Brig. Gen. Randall Gibson's Louisiana Brigade, Brig. Gen. James Holtzclaw's Alabama Brigade, and Brig. Gen. Matt Ector's Texas and North Carolina Brigade. As members of the Army of Tennessee, these brigades had been fortunate to miss the battle of Franklin the previous November, but had not been so lucky in Nashville. They were entrenching again, waiting for the inevitable blue tide to roll toward their works.

The dapper-looking Randal Gibson was given command of the garrison, and quickly began trying to fortify his position. The defenses at Spanish Fort were weak, consisting of the ancient Spanish Fort and two other redoubts, Fort McDermott and Fort Blair. Gibson set about entrenching a semicircle around Spanish Fort, linking in the existing forts and adding more. The Confederates raced to dig and fortify as Canby's column advanced from Fort Morgan, accompanied in the Bay by a small force of ironclads.

Arriving on March 27, Canby began a siege. For thirteen days, Gibson's men withstood bombardment from land and sea.

Finally, on April 8, the garrison's time was up. Canby ordered an assault to carry the Confederate position.

Among the men in Gibson's beleaguered garrison were the tiny remains of the 5th Company of Washington Artillery from New Orleans. They had seen much since their first combat almost exactly three years earlier at Shiloh, including losing all of their guns in the Tennessee Campaign. Now they occupied Fort Blair and prepared to see the hell of battle again. Among the gunners was Philip D. Stephenson, who later took pen in hand to recount his final engagement:

> The assault did not come until about 3 p.m., but from dawn they had rained upon us from front and flank and rear, from field guns, siege guns, ship guns, and mortars such a tempest of shot and shell that defies description. Think of seventy-five or a hundred guns massed in that contracted semi circle around us. Think of those huge mortars belching forth their monstrous contents. Think of the fleet in our rear pouring its fire into our backs.

Suddenly that demonic storm burst forth and it ceased not for a moment through all that interminable day. The very air was hot. The din was so awful it distracted our senses. We could hardly hear each other speak. The cracking of musketry, the unbroken roaring of artillery, the yelling, the shrieking and exploding of the shells, the bellowing boom of the mortars, the dense shroud of sulphurous smoke thickening around us. It was though 'The Pit' had yawned and the uproar of the damned was about us. Men hopped about, raving, blood bursting from ears and nostrils, driven crazy by concussion. They did all this to get us in a proper frame of mind for their assault. 'Tis the usual tactics.

It was utterly idle to try to return that fire. After a few rounds we did not attempt to do so. We stood around sheltering ourselves as best we could. Our works were no longer a protection to us except against the fire in front, but that we did not mind. Our thoughts were of the fire from the rear, and, from above all, of those huge descending bombs. Now occurred a strange scene. We deserted the cover of our works and scattered in the open space behind them. There, exposed to the full range of all the rest of that fearful fire, we devoted ourselves entirely to the work of dodging those mortar shells, and they were dodgeable. . . .

About 3 p.m. we heard that familiar cry, 'Here they come!' So we sprang to our places. The long looked for assault had begun.

But it was a feeble affair where we were and evidently a feint. The main attack was on our extreme left, where we had had no time to extend any works and trusted to the impenetrable marsh. They got through that marsh, however, and pushed back the feeble picket line we had there, got to the bay between us and Blakeley, thus cutting us off. There they planted a battery and charged down our line around the semi circle, driving our slender force before them until they got to the fort on our left which they captured. There they stopped! It was only a few hundred yards from us, and we could see them moving about in the moonlight. Why they did not come right on and take us too we could never understand.

Night came at last. It brought silence and a moment to breathe and rest. Oh how delicious, how inexpressibly comforting is the coming of night to the soldier in war. But it gave respite only by a change of scene. With the dusky outlines of our enemies in full view at the captured fort above us, and with all our line beyond there in their possession, we prepared to silently escape. . . . About 10 o'clock, after spiking our guns, we left our works and made directly for the beach on a run. . . . We reached the edge of the steep bluffs overlooking the bay and caught up with our men. What next? Beyond the head of the column seemed to melt gradually into the earth, and as we moved up to supply their place we understood their disappearance. The face of the bluff was precipitous and creased with great fissures opening out upon the water. The head of the column had disappeared down one of these! We followed pell mell, right down the almost perpendicular sides of the gorge clinging to vines, saplings, rocks, anything to keep our hold. And there to our amazement we found the beginning of a treadway, one or two planks wide. At the word, all shoes and boots were off and we stood in our stockings or naked feet in single line upon that narrow treadway. . . .

By the time Canby's men moved in, they found the Confederates had slipped the noose. Stephenson and his comrades had made their escape from the doomed Spanish Fort.

1. Walking the Battlefield at Fort Blakeley, Mobile, Alabama

by Sheritta Bitikofer

Originally published as a guest post at Emerging Civil War on June 24, 2021

On the evening of April 9, 186—the same day as Robert E. Lee's surrender at Appomattox Court House in Virginia—another battle was taking place on the opposite side of the Confederacy.

For a week, 16,000 Union soldiers in the Army of West Mississippi under Maj. Gen. E. R. S. Canby's command laid siege to the three-mile-long entrenchments occupied by 3,500 Confederates from the District of the Gulf under Maj. Gen. Dabney H. Maury on the Eastern Shore of Mobile Bay, Alabama.

Nine redoubts connected by earthworks encircled Blakeley, a once-booming port town that competed in trade with Mobile along the banks of the Blakeley River. These redoubts were constructed by enslaved labor provided from Mobile and the surrounding areas as well as United States Colored Troops who had been taken prisoner from further north during Lt. Gen. John Bell Hood's Tennessee Campaign between September and December of 1864.[1]

---

1 William Lee White, *Let Us Die like Men: The Battle of Franklin, November 30, 1864* (El Dorado Hills, CA: Savas Beatie, 2017), 29.

OPPOSITE: HISTORIC BLAKELEY STATE PARK—Historic Blakeley State Park outside Mobile, Alabama, is an excellent success story for the way it embraces a multi-use philosophy in order to preserve its historic resources. Miles of trails offer access to Federal and Confederate works, with excellent interpretation along the way. Visit https://www.blakeleypark.com/.

In front of the redoubts and earthworks was an impressive system of *abatis* and *cheveaux-de-fris*—a mobile defensive obstacle constructed of sharpened poles arranged along a center beam. Additionally, there was a wall of fallen tree limbs, brush, and a network of wire strung between pine stumps to trip up any attacking force. If this weren't enough, torpedoes— what we would consider today as land mines—were buried across the fields.

Ahead of each redoubt was a wide, dry ditch that would have to be crossed before the steep walls of the fortifications could be scaled. All the while, artillery pounded away at the invading forces. Up to the end of the siege, the Confederate engineers continued strengthening any weaknesses in their works, including constructing bombproofs to protect from Union artillery.[2]

In this first week of April, the Union soldiers progressively inched closer to the Confederate works. They would dig zigzag approaches during the night toward previously established shallow rifle pits. There, they created a new line of entrenchments.[3] By the last day of the siege, Federals had made three lines, closing within 400 yards of the works—and closer in some places—therefore easily visible to the Confederates. This final Federal line stretched for four miles, arching around the Confederate line.

Meanwhile, both sides kept up a continuous firefight, lobbing shells and engaging in sorties. Confederate Maj. Gen. St. John Richardson Lidell, commanding the Eastern Division of the District of the Gulf, was fully aware of the approaching Federal troops and made efforts to reveal their nightly digging. He told his subordinates, "I want to light up the front of our works, in order to see their dispositions and allow the artillery to be used in effect."[4] The Confederates began throwing "fire-balls," shells coated with

---

2 Mike Bunn, *The Assault on Fort Blakeley: The Thunder and Lightning of Battle* (Mount Pleasant, SC: History Press, 2021), 24-25.

3 Letters of Major Ephraim Brown, 114th Ohio, April 10 and April 15, 1865, original in Ohio Historical Society; Merriam, "Capture of Mobile," vol. 3, 230-50 – Henry C. Merriam of the 73rd USCT describing the use and construction of zigzag approaches.

4 Lidell Dispatches, April 5 and 8, 1865, Nicolson Collection at Historic Mobile Preservation Society Library on Oakleigh Campus, Mobile, Alabama.

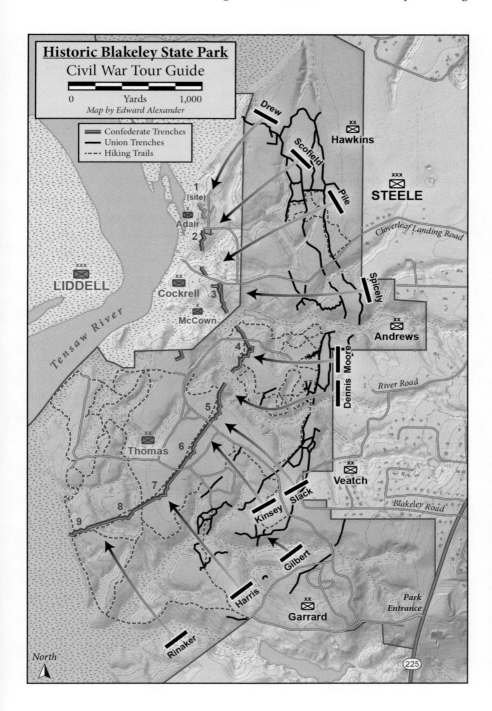

Historic Blakeley State Park
Civil War Tour Guide

0   Yards   1,000
Map by Edward Alexander

━━━ Confederate Trenches
──── Union Trenches
┄┄┄ Hiking Trails

270 War in the Western Theater

calcium oxide, or quicklime, that was ignited and fired from the mortars that looked like massive Roman candles.[5]

The Federals were not deterred and began work on a new set of zigzags from their third parallel. However, some unsettling news was filtered through the command. Five miles south, another siege had been taking place simultaneously around Spanish Fort, a garrison occupied by troops under the command of Brig. Gen. Randall Gibson. On the night of April 8th, the Confederates began to abandon the fort, fleeing toward Mobile. By the morning of April 9th, Federal soldiers had stormed the fort, only to realize it was abandoned. Federal officers around Blakeley feared that the Confederates within the entrenchments would vacate and make a dash for Mobile.

Canby passed the order that a sweeping, united charge would occur at 5:30 p.m. on April 9th. The charge was not executed simultaneously, as some units were slightly delayed.

The majority commenced their charge around 5:45 p.m., beginning with the deployment of skirmishers to flush out the Confederate rifle pits. This was followed by a charge toward the intimidating fortress before them. Troops primarily from Indiana, Illinois, Iowa, and Ohio—the 2nd and 3rd Brigades of the 2nd Division, XIII Corps under Brig. Gen. Christopher Andrews—flooded the field in front of Redoubt Four.

It was a horrendous task. Soldiers saw comrades shot down and blown to pieces. "Now, every cannon of the enemy had on his line, and every rifle, poured forth their deadly missiles on our advancing men," recalled Capt. J. S. Clark of the 34th Iowa Infantry. "Tempests of bullets, pieces of bursting shell, grape and cannister filled the air and whistled around our ears. We were met by deadly, unseen and unknown dangers in sunken torpedoes, which, when trodden upon, exploded stripping the flesh from the legs and wounding terribly those not killed outright. Fallen trees, abatis and wire stretched along the near ground, impeded our progress and exposed us longer to the enemy's destructive fire."[6]

Today, the park is covered in a pine forest. However, during the battle, the land had been cleared in front of the earthworks, enabling those men

5 Bunn, 28.

6 Clark, *Life in the Middle West*, 125–126.

charging Redoubt Four to be aware of what was happening across the lines. To their right, they could hear the 1st Division, composed of three brigades of U.S. Colored Troops, storming Redoubts Two and One. Sergeant Carlos W. Colby of the 97th Illinois remembered, "I had the grand and thrilling sight of a charge of a colored brigade off to the right. . . . As the storming column passed over the works, I could distinctly hear their yell, 'Fort Pillow, Fort Pillow.'"[7]

Two dipping ravines directly in front of Redoubt Four, and imperceptible from the third parallel, compounded their struggle against the abatis, the torpedoes, and the deadly fire of the enemy. Those within the rifle pits or perhaps those who worked on the last zigzag approach might have seen this change in the terrain, but for many, it was one more unexpected impediment. Ravines and swales also mark this northern portion of the battlefield in front of the neighboring redoubts, providing temporary cover or a killing zone for those charging.

Despite the odds, this blue tidal wave, 16,000 strong, managed to overwhelm the fortifications, engaging in fierce hand-to-hand after mounting the works. Lieutenant Colonel John Charles Black of the 37th Illinois poetically wrote after the battle, "Fifteen minutes passed in the breathless charge and battle noises were hushed while wild cries of triumph rung over the conquered wall. The rag was down and the last rays of the sun shone full on Old Glory waving over Blakeley Batteries. Oh, the life, the joy, the madness of that hour. Men shouted sung and cheered. They laughed and whooped and hugged each other, stern veterans who a short time before had parted not expecting again to meet oer the whither shore."[8]

The Confederates who didn't surrender either tried to reform in the thicket beyond their works or ran to the river. A few fled across the river to Mobile, while others were captured or drowned trying to evade. Confederates in Redoubts Two and One, where the USCT had charged, feared their captors would not treat them fairly and rushed to the neighboring redoubts to surrender to white troops instead.

7 Bilby, "Memoirs of Military Service," 24-29.

8 Letter of Colonel Charles Black, April 12, 1865, original in Illinois State Historical Library.

The entire charge—the last great attack of the Civil War—took less than half an hour. Thirteen Medals of Honor were awarded for the action there. Four were given to soldiers who participated in the charge against Redoubts Four and Three.[9]

Fort Blakeley is one of the best-preserved Civil War battlefields in the deep south, maintained by Historic Blakeley State Park. Several trails follow the former entrenchments, and all but three redoubts are accessible on the park's property. Along "Breastwork Trail," a visitor can walk from Confederate Redoubt Nine to Redoubt Five, with each regiment's location marked by helpful signs. "Siege Line Trail" follows the Union earthworks established in front of Redoubt Five and takes the hiker directly to Redoubt Four, which has been recreated on the original site of the Confederate fortification for educational and historical interpretation. This sector of the park, known as "The Battlefield," has been meticulously reconstructed, depicting what the 1864 battlefield would have looked like to the common soldier.

Redoubt Four is authenitically rebuilt, and a small Union fortification has also been recreated on a portion of the original trenchworks. The last set of zigzag approaches and Union and Confederate rifle pits have also been preserved. The system of abatis has been reestablished, complete with the line of brush and *cheveaux-de-fris*. Pine tree stumps remain, giving a complete picture of what the Federals would have seen as they charged on April 9th. A visitor can walk from one end of the battlefield to the other, following in the soldier's footsteps who gave their all in storming the last defenses of Mobile.

Fort Blakeley is stunningly well preserved and maintained by the dedicated staff and volunteers who see the historic value of what lies in their backyard. Because of their hard work, historians and curious hikers can walk the battlefields and read survivor's testimonies. Their words come alive as one traces their progress to Redoubt Four, and for just a moment, one can almost hear the thunder of battle carried on the winds.

9 Bunn, 47.

The Last Confederate Fort and the Last Confederate General

by William Lee White

*Originally published as a blog post at Emerging Civil War
on April 16, 2015*

Easter morning, April 16, 1865, dawned unseasonably cool in the little town of West Point, Georgia. News of President Lincoln's assassination and the surrender of Lee's army were making their way like lightning through the land. However, in West Point, more pressing and immediate concerns took precedence.

The town bustled with activity. The rail lines that ran into the town to cross the river were choked with a bottleneck of traffic that filled all four side tracks with freight cars, and a train a quarter of a mile long stood still along the main track. The wagon bridge was also full of fleeing vehicles carrying military stores and civilian property. Union Raiders, part of Gen. James Wilson's Union Cavalry Corps, rode that way.

Wilson's men crossed the Tennessee River on March 22nd, intending to destroy what remained of the Confederacy's military-industrial complex. Wilson destroyed ironworks in central Alabama and wrecked the Selma Arsenal, giving Nathan Bedford Forrest his last battle and defeat there on

April 2. Wilson then rode east, capturing the former Confederate capital at Montgomery on April 12th. Now, Wilson aimed for Georgia.

Nature presented a barrier, the Chattahoochee River. There were options available: the bridges at Columbus and West Point, 35 miles to the north.

Wilson led the bulk of his command directly toward the manufacturing center of Columbus. He sent one brigade, that of Col. Oscar LaGrange, to seize the crossings at West Point in case the defenses at Columbus were too strong.

The fall of Montgomery and the Union advance set a panic in West Point, and the options for the post commander, Brig. Gen. Robert C. Tyler looked grim. A line of trenches surrounded the town, and a redoubt sporting three cannons, known as Fort Tyler, dominated the town from the northwest side. Fort Tyler was approximately 30 yards square, with walls four feet high, eight feet thick, and fronted by a ditch ten feet deep and a line of thick abatis. A palisade was constructed to cover the fort's southern entrance, but the defenders had no head logs for protection, which would prove fatal for many defenders. Despite its position and armament, the fort was dubbed "a slaughter pen" by one Confederate officer.

To man his defenses, Tyler did not have much: approximately 120 men consisting of soldiers on their way to their commands in North Carolina, refugees from Selma, hospital patients, and the local home guard. These forces were described by one participant as "a promiscuous and most voluntary gathering." This force would have to face more than 3,000 veteran cavalrymen of LaGrange's command. Despite the odds, Tyler chose to fight.

LaGrange's command approached the town around 10:00 a.m. and began skirmishing with Tyler's outposts. He pushed back through town, fighting from building to building, as the 18th Indiana Battery deployed and opened fire on Fort Tyler, pounding the earthen ramparts. As the Indianan's guns roared, LaGrange's troopers moved toward the fort. LaGrange ordered three of his regiments, the 1st Wisconsin, 7th Kentucky, and 2nd Indiana, to dismount and engage the fort's defenders. Meanwhile, the 4th Indiana remained mounted, and at the right moment, would charge under the fort's guns, capturing the wagon bridge before it could be destroyed.

By mid-afternoon, the time was right, and the 4th charged. They took the bridge as their dismounted brethren occupied nearby buildings or took whatever cover they could, beginning a sharpshooting contest with the fort's defenders. Among the first to fall was General Tyler. Shot three times, he fell near the fort's entrance. He was the last Confederate general to die in the war.

As the sun set, LaGrange decided it was time to capture the fort, and ordered his men forward. One Wisconsin officer later described it:

> Our boys are rapidly approaching the works. There they go into the ditch; now up on the embankment! There they lie within 10 feet of the enemy, waiting for the rest of the brigade to get up close as they are. While in the ditch lighted fuse shells are thrown over among our boys, but they prove boomerangs in every instance, for our boys pitch them back into the fort, where they explode . . . then they threw over great rocks. . . . The Bugler is sounding the charge. Up they spring to the top of the embankment like a swarm of bees. Up goes the white flag, they have surrendered!

Thus, General Tyler and the fort fell—the last fort and general to fall in the war. LaGrange secured his crossing even as Wilson made his own at Columbus.

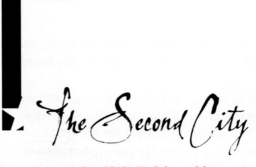

1. The Second City

by Chris Kolakowski

*Originally published as a blog post at Emerging Civil War
on March 13, 2017*

The Civil War defined America—that statement is heard often in many quarters. We use that phrase in ECW's tagline. Many effects of that conflict are quite visible in today's America, while others are not as apparent. An example of the latter is a legacy of the Civil War that can be found on maps of the Great Lakes region of the United States—Chicago as the Second City of the USA.[1]

In 1860, the United States was growing and ever-expanding westward. New York City was the fulcrum of the U.S. economy and its largest and most important city. It also served as a connector on the East Coast between the interior and international destinations. However, there was a horse race among four interior cities to become the Second City—the primary gateway city to the West. New Orleans, Chicago, St. Louis, and Louisville all were on the lists, although Louisville was fading. It will be noted that three of these cities were dependent on rivers; Chicago was not.

---

1 Information in this post is drawn from William Cronon, *Nature's Metropolis: Chicago and the Great West* (New York: W.W. Norton 1992) and maps available from the U.S. Department of Transportation.

Chicago in 1860, on the eve of the Republican National Convention that would nominate Lincoln for the presidency. *Library of Congress*

The Civil War decided the race. The war, and the closing of the Mississippi River, gave the crown to Chicago as Second City. During and after the war, Chicago could maintain its economic position (the others lost ground) and leverage its access to the Great Lakes trade route and Erie Canal/St. Lawrence River to keep up commerce. Its key location at the base of Lake Michigan also put the city astride the great westward land corridors. Chicago thus became the gateway to the West.

The effect of this can be seen in a 1926 map of the New York Central Railroad and the railways it connects to *(see following page)*. Note all those that concentrate at Chicago—more than St. Louis.

This legacy remains visible on modern transportation maps. The viewer will see it by looking at a general overview of the Interstate Highway system *(see following page)*. Six highways (I-55, I-57, I-80, I-88, I-90, and I-94) all pass through or around Chicago. Two of the three transcontinental interstates—I-10, I-80, and I-90—pass through Chicago.

These road and rail corridors still operate today. Transcontinental routes of intermodal rail freight movement and truck traffic still primarily move from west to east via Chicago toward New York and the Northeast.

These maps demonstrate that Chicago remains the major east-west transportation hub in the middle of the country. Although Los Angeles

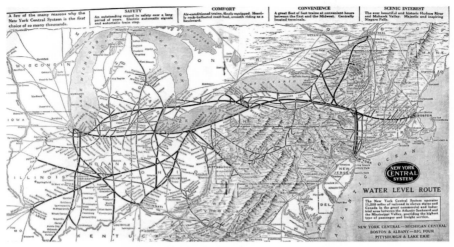

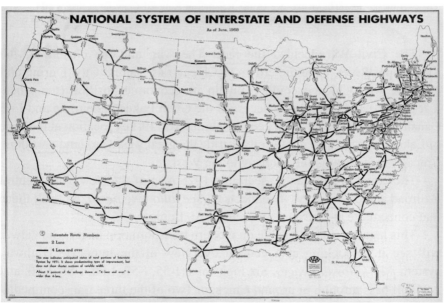

is now the second-largest city in the United States, Chicago remains the primary connector between east and west. The Civil War gave the Windy City that position, one that it holds today—an enduring legacy of the Civil War.

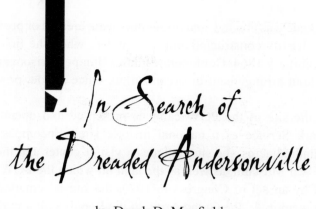

In Search of the Dreaded Andersonville

by Derek D. Maxfield

Originally published as a blog post at Emerging Civil War on August 1, 2019

I have seen the ugly photos of the crowded pen. Like many others, I have recoiled in horror at seeing the skeletal men released from the Andersonville Prisoner of War (POW) Camp. Now it was time for me to see the place for myself. I would have to go in search of Camp Sumter.

My path to Americus, Georgia, began in an unlikely place: Elmira, New York. After spending a few years writing about the Union POW camp on the Chemung River in southern New York and reading numerous accounts alleging that Elmira was the "Andersonville of the North," I determined that I would have to go to Georgia.

Situated in south-central Georgia, about 125 miles south of Atlanta, Camp Sumter, the formal name given to the Andersonville pen, would become the most infamous of all Civil War POW camps. It had a death rate approaching 30% and was the largest of the camps. At its peak, Camp Sumter held around 30,000 prisoners of war.

Although the original plan called for the construction of barracks on sixteen acres, Confederate officials quickly abandoned the idea. Instead, a double stockade was erected, and no shelters were created or provided. The facility was hastily constructed and incomplete when the first prisoners arrived in February 1864. Confederate guards dumped prisoners in helter-skelter, without arrangement or organization. Once inside, prisoners had to improvise.

Today, the site of the POW camp is preserved and operated by the National Park Service as a national historic site.[1] Encompassing more than five-hundred acres, the site includes a visitor center and the National Prisoner of War Museum, as well as the land on which the POW camp sat. Established by an act of Congress in 1970, the site is remarkable for its history as a memorial. The Grand Army of the Republic first purchased the in May 1890. In 1910, the GAR gave the site to the United States, and the Department of the Army administered it for more than half a century.

I began at the visitor center and museum. It was a fascinating exhibit dedicated to the story of prisoners of all wars. However, I was surprised that there was not more attention to Civil War POWs, and disappointed that there were only one or two pictures from the Elmira camp. Still, the museum is something everyone should see.

I was anxious to get out to the site of the camp itself. I have always felt that reading about something is inadequate for understanding; you must stand on the ground. This has been especially important to my understanding of Vicksburg, Chattanooga, and Fredericksburg.

Surrounded by a simple driving loop, the stockade site is situated on forty acres of sloping ground. The high ground features some shade and trees, although while the camp held POWs, there were very few.

A steep decline leads to marshy ground. In this area, a sluggish stream ran through the center of the camp. Deadly to drink from at the time, it is now home to venomous serpents, as indicated by a warning sign for visitors.

Near the compound's center, a replica palisade, guard tower, and gate give the visitor a feel for the height and character of the fence. Nearby is what appears to be a temple, tasteful, yet oddly out of place. This is Providence Spring. According to camp legend, this was the site of a miracle. In 1864, when the inmates were suffering in the summer's stifling heat, a storm caused a spring to suddenly burst from the earth—cold, clear, and pure. Andersonville survivors remembered this as divine intervention. Today, a

---

1 To learn more, visit: https://www.nps.gov/ande/index.htm.

The National Park Service uses this image at Andersonville to point out the prisons within the prison: not only were prisoners hemmed in by the stockade but also by the sheer number of bodies around them, which served to further confine their ability to move. *Library of Congress*

granite and marble building marks the place. Ironically, a nearby sign warns that the water is "unfit for human consumption."

At the far end of the loop, another line of palisade stands with a handful of recreated shelters—called shebangs—rigged by prisoners as shelter from the brutal sun. The run-down feel of this display is particularly effective.

All told, visiting the site of the compound was worthwhile and helpful in visualizing the lay of the land. I was surprised by the steepness of the slopes, particularly on the nearside of the stockade. During my visit in May, it was ninety-five degrees. Standing on that ground, I was struck by the fiercest of the Georgia sun. It occurred to me that Union prisoners battled an unrelenting heat here, while Elmira was literally the polar opposite—an unmerciful cold.

No visit would be complete without a visit to the National Cemetery. There is no more startling reminder of the deadliness of Andersonville. Of the nearly 40,000 men that were housed in the Georgia pen, 12,919 died. The cemetery was all decked out in red, white, and blue to prepare for Memorial Day. It was a stirring sight.

My visit to Georgia was an important exercise. Seeing the ground and getting a feel for the place gave me perspective to consider the comparison

"Andersonville becomes an object lesson in patriotism. To this retired and beautiful spot will thousands resort in the long years to come, to learn again and again lessons of heroic sacrifice made by those who so quietly sleep in these long rows of graves." — Robert H. Kellogg, Andersonville survivor, quoted on the NPS webpage for Andersonville National Cemetery. *Chris Mackowski*

between the pens in Andersonville and Elmira. For one, it reinforced the argument in my book *Hellmira: The Union's Most Infamous Civil War Prison Camp–Elmira, NY:* that Civil War prison camps—North and South—represented a great humanitarian failure. Both sides should have done better to see to the welfare of the human beings in their charge.

I don't think it's productive for us today to participate in a blame game over prison camps. Do I think Andersonville was worse than Elmira? Yes. However, it is possible that Salisbury, North Carolina, might have been worse. We don't have the records to back that up. Elmira represents a tragedy that was eminently avoidable because the resources were available—unlike at Andersonville—to take better care of the inmates. Regardless, a program of retaliation by the Union War Department created much of the suffering at the Elmira camp.

Around 3,000 Confederate soldiers died in captivity along the banks of the Chemung River. The death rate was about 24%, which was the highest of any Union prison camp. Some loss was unavoidable due to disease. Yet, some could have been avoided, although there is no telling how much. We should have done better, without retaliating for Confederate treatment of Union POWs.

Anyone interested in making sense of the Civil War should visit Andersonville. The excellent museum and a visit to the ground where the prisoners were held is a moving experience. It reminds us of the scale of the humanitarian disaster at the prison camps, showing a new perspective on the loss of human life because of the war. We know 700,000 soldiers perished in the war. However, few think about the 56,000 who died in captivity. It is a disturbing tale of man's inhumanity to man, something we should not forget.

Space in the Western Theater

by Phillip S. Greenwalt

Originally published as a blog post at Emerging Civil War on October 1, 2020

Recently, I had the opportunity to visit a few battlefields on my bucket list: Fort Donelson, Shiloh, and Vicksburg. Three battlefields in two states, separated by a heck of a lot of distance. My ultimate destination would be my home in Florida. When charting the journey, which departed from the Baltimore suburbs and heading west in a huge semicircle, I considered that I would be covering a lot of ground.

After traveling up the beautiful Shenandoah Valley as far as Harrisonburg—the geography of the Valley of Virginia is opposite cardinal directions, so traveling "up the Valley" means going south—I turned into the mountains, and then West Virginia. I took in the sites associated with the battle of McDowell, which typified one side bonus of a battlefield trip exploration: finding other historic sites, battlefields, or graveyards.

I cut through the Mountain State and spent the night in Lexington, Kentucky. I then drove the entire Bluegrass State, heading southwest toward Paducah, where I would pick up the trail for the Fort Henry-Donelson Campaign.

Then a thought struck me. Space. How much space—miles, distance, however you want to term it—there is in this part of the country. As I traveled into the northwestern corner of Tennessee, I realized I had driven almost the breadth of Confederate Gen. Albert S. Johnston's initial defensive line, from one side of the state of Kentucky to the other side.

The site of Fort Henry, beneath the waves of the Tennessee River, offers a wide-open panorama as seen from the Land Between the Lakes National Recreation Area. *Chris Mackowski*

I drove at 65—okay, 75—miles per hour in an air-conditioned car, and I could stop for provisions anywhere I wanted, and I could even buy some bourbon if I wanted. However, Johnston, in 1861–62, was tasked with constructing a defensive line; finding a headquarters; and dealing with subordinate officers, politicians, and the Confederate government in far-off Richmond, Virginia. He was trying to impose confidence, showing he could defend the geographic middle of his fledgling nation.

I did not envy him. And when I consider that his men had to walk all this distance I was able to drive, I envied them even less.

I spent the day in the Fort Henry-Heiman-Donelson area, which I had mostly to myself—except for some skittish deer in the interior of Fort Donelson. As I walked the grounds, I could really envision what transpired there in February 1862. I was trotting on the same ground Ulysses S. Grant walked and rode on his way to overall command of the United States Army and his role as architect of the U.S. victory. Talk about the power of place!

After soaking in the views of the Tennessee and Cumberland Rivers, I ventured down to Shiloh. On the way, I stumbled upon the Parker's Crossroads Battlefield, conveniently located just off the exit of I-40 that one takes to travel to Shiloh National Military Park. This was another great, unexpected discovery.

From there, I once again picked up the trail of Johnston, making Corinth, Mississippi, my first priority and from their following the Confederate route to Shiloh, which meant I backtracked some. However, as history enthusiasts know, if you are going to go "battlefielding," you might as well do it following the route of one side or the other in its entirety, right?

I tried to put myself into the soldiers' shoes making that trek, while thinking about what Johnston was feeling. He was proverbially "rolling the dice," akin to what Robert E. Lee would do in the Eastern Theater. He took a chance and placed his confidence in one climactic battle to reverse Confederate fortunes.

If you have not been to Shiloh, I highly recommend prioritizing it for your next history trip. Yes, it is out of the way. However, the battlefield is well preserved, the staff and visitor center are great at orientation, and, for us book aficionados, the Eastern National bookshop has a great selection.

I spent an entire day hiking, riding, reading, and trying to comprehend the action in that corner of the Volunteer State: from visiting Johnston's death site, to locating where a few Floridians fought—which was a pleasant surprise since I had temporarily forgotten that the 1st Florida was there—to spending time marveling at the Hornet's Nest and the steadfastness of the Union soldiers who made that valiant stand. I finished near the Pittsburg Landing site, contemplating the mental fortitude of Ulysses S. Grant.

About Grant: what a difference from when I followed his footsteps in northwestern Tennessee in the Fort Donelson engagement/siege to his experiences at Shiloh.

I bid adieu to Tennessee, after a quick stop in Memphis to try and catch a glimpse of Graceland and snag some barbecue. I decided to drive to Jackson, Mississippi, to set myself up for the Vicksburg Campaign, or what I could fit in the one day I had left before turning southeast for the road back to south Florida.

Unfortunately, the rain moved in, and I had to cut Vicksburg short. I glimpsed the siege lines between torrential downpours. The vastness of the siege lines impressed me, and so did their condition. They're still in very

Little remains of the final surrender site east of the Mississippi River. *Chris Mackowski*

respectable shape even after the passage of sixteen decades. The ground both sides had to cover, advance across, or defend left me amazed at all this siege entailed. I decided I should dedicate much more time to this part of Mississippi to cover the terrain more fully, and I'd like to read more into the campaign, as well (I always need more books to add to the ever-growing "to-read list").

I made one final stop, at a small town in southeastern Alabama, a short distance north of Mobile: Citronelle, the site of Lt. Gen. Richard Taylor's surrender in May 1865, the last organized infantry force east of the Mississippi River to lay down their arms. I last ran into Taylor back in the Shenandoah Valley in the early months of 1862, and look how far he'd traveled in the three years since. Wow. That's a lot of miles and a lot of change.

While Citronelle is off the beaten path, it's worth a quick stop if you're ever in the Mobile area. The juxtaposition between Appomattox, Bennett Place, and Citronelle was really noticeable. For one thing, it was really lonely out there!

I imagined the Confederate troops in this district marching in to lay down their arms and accoutrements. Although far from the main armies of the Confederacy, they had been just as important to keeping the dream of Southern independence alive. Did they know they were the last land forces to surrender east of the Mississippi? Just food for thought as I became food for some pesky mosquitos.

A lot of space, time, and appreciation for the difficult task Johnston—and, in essence, the Confederate government—faced devising a defensive scheme in the "west."

Contributors' Notes

Emerging Civil War is the collaborative effort of more than thirty historians committed to sharing the story of the Civil War in an accessible way. Founded in 2011 by Chris Mackowski, Jake Struhelka, and Kristopher D. White, Emerging Civil War features public and academic historians of diverse backgrounds and interests, while also providing a platform for emerging voices in the field. Initiatives include the award-winning Emerging Civil War Series of books published by Savas Beatie, LLC; the "Engaging the Civil War" Series published by Southern Illinois University Press; an annual symposium; a speakers bureau; and a daily blog: www.emergingcivilwar.com.

Emerging Civil War is recognized by the I.R.S. as a 501(c)3 not-for-profit corporation.

* * *

Edward Alexander is a freelance cartographer at Make Me a Map, LLC. He is a regular contributor for Emerging Civil War and the author of *Dawn of Victory: Breakthrough at Petersburg* in the Emerging Civil War Series. Edward has previously worked at Pamplin Historical Park and Richmond National Battlefield Park. He has written for the Emerging Civil War blog since March 2013.

Sarah Kay Bierle, author, speaker, and researcher focusing on the American Civil War, graduated from Thomas Edison State University with a BA in History, volunteers as the managing editor at Emerging Civil War, and works in the education department of the American Battlefield Trust.

Sheritta Bitikofer is a lifelong student of history. She's currently in pursuit of her undergraduate degree in American History with American Public University. Since 2016, she's published over a dozen historical fiction novels and novellas that cover many eras of history from Tudor England to the American Prohibition. She also works part-time with the University of West Florida's Historic Trust in their archives and collections department.

Carson Butler, a Gettysburg College graduate majoring in history and minoring in Civil War era studies and public history, has worked as a summer intern with the National Park Service at Appomattox Court House NHP, Vicksburg NMP, and Fredericksburg and Spotsylvania NMP. Currently, he leads a Facebook group, "Little will be said or written about the private soldier…", focused on sharing untold stories of the American Civil War. Carson has been contributing to the Emerging Civil War blog since December 2020.

Neil P. Chatelain teaches history at Lone Star College-North Harris and Carl Wunsche Sr. High School in Spring, Texas. The former US Navy Surface Warfare Officer graduated from the University of New Orleans, the University of Houston, and the University of Louisiana-Monroe. Neil authored *Defending the Arteries of Rebellion* and *Fought Like Devils*. His first guest post on the Emerging Civil War Blog appeared on July 10, 2017, and his first post as a member on September 3, 2021.

Sean Michael Chick is a New Orleans native. He holds an undergraduate degree from the University of New Orleans and a Master of Arts from Southeastern Louisiana University. He is currently a New Orleans tour guide, giving one of the only guided tours of the French Quarter concentrating on the American Civil War and slavery. His first book was *The Battle of Petersburg, June 15-18, 1864*. He joined the Emerging Civil War blog in the summer of 2017 after making several guest contributions to the blog.

Daniel T. Davis is a graduate of Longwood University with a bachelor's degree in Public History. He has worked as a Ranger/Historian at Appomattox Court House National Historic Site and Fredericksburg and Spotsylvania National Military Park. Dan is the author or co-author of numerous books and articles on the Civil War. He is the co-author, with Phillip S. Greenwalt of *Hurricane from the Heavens: The Battle of Cold Harbor, May 26-June 5, 1864* and the author of *Most Desperate Acts of Gallantry: George A. Custer in the Civil War*. Dan is the education manager with the American Battlefield Trust and resides in Fredericksburg, Virginia.

David T. Dixon is the author of more than a dozen published articles on Georgia's Civil War history. His most recent book is *Radical Warrior: August Willich's Journey from German Revolutionary to Union General* (Univ. of Tennessee Press, 2020).

Robert M. Dunkerly (Bert) is a historian, award-winning author, and speaker who is actively involved in historic preservation and research. He holds a degree in History from St. Vincent College and a Masters in Historic Preservation from Middle Tennessee State University. He has worked at 13 historic sites, written 11 books and over 20 articles. Among his books in the ECW series is *No Turning Back: A Guide to the 1864 Overland Campaign*. Dunkerly is currently a Park Ranger at Richmond National Battlefield Park.

Phillip S. Greenwalt is a historian with Emerging Civil War and the co-founder of Emerging Revolutionary War. He is the author of five books on the American Revolution and American Civil War. He is currently a park ranger with the National Park Service.

In 1990, **Chris Heisey** began photographing American battlefields. He has published images in more than 250 worldwide publications and media venues, and his images have garnered numerous awards including four national merit awards. He has collaborated on three previous books: *In the Footsteps of Grant and Lee* with Gordon Rhea; *Gettysburg: This Hallowed Ground*; and *Gettysburg: The Living and The Dead* with Kent Gramm. He started writing and contributing photography with Emerging Civil War in June 2020.

Robert Lee Hodge, a living historian well known in reenacting circles for his devotion to accuracy, has also worked passionately in the preservation community for nearly three decades. In 1999, Rob came to national prominence upon the publication of Tony Horwitz's Confederates in the Attic; Rob appeared as a major character in the book and also appeared on its cover.

Dwight Hughes is a retired U. S. Navy officer, Vietnam War veteran, and public historian who speaks and writes on Civil War naval history. He is author of two books and a contributing author at the Emerging Civil War blog. Dwight has presented at numerous Civil War roundtables, historical conferences, and other venues. You can find out more about Dwight's works at https://civilwarnavyhistory. com. His first guest post on the ECW blog was in December 2014, and since that time has contributed more than 66 posts.

Patrick Kelly-Fischer graduated from Bard College in 2009 with a B.A. in Political Studies. Originally from upstate NY, Pat now lives in Denver, where he works for a network of nonprofits. He began writing for Emerging Civil War in 2021.

Christopher L. Kolakowski has spent his career interpreting and preserving American military history, and is currently director of the Wisconsin Veterans Museum in Madison. He has written and spoken on various aspects of military history from 1775 to the present, including five books on the Civil War and World War II. He started blogging for Emerging Civil War in May 2013, and served as ECW's chief historian from 2017 to 2021.

JoAnna M. McDonald, PhD, is a historian, writer, and public speaker. She has worked for federal and state governments, as well as in the defense and television industries. Author of eleven books on the Civil War and WWII, as well as numerous journal and newsletter articles regarding U.S. Marine Corps history, JoAnna's next book is *R. E. Lee's Grand Strategy & Strategic Leadership: Caught in a Paradoxical Paradigm.*

Chris Mackowski, PhD, is the editor-in-chief and co-founder of Emerging Civil War. He is the series editor of the award-winning Emerging Civil War Series, and author, co-author, or editor of more than twenty-five books. Chris is a professor of journalism and mass communication in the Jandoli School of Communication at St. Bonaventure University in Allegany, New York, and historian-in-residence at Stevenson Ridge, a historic property on the Spotsylvania battlefield in central Virginia.

Derek D. Maxfield is an associate professor of history at Genesee Community College in Batavia, New York. Author of *Hellmira: The Union's Most Infamous Civil War Prison Camp—Elmira, NY,* and *Man of Fire: William Tecumseh Sherman in the Civil War*, Maxfield has written for Emerging Civil War since 2015. In 2019, he was honored with the SUNY Chancellor's Award for Excellence in Teaching, and in 2013, he was awarded the SUNY Chancellor's Award for Excellence in Scholarship and Creative Activities.

Visits to Shiloh as a Boy Scout led **Greg Mertz** to become fascinated with both the Civil War and parks. He worked for four years at Gettysburg National Military Park and the Eisenhower National Historic Site, and then transferred to Fredericksburg and Spotsylvania National Military Park where he worked for 36 years—27 years as the Supervisory Historian, managing the park's visitor services. He authored the ECW Series book *Attack at Daylight and Whip Them: The Battle of Shiloh, April 6-7, 1862.*

Kevin P. Pawlak is a Historic Site Manager for Prince William County's Historic Preservation Division and serves as a Certified Battlefield Guide at Antietam National Battlefield and Harpers Ferry National Historical Park. Kevin is the author or co-author of five books. He has been a member of Emerging Civil War since May 2016.

David A. Powell is a graduate of the Virginia Military Institute (1983) with a BA in History. He has published numerous articles and more than fifteen historical simulations. For the past fifteen years, David's focus has been on Chickamauga, and he is nationally recognized for his tours of that important battlefield. David, his wife Anne, and their three bloodhounds live and work in the northwest suburbs of Chicago, Illinois. He started blogging with ECW in September 2017.

Ryan T. Quint graduated with a BA in History from the University of Mary Washington. He has worked for a number of museums, including the George Washington Foundation, Colonial Williamsburg, Richmond National Battlefield Park, and the Fredericksburg & Spotsylvania National Military Park. His book, *Determined to Stand and Fight: The Battle of Monocacy, July 9, 1864,* was published as part of the Emerging Civil War Series in 2017. Ryan has written for the Emerging Civil War since July 2013.

Angela M. Riotto is a military historian who specializes in the American Civil War era, prisoners of war, memory studies, and gender studies. She received her Ph.D. in American History at the University of Akron. She has worked as an assistant professor of military history at the U.S. Army Command and General Staff College in Fort Leavenworth, Kansas, and on Army University Press's films team, producing documentary films to teach U.S. military history and current U.S. Army doctrine. She is working on a book, *Beyond the Prison Pen: Union and Confederate Former Prisoners of War and their Narratives of Captivity, 1861-1930.* She has written for ECW since April 2020.

Theodore P. Savas is the co-founder and director of Savas Beatie. He holds a B.A. in American history and a Juris Doctorate from The University of Iowa College of Law (With Distinction). Ted is the author or editor of many books published in multiple languages, including (with J. David Dameron) *A Guide to the Battles of the American Revolution, Hunt and Kill: U-505 and the U-Boat War in the Atlantic,* and *Silent Hunters: German U-boat Commanders of World War II,* as well as scores of articles in journals, magazines, and newspapers. His hobbies include scuba diving, smoking good cigars, drinking quality gin, and playing bass and keyboards in the hard rock band Arminius.

Brian Swartz is a 36-year veteran newspaper journalist and a historian focusing on Maine's and Mainers' involvement in the Civil War. He has published several history books, including a Joshua Chamberlain biography for the Emerging Civil War Series. Besides contributing posts to Emerging Civil War, he writes for a newspaper and other publications in Maine. His own blog posts can be found at www.maineatwar.bdnblogs.com.

Kristen M. Trout is the museum director at the Missouri Civil War Museum in St. Louis. She received her BA in History and Civil War Era Studies at Gettysburg College, and her MA in Nonprofit Leadership from Webster University. Trout has worked with the American Battlefield Trust, the Civil War Institute, the Gettysburg Foundation, and the National Park Service. A native of Missouri, Trout's focus of research is the Civil War in Missouri. She has been a contributor with Emerging Civil War since July 2018.

Ashley Webb is the curator of collections and exhibitions with the Historical Society of Western Virginia in Roanoke, Virginia. She also acts as the registrar for the Moss Arts Center at Virginia Tech and is a museum collections specialist and dress historian with Bustle Textiles. She received her BA in History and Anthropology from Longwood University and holds an MA in Museum Studies from Bournemouth University, England. She is the author of *Botetourt County: 250+1 Years of Delight*, highlighting the history and material culture of Botetourt County, Virginia, through the decorative arts.

Dan Welch is a public school teacher and seasonal Park Ranger at Gettysburg National Military Park. Dan received his B.A. in Instrumental Music Education from Youngstown State University and an M.A. in Military History with a Civil War Era concentration from American Military University. He is the co-author of *The Last Road North: A Guide to the Gettysburg Campaign, 1863*. He has been a contributing member at Emerging Civil War for over six years.

Kristopher D. White is the deputy director of education at the American Battlefield Trust and the co-founder of Emerging Civil War, the Emerging Civil War Series, and ECW's Engaging the Civil War Series. White is a graduate of Norwich University with an M.A. in Military History, and a graduate of California University of Pennsylvania with a B.A. in History. For nearly five years he served as a ranger-historian at Fredericksburg and Spotsylvania National Military Park.

William Lee White is a park ranger at Chickamauga and Chattanooga National Military Park, where he gives tours and other programs. He is the author of *Bushwhacking on a Grand Scale: The Battle of Chickamauga, Let Us Die Like Men: The Battle of Franklin*, both part of the Emerging Civil War Series, as well as several articles and essays on topics related to the Western Theater. He also edited *Great Things Are Expected of Us: The Letters of Colonel C. Irvine Walker, 10th South Carolina Infantry CSA*. He has contributed to Emerging Civil War since 2013.

Postscript

The Theaters of the Civil War

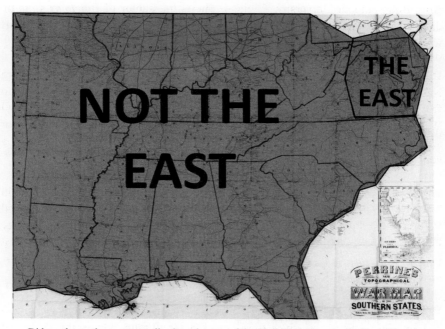

Did you know there are actually *three* theaters of the Civil War? They are the East (Virginia through Pennsylvania); the West (everything between the Appalachians and the Mississippi River); and the Trans-Mississippi (everything west of the river). However, many Civil War buffs in the East can name only two: the East (with its capital city, Gettysburg) and Not the East (with its capital city, Vicksburg-Which-Surrendered-the-Same-Weekend-as-Gettysburg). *Garry Adelman*

I Index

Cities are listed as subheads under the state where each is located. For instance, find "Richmond" as a subhead under "Virginia". Battlefield features are listed as subheads under the battlefields where they're located. For instance, find "Craven House" as a subhead under "Chattanooga."

Corps are listed as subheads under the army in which they served. Regiments are listed as subheads under the state from which they originated.

Also from the
Emerging Civil War
10th Anniversary Series

**For a complete list of Emerging Civil War titles,
visit www.emergingcivilwar.com.**

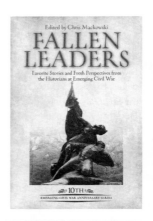

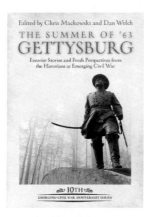

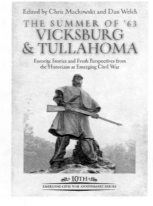

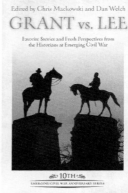

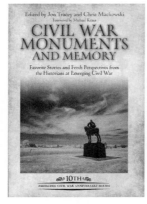

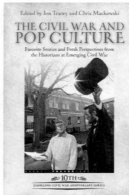

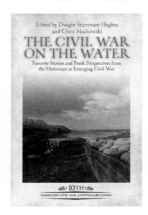

www.emergingcivilwar.com